PAKISTAN ARMY

LEGISLATOR, JUDGE AND EXECUTIONER

U C JHA

KNOWLEDGE WORLD
KW Publishers Pvt Ltd
New Delhi

ISBN 978-93-83649-96-9

Published in India by Kalpana Shukla

KNOWLEDGE WORLD

KW Publishers Pvt Ltd
4676/21, First Floor, Ansari Road, Daryaganj, New Delhi 110002
Phone: +91 11 23263498/43528107
Email: knowledgeworld@kwpub.com • www.kwpub.com

2011 FPBA BEST PUBLISHERS AWARD (ENGLISH)

Printed and Bound by Sapra Brothers.

Contents

Preface

A brutal terrorist attack on Army Public School in Peshawar on December 16, 2014, which left 153 dead, most of them schoolchildren, led to the handing over the reign of the internal security to the military in Pakistan. Earlier in June 2014, Operation *Zarb-e-Azb* (Sharp and Cutting) was launched against the *Tehreek-e-Taliban Pakistan (TTP)* by the Pakistan Army and the Air Force. The military forces used heavy fire-power deploying fighter aircraft, helicopter gunship and artillery to destroy terrorist hideouts. The indiscriminate use of force caused large scale collateral damage. According to *TTP* spokesperson, the killings of school children in Peshawar were meant to avenge the deaths of innocent people in air strikes and artillery bombing during the ongoing military operation.

Since its independence on August 14, 1947, the military has governed the country on several occasions through coups and ruled for nearly half of Pakistan's history (1958-70; 1977-88; 1999-2008). In the remaining half, the military has ruled the country by proxy. Its ruling was legitimised by the failed judiciary and the apathy of the population. In spite of its losing four wars and unsuccessfully combating militancy, the military in Pakistan continues to enjoy widespread respect. The democratically elected governments in Pakistan have always functioned under the fear of military take over. A few political leaders did try to rein the military but remained unsuccessful. A number of military officer as well as civilians feel that there was nothing wrong in uprooting a corrupt government that has not only abused public authority, but also undermined national interests.

After the December 2014 attack on the Army Public School, Pakistan's Prime Minister Nawaz Sharif vowed, "We will continue war against terror till every terrorist has been wiped out from Pakistan." Under pressure from the army, the Pakistan government unveiled a strategic 20-point National Action Plan (NAP) to deal with terrorism in the country. The army had a major role in the drafting to the NAP, which designated prominent role for it at various levels of hierarchy in the states. The Constitutional Amendments were made in hurry, which authorised the military to establish special summary military courts to handle cases of terrorism for a period of two years, ending January 2017. In order to deter crime and terror, the government also lifted the moratorium on the executions to hang people who were on the death-row.

In spite of making tall claims by the military, the terrorist strikes have not ceased in Pakistan. Violence, abuse, and social and religious intolerance by militant organisations and other nongovernmental actors contribute to a culture of lawlessness in the provinces of Baluchistan, Sindh, Khyber Pakhtunkhwa (formerly known as the North West Frontier Province), the FATA and elsewhere in Pakistan. The military is itself responsible for many acts of violence within country and beyond its international borders. The most serious human rights violations allegedly committed by the military and security forces have been extrajudicial and targeted killings, sectarian violence, disappearances, and torture. Lack of government accountability is a main problem, as abuses often go unpunished, fostering a culture of impunity. Millions of people in Pakistan, therefore, continue to live with little or no redress for violations of their human rights.

The Pakistan military, besides defending the 'State' against external aggressions, has played myriad roles in the internal affairs of the country. Every Martial Law Regime abrogated or suspended the Constitution of Pakistan and promulgated new legal order either under the title of Laws (Continuance in Force) Order or under the name of Provisional Constitution Order (PCO). The military regimes have enacted draconian counter terrorism legislations. They have played dominant role in the internal security affairs of the country and held assertive opinion on the issues of foreign relations. The civilian as well as military legal systems were amended by various military regimes to try civilians by military Court Martial which denied them any rights to fair trial. The adventures in economic activities has turned Pakistani military into a giant financial company, extracting patronage from the state and distributing it to its members. This has also led to large scale corruption in the military hierarchy.

In April 2016, the Army Chief has ordered administrative dismissal of a few high ranking military officers. After names of some members of Prime Minister Nawaz Sharif's family appeared in the recent Panama Papers leak, there are reports that the Army Chief has asked the Prime Minister to appoint an independent judicial commission for investigations about the offshore investments. Every military in the world prepares contingency plans to meet any emergent situation. In the case of Pakistan, the army has a unique contingency plan, "How to Execute Swift Military Takeover"; which has been tried out successfully four times. There are speculations that the Pakistan's army is getting ready to take over the government for a fifth time to play its self-acquired additional role of defending national integrity.

This book is about Pakistan military. Military rulers as Martial Law Administrators and the President have "abrogated", "suspended", or held "in abeyance" the Constitution of the Islamic Republic of Pakistan. They have undermined the independence of the judiciary and attacked other rights and freedoms guaranteed by the Constitution. The book covers certain legal aspects of the functioning of Pakistan military, their obligations under the IHL while they were deployed in international and non-international (or internal) armed conflict. It dwells upon the efficacy of the military justice system to try civilians through summary military courts in Pakistan. It also examines the efficacy of the military justice system to prosecute military accused who are alleged to have committed war crimes and crimes against humanity during the armed conflict.

Chapter I of the book is introductory; it provides a brief about the military, the constitution and its abrogation under the military regimes, and the civilian court system in Pakistan. In order to overcome the problems experienced by the anti-terrorism courts (ATCs) in the past, the military has established Field General Court Martial (FGCM) for the trial of civilians. The existing military justice system and an overview of the trial by a FGCM under the Pakistan's Army Act have been covered in Chapter II. Pakistan has traditionally relied on special security laws. The 1997 Anti-Terrorist Act, the 1998 Armed Forces (Acting in Aid of Civil Power) Ordinance, and the 2014 Pakistan Protection Act have been discussed in Chapter III. Chapter IV critically examines whether the military courts, in particular trial under FGCM meet the international standards of a right to fair trial.

In January 2015, the National Assembly of Pakistan and the Senate approved the 21st Constitutional Amendment Bill and Pakistan Army Act 1952 (Amendment) Bill 2015 unopposed. It amended the Article 175 and the First Schedule of the Constitution to provide constitutional cover for extending the jurisdiction to military courts for the trial of civilians suspected to be involved in terrorism. These Constitutional Amendments were challenged; however, the Supreme court up held that the amendments do not violate the basic structure of the Constitution of Pakistan. Chapter V of the book discusses the Fundamental Rights contained in the Constitution and critically analyses the verdict of the Supreme Court which has legitimised the trial of civilians by the military courts. There are allegations that the Pakistan military and security forces as well as non-state armed groups have committed serious violations of IHL and gross human rights law in the internal armed conflict. The allegations of enforced disappearances have been discussed in Chapter VI, as Pakistan is bound by rules against enforced disappearance under the Pakistan Penal Code, 1860.

The Pakistan military has fought four major wars and has been actively involved in the non-international armed conflict. Pakistan has also signed and ratified the four Geneva Conventions of 1949, giving protection to victims of an armed conflict. Chapter VII covers the obligations of the Pakistan armed forces under the International Humanitarian Law and analyses whether the concepts such as 'command responsibility', the 'war crimes' have been incorporated in the military legal systems of Pakistan. Chapter VIII is concluding one and makes certain suggestions for the military and its systems of governance as the ethnic rivalries and widespread violence are not likely to be resolved in the near future in Pakistan.

I am grateful to Prof Eugene R. Fidell and Global Military Justice Reform blog <http://globalmjreform.blogspot.in/> which I have been visiting regularly for postings relating to military justice in Pakistan. I sincerely thank KW Publishers for their professional assistance in bringing out this book.

U C Jha

1

Introduction

Pakistan was created in 1947 in the name of the Muslims of British India.[1] It had two wings: West Pakistan and East Pakistan separated by nearly 1000 miles. In 1971 East Pakistan became the independent state of Bangladesh. The official religion of Pakistan is Islam, and about 97 percent of the population is Muslim.[2] Other religions include Ahmadiyah, Christianity and Hinduism. Pakistan is a federation of four provinces: Punjab, Sind, Balochistan and the North West Frontier Province. Governors appointed by the President head the provinces. Each province has its own distinctive ethnic, linguistic and cultural identity. In addition, the seven Federally Administered Tribal Areas (FATA) and the Islamabad Capital City are under the jurisdiction of the Federal Government. The official languages are Urdu and English. Fifty seven percent of the population lives in Punjab which is the most developed province and from which the Pakistan armed forces have traditionally been recruited.[3] Pakistan shares its border with Iran, Afghanistan and India and in south it's border extends to the Arabian Sea. Pakistan's geo-strategic importance has attracted international attention.

Pakistan Armed Forces

Post-partition, the British Indian Army was divided between the successor states-India and Pakistan. While Pakistan is the 36th largest country in the world in terms of total land area, its armed forces have been ranked as the 11th strongest military in the world.[4] It has nearly 1.3 million men and women in uniform.[5] The Pakistani Army forms the bulk of Pakistan's Armed Forces, and its Chief is the key player in Pakistan's external and internal security matters and the country's power politics.[6] In the last seven decades, Pakistan has fought four major wars and lost significant part of its territory to a secessionist movement. It has served as a frontline state for a superpower proxy confrontation, and suffered major militant insurgencies and terrorist campaigns. Since 1960, Pakistan has been a significant contributor to the UN peacekeeping operations. It has contributed more than 160,000 troops to-date in 41 missions spread over 23 countries in almost all continents. At present more than 7,600 military and police personnel of all ranks are deployed in six UN missions.[7]

Pakistan's Military Intelligence Agency, the Inter-Service Intelligence (ISI), established in 1948, is headed by a Lieutenant General appointed by the Army Chief. About 80 percent of the ISI is drawn from the Pakistan's three military services, mostly from the army. The ISI is a powerful political force in the country and is responsible for foreign intelligence. During the Afghanistan insurgency, the ISI grew enormously and its functional domain today include domestic matters[8] as well as extremists groups.[9] The other intelligence services in Pakistan are civilian Intelligence Bureau (IB) and Military Intelligence (MI).

Since the start of the conflict in Afghanistan in 2001, the military of Pakistan have been countering *Taliban* and *Al-Qaeda* militants across the seven tribal agencies along the Afghanistan border (FATA). Nearly 150,000 troops remain deployed in the FATA region, alongside 30,000 troops of paramilitary Frontier Corps. The Army Aviation Corps as well as the Air Force aircraft have been used in the internal armed conflict. The resistance put up by *Tehrik-e-Taliban* Pakistan and associated groups presents the biggest challenge to the Pakistan military. In order to assist the Pakistan military in counter-insurgency and internal security operations, the USA has made several financial allocations. In addition, the USA has continued to use armed drones to attack suspected militants in FATA.[10]

The Pakistan's military has overshadowed state's civil institutions and evolved into an institution of disproportionate strength and importance.[11] The military's dominant presence in Pakistani society is often matched by an equally underdeveloped civilian government.[12] The military regime in Pakistan has ruled the country for nearly half the period of its existence and has either abrogated or suspended the Constitution on several occasions.[13]

Constitution Abrogation Under Military Regimes

During the last 70 years, Pakistan has followed one provisional constitution, three permanent Constitutions and one interim Constitution. The Constituent Assembly took seven years to frame the first Constitution of Pakistan. Delay in framing of the Constitution was mainly because of the lack of consensus on the role of religion in the new state. The Constitution came into being on March 23, 1956 and Pakistan became an Islamic Republic. Between 1953 and 1958 seven Prime Ministers were nominated and removed. The political system was made more fragile by the formation of an officially sponsored Republic Party. In October 1958, the Constitution was abrogated when the President dismissed the central and provincial governments and declared Martial Law.[14] This set precedence for the military to assert itself in the country's political affairs.[15]

On imposition of Martial Law, state power came into the hands of President Iskander Mirza, and General Ayub who had been appointed as Chief Martial Law Administrator (CMLA).[16] The disputes on sharing power between the two military personnel emerged soon, resulting in Ayub assuming complete control on state affairs. Ayub Khan, as CMLA, then staged another coup also in October 1958, forced Mirza out of power, and assumed the presidency. Mirza was arrested and sent to exile to Great Britain where he later died. The Supreme Court upheld the Martial Law and the Laws (Continuance in Force) Order.[17] On February 17, 1960, Ayub appointed a Constitution Commission to examine the causes of failure of parliamentary government. On May 6, 1961, the Commission's Report encompassing various issues of constitutional importance was submitted. Ayub's 42-months long Martial Law Regime ended on the Promulgation of the Constitution in 1962.[18] The main emphasis of the 1962 Constitution was on a strong executive, expressed through the office of the President.

Under Article 225 of the 1962 Constitution, the Presidential Proclamation of 1958 imposing martial law was revoked. The proceedings pending before any special military court stood transferred to the criminal courts which had the jurisdiction to try the offence under ordinary law.[19] The pending petitions for review of sentences awarded by military courts were to be disposed of by the military commanders, depending upon the length and gravity of the sentences. These authorities could also entertain petitions for annulment and commutation of sentences already awarded by the military courts. All sentences passed during martial law by a martial law authority were deemed to have been passed lawfully were to be carried out into execution. Complete protection was given to all actions done and proceedings taken during the period by any martial law authority and none of these actions or proceedings could be called into question. An indemnity was also provided to all actions and proceedings in connection with the administration of martial law.[20]

There was serious criticism about the curtailment of the powers of court in protecting Fundamental Rights of citizens. Ayub responded by introducing a Bill on Fundamental Rights in the National Assembly in March 1963 which made these rights justiciable.[21] Article 88 of the Constitution gave power to the judiciary to act as guardian over actions of executive in Pakistan. The new amendment made the judicial review over legislative act permissible. Thus no legislature in Pakistan could pass a bill which was inconsistent with the Fundamental Rights as laid down in the Constitution and the judiciary was empowered to scrutinise and pass judgment upon the validity of any enactment either of the executive or the legislature. During the Ayub regime from 1958 to 1969, retired military officers occupied the top posts of public and private institutions. The Constitution institutionalised the institution of military into politics for 24 years by prescribing that the President or the Defence Minister must be person who had held a rank not lower than that of Lieutenant General in the army or equivalent in the air force or navy.[22]

The defeat in the 1965 War and ensuing Tashkent Declaration were not acceptable to Pakistan's public. It led to demonstrations throughout Pakistan. The Ayub's regime was charged with corruption, nepotism, graft, and administrative incompetence and the protesters demanded Ayub's resignation. Ayub, neglected by the military, bureaucrats and police resigned on March 25, 1969.

The Pakistan Army's Commander-in-Chief Agha Mohammad Yahya Khan took up the reins and immediately re-imposed Martial

Law throughout the country. The Constitution was abrogated again, the National and Provincial Legislatures dissolved, and all political parties were banned. Yahya assumed the office of Chief martial law Administrator (CMLA) and appointed Deputy Army Chief, Air Force Chief, and Naval Chief as Deputy CMLAs. Twenty-five martial law regulations were issued on the same day listing offences, punishments and trial procedures. It allowed the continuance in force all courts and tribunals, all offices and authorities under the Constitution subject to the discretion of the CMLA.

On April 4, 1969, a Provisional Constitution Order was promulgated by the CLMA wherein it was provided that, notwithstanding the abrogation of the Constitution, the state of Pakistan would be governed as nearly as may be possible under the last Constitution. The CLMA was to be the President of Pakistan and would perform all functions assigned to the President under the last Constitution. No judgment, decree, writ order, or process could be made or issued by any court or tribunal against the CMLA or Deputy CMLA or any authority exercising powers or jurisdiction under them. No court or tribunal could question the proclamation, or any martial law regulation or order, or any sentence or order of special or summary military courts. Appeals to the Supreme Court could only lie against any judgment, final order or sentence of a high court that awarded the death sentence or transportation for life, reviewing an order of acquittal or cases involving substantial questions of law. Yahya Khan believed that the military was the only legal and effective instrument to take over the country.

After the defeat and surrender in the 1971 India-Pakistan War, the army was discredited. Yahya was advised by his military colleagues to hand over the power to Zulfikar Ali Bhutto, whose party, the PPP, had emerged as the majority party in the erstwhile West Pakistan. In December 1971, Bhutto though a civilian, was handed over the power as President and Chief Martial law Administrator. Bhutto appointed a commission of enquiry headed by the then Chief Justice of Pakistan to look into the circumstances that led to the military debacle in East Pakistan and surrender in West Pakistan. The Service Chiefs were replaced and their designation was changed from Commander in-Chief to Chief. The President became the sole Commander-in-Chief of the Armed Forces.

The third Constitution of Pakistan came into being in 1973. For the first time the functions of the military were defined in the constitution, which stated that the military was required to "defend the country against-external aggression or threat of war and, subject to law, act in aid of civil power when called upon to do so".[23] The new Constitution stated that anyone who abrogated or attempted or conspire to abrogate or subvert the Constitution shall be guilty of high treason.[24]

In July 1977, General Zia ul-Haq, Chief of the Army Staff, became Chief Martial Law Administrator and suspended the Constitution. Bhutto, his chief opponent, was tried and sentenced to death in 1978 on the charge of conspiring to murder a political opponent. The Supreme Court upheld the sentence, and Bhutto was hanged in April 1979. Zia issued a Provisional Constitution Order (PCO) that not only gave the military regime the right to rule but also the right to amend the Constitution at will. Zia governed Pakistan with three titles: the Chief of the Army Staff (COAS), CMLA, and President. Under Zia military personnel were appointed not only as officers in key Ministries like Defence, Information, Interior, Communications, Housing and Labour; a number of them were also appointed as Joint Secretaries. He formed a Military Council of Chairman of the Joint Chiefs of Staff Committee and the three service chiefs of staff. The country was divided into five military zones under the command of five serving men. In 1981, seven Ministers were retired army officers. Even when the civilian bureaucracy was co-opted into the Federal Cabinet that year, it was as a junior partner. However, the public had shown disdain for the military rule.[25]

Zia died in an air crash in August 1988 and left Pakistan without a President, Prime Minister, or National or Provincial Assemblies. Ghulam Ishaq Khan, the chairman of the Senate, which had not been dissolved by Zia, and next in the constitutional line of succession, took over as interim President in December. Elections were held, Mrs Benazir Bhutto became Prime Minister, and Ishaq Khan was subsequently elected as President of Pakistan. After the ouster of Benazir's Government, elections were held in October 1990 and Nawaz Sharif was elected as

Prime Minister on November 1, 1990. Nawaz's Government remained in power till April 1993, when President Ghulam Ishaq Khan dissolved the National Assembly, once again exercising his power through the Eighth Amendment. On May 26, 1993, the Supreme Court of Pakistan declared the Presidential Order of the Assemblies' dissolution as unconstitutional and ruled for restoring the Nawaz Government and the National Assembly. However, because of the serious difference between the President and the Prime Minister, both resigned from their offices on July 18, 1993. Moin Qureshi, a top World Bank Official, was appointed as the caretaker President.

Benazir Bhutto returned to power for the second time in 1993. However, she was dismissed on charges of corruption and mismanagement on November 5, 1996 under the Article 58(2)b of the Eighth Amendment. After the elections of 1997, Nawaz Sharif was re-elected as Prime Minister. In 1998, during the Nawaz's government, the law and order situation gradually deteriorated and sectarian killings took place all over the country. In order to crack down on MQM, Pakistan Armed Forces (Acting in Aid of the Civil Power) Ordinance, 1998 was promulgated on November 20, 1998. The Ordinance allowed establishment of military courts for trial of civilian charged with offences mentioned in the schedule to the ordinance. The MQM challenged the Ordinance under article 184 (3) of the Constitution as a violation of the Constitution. The Supreme Court held that the said Ordinance was unconstitutional and that the cases in which sentence has already been awarded but not yet executed would stand set aside and the cases should stand transferred to the Anti Terrorist Courts. However, the sentence passed and punishment already awarded and executed would be treated as closed.[26]

While General Musharraf, the COAS, was in Sri Lanka on an official visit, Nawaz Sharif tried to promote Lt. Gen. Ziauddin to the rank of General and appoint him as COAS. On October 12, 1999, Pakistan's armed forces staged a military coup against the government of Sharif. With this Pakistan entered its 25th year of military rule. The next day, General Pervez Musharraf announced that the armed forces have taken control of the affairs of the government to prevent any further destabilisation of the country. Musharraf proclaimed emergency throughout Pakistan and assume the charge of the Chief Executive. However, he did not abrogate the constitution; it was held in abeyance. The National Assembly, the senate, and the four Provincial Assemblies were suspended. A Provisional Constitutional Order (PCO) was promulgated which provided that notwithstanding the abeyance of the Constitution, Pakistan would be governed as nearly as may be, in accordance with the Constitution.[27] All courts in existence would continue to function and to exercise their respective powers and jurisdiction provided that the Supreme Court and the High Courts or any other court would not have the power to make any order against the Chief Executive or any person exercising power or jurisdiction under his authority. The President was to act on the advice of the Chief Executive. Musharraf did not impose Martial Law and declared that the armed forces had no intention to stay in charge any longer than is absolutely necessary to pave the way for true democracy to flourish in Pakistan.

On November 03, 2007, Musharraf proclaimed emergency in his capacity as Chief of the Army Staff. In his proclamation, he gave suicide bombings, terrorist attacks on law enforcement agencies and fight against terrorism as some of the reasons for imposing the same. Other reasons included interference by judiciary in government policies, release of hardcore criminals, judges overstepping the limits of judicial authority and taking over executive and legislative functions. He also ordered that the Constitution would remain in abeyance. On November 28, 2007, Musharraf handed over command of the army to General Ashfaq Parvez Kayani and the next day he took oath as civilian President. In 2007, the 1973 Constitution was revived, albeit with various amendments made during the Musharraf's regime. In order to avoid the impeachment process, Musharraf announced his resignation from the office of President on August 18, 2008; thus ending his nine-year of military-cum-civilian rule. The constitutional amendments made during Musharraf regime were reversed in April 2010 by the government that transferred key powers from the President to the Provinces and extended Fundamental Rights to include the right to education and information.

The Court System in Pakistan

The administration of justice in Pakistan is categorised into the superior judiciary and subordinate judiciary. The superior judicial system established by the Constitution and comprises the Supreme Court, High Courts and Federal Shariat Court. The Supreme Court is the apex court of Pakistan and consists of a Chief Justice, known as the Chief Justice of Pakistan, and 17 Judges. The Supreme Court has limited original and extensive appellate jurisdiction. A special bench of the Supreme Court known as the Shariat Appellate Bench hears appeals from the orders/ judgments of the Federal Shariat Court, established in 1979. The Supreme Court has important powers with regard to enforcement of Fundamental Rights. Judges of the Supreme Court hold office till the age of 65 and are appointed by the President in consultation with the Chief Justice of Pakistan.

There are five High Courts in Pakistan, one for each Province and one for the Islamabad Capital Territory, serving as appellate courts on most civil and criminal matters. The High Courts have a principal seat and one or more benches. The Lahore High Court has three added benches at Rawalpindi, Multan and Bahawalpur. High Courts have extensive appellate and substantial original jurisdiction. They have powers to issue orders in the nature of writs. High Courts are also entrusted with powers of superintendence and control over most courts.

The Federal Shariat Court comprises of not more than eight Judges including the Chief Justice. The Court has appellate and revisionary jurisdiction in *Hudood* cases and jurisdiction to review laws to find out their compatibility with injunctions of Islam. Sharia courts continue to exist, but the government no longer refers cases to them.

The subordinate courts of general jurisdiction deal with the civil and criminal law in Pakistan. These courts have jurisdiction over all civil, criminal, and administrative matters unless provided otherwise by legislative enactment. The subordinate courts are subject to the supervisory control of the High Courts.[28] Criminal courts of general jurisdiction are set up under the Code of Criminal Procedure, 1898. These courts can try all cases arising out of the Pakistan Penal Code, 1860. Criminal courts are of two types: Sessions Court and Courts of

Magistrates. The Sessions Court comprises one Sessions Judge who is in charge of the administration of the court and varying number of Additional and Assistant Sessions Judges. Additional Sessions Judges have same judicial powers as the Sessions Judge. Sessions judges are invariably District Judges and are known as District and Sessions Judges.

The jurisdiction of the superior courts does not extend to the Federally Administered Tribal Areas (FATA), thus denying citizen's access in the enforcement of Fundamental Rights guaranteed in the Constitution. A traditional jirga (tribal council) deals with issues affecting those in tribal areas including land and property disputes, inheritance, alleged violations of honour, and intra-tribal/inter-tribal killings. Jirga is considered as the most preferred form of informal or parallel justice/dispute resolution mechanism in many Pakhtun dominated areas of Pakistan. Jirgas consists of men-only; however, in 2013, an all-female jirga was convened in Swat Valley, Khyber Pakhtunkhwa. The decisions of Jirga may result in the violation of human rights, especially the rights of women and ethnic/ religious minorities. Jirgas have been infamous for imposing a large number of death sentences, and the forced exchange of brides between tribes. Though the Sindh High Court and the government have imposed a ban on holding jirgas in the province, the implementation has not been very effective.

The Court Martial, which is only a temporary tribunal, constituted under the Army Act, 1952, the Air Force Act, 1953, and the Navy Ordinance, 1961 are special courts for maintaining discipline amongst the members of the three wings of the armed forces. The military legal system has been often amended to try civilians by the Court Martial, both during the Martial Law Regimes and also when the democratic government was in power in Pakistan.

The Constitution and Judicial Independence

The necessity of judicial independence is recognised universally.[29] The Constitution of the Islamic Republic of Pakistan provides for the establishment of a judiciary which is independent from the other two branches of government and whose Judges can only be removed or disciplined in accordance with the procedures contained in the Constitution itself.[30] The principle of independence of judiciary has been established in a number of the judgments by the superior courts in Pakistan.[31] The Supreme Court in the case of *Zafar Ali Shah v General Pervez Musharraf* [32] held that judiciary has to be properly organised, effective and efficient enough to quickly redress and resolve public claims and grievances, and also to be strong enough to dispense justice fairly and impartially. The manner of appointment of the superior court judges has a close nexus with the independence of the judiciary and cannot be separated from each other.[33] The related issues which need consideration in respect of the judicial independence are the manner of removal, promotion and transfer of the judges. It includes the term of office of the judges, a protection from involuntary transfers, an adequate emolument, and the proper conditions of service, pensions and the age of retirement.[34] However, in the case of Pakistan, whether it was governed by civil or military regime, none of the governments wanted an independent judiciary. The constitutional provisions relating to independence of judiciary in Pakistan have been violently abrogated both during the civilian and the military regimes.

Making preference for pliable judges over independent; civil as well as military executive have kept judiciary under pressure and made it subservient to executive's powers. Every government in Pakistan has tried to get favourable decisions from the courts and adopted various tactics to put pressure on the judges. The humiliation and intimidation of the judges by the government are not limited only to the superior judiciary; the lower judiciary has also been treated badly by the executive. The judicial history of Pakistan indicates that Governor General Ghulam Muhammad and two former Prime Ministers namely Zulfikar Ali Bhutto and Benazir Bhutto, and Present Prime Minister Nawaz Sharif have severely damaged the institution of judiciary. They ridiculed the judiciary whenever it gave decisions against the government in power. Each Martial Law Regime has clipped the wings of the judiciary. The military regimes have arbitrarily removed the judges and degraded the dignity of the judiciary by interfering in the proceedings of the court. Every successive Martial Law governments has followed the foot prints of its predecessors and adopted new trend for controlling judiciary.

Under the military regimes, the higher judiciary was allowed to function but was deprived of the power to challenge the military government or to pass any order/judgment against military dictators. During first three Martial Law Regimes of 1958, 1969 and 1977, parallel military courts of criminal jurisdiction were set up. These courts were empowered to punish any person for the violation of Martial Law regulations or orders and also for offences under ordinary law. Appeals against any decision or order of the military courts were not allowed to any court including the higher courts in Pakistan. In case any court showed courage to review the actions taken by Martial Law Regime or questioned judgments of military the military regimes reacted by restricting the powers of the courts.[35] This made the judiciary very cautious while exercising the power of judicial review and they desisted in questioning Martial Law regulations and orders.

The military regimes manipulated the system of appointment of judges on personal or political consideration. The appointments of the judges in the superior courts have been arbitrary, thus undermining the independence of the judiciary. For this direct and blatant assault on judiciary, every military regime in Pakistan from General Ayub Khan to Pervez Musharraf is blameworthy. The Martial Law administrators removed unwanted judges of the superior courts sometimes by adopting the constitutional procedure or by issuing arbitrary orders.[36] Manipulation of the judges for getting favourable decisions has been has been the practice of every successive military government. In November 2007, General Musharraf made a coup against the judiciary to stop the Supreme Court from giving a judgment in the cases challenging his eligibility for the Presidential election.[37] He arbitrarily removed 12 of 17 Judges and reconstituted the "Supreme Court" of his choice to get favourable verdict.

The Supreme Court of Pakistan has suffered the most in terms of integrity and prestige. This legacy of the Court has been continuing. In 2015, while considering judicial review of the 18th and 21st Constitutional Amendments and amendments in the military legal systems for the trial of civilians accused of terrorism related offences, the Supreme Court chose the middle path. The Supreme Court, while considering the judicial challenge to the military courts, had earlier suspended the death sentences awarded to convicted terrorists. Since the Court has validated the two Constitutional Amendments, it has removed the moratorium on implementing the death sentences passed earlier by the military courts.[38]

Constitutional Framework and Human Rights

The Constitution of Pakistan contains a comprehensive chapter on Fundamental Rights. According to Article 8, any law, or any custom or usage having the force of law, in so far as it is inconsistent with the rights conferred by this Chapter, shall, to the extent of such inconsistency, be void. The Constitution specifies, however, that this does not apply to any law relating to members of the Armed Forces, or of the police or of such other forces as are charged with the maintenance of public order, for the purpose of ensuring the proper discharge of their duties or the maintenance of discipline among them.

Article 10A results from the 18th amendment and provides for the right to fair trial: For the determination of his civil rights and obligations or in any criminal charge against him a person shall be entitled to a fair trial and due process. Article 9 of the Constitution provides that no person shall be deprived of his life or liberty save in accordance with law. Article 10 provides for a series of safeguards in the case of arrest or detention. It states that "no person who is arrested shall be detained in custody without being informed, as soon as may be, of the grounds of such arrest, nor shall be denied the right to consult and be defended by a legal practitioner of his choice." Further, it provides for the right of any person arrested and detained in custody "to be produced before a magistrate before a period of twenty four hours of such arrest, excluding the time necessary for the journey from the place of arrest to the court of the nearest magistrate, and no such person shall be detained in custody beyond the said period without the authority of a magistrate." However, paragraph 3 of Article 10 provides that clauses 1 and 2 do not apply to "any person who is arrested or detained under any law providing for preventive detention." Clauses 4 to 9 of Article 10 describe a system of "preventive detention" applicable to "persons acting in a manner prejudicial to the integrity, security of defence of Pakistan or any part thereof, or external affairs of Pakistan, or public order, or the maintenance of supplies or services", under which such persons may be detained for "a period exceeding three months" under the supervision of a review board.

Military in Business

The Pakistan military is a complex organisation that has significant influence on country's economy. It is unique in the sense that it runs an economic business empire like no other army in the world.[39] In addition to the prominent political role that the military plays in Pakistan, it is also a leading economic power in the country. Five giant conglomerates, known as 'welfare foundations' of the military, run thousands of businesses, ranging from street corner petrol pumps to sprawling industrial plants.[40] The military-run enterprises include banks, fertilizer factories, cereal factories, cement factories, construction and real estate companies, transport companies, insurance companies, universities and bakeries. The transport company, National Logistic Cell (NLC), was created in 1978 and is the largest goods transportation company in the country having a fleet of nearly 2,000 vehicles.

The military's penetration into society was started soon after the Independence in 1947, and had accelerated under the various military regimes.[41] The military personnel were appointed to posts earlier held by the civilians. It was primarily done to increase the military's influence over the civil administration, as well as to accrue financial gains.[42] President Pervez Musharraf was responsible for appointing 1,200 officers into key positions in public organisations such as universities and training colleges. The military claimed that it can run these institutions better than the incompetent and corrupt civilians.[43] The military's meddling has made civilian institutions in Pakistan even weaker. It has left the civil service corrupt and demoralised.[44]

According to Pakistan People's Party (PPP)'s Senator Farhatullah Babar, military's business activities have not only been kept out of the public view and parliamentary oversight but have also escaped government accountability procedures. There was need to look into state subsidies and other support provided to entities by military's economic foundations and examine their adverse impact on the growth of free market economy.[45] A former senior military officer[46] has rationalised the military's commercial and business activities stating that the funds generated by the commercial ventures are used entirely for welfare measures.[47] According to him, the earnings of Fauji Foundation are utilised for the welfare of 1.3 million ex-servicemen and over 33,000 are being added every year; and criticism of military's economic venture has increased due to the freedom granted to the media.[48]

Retired military officers run most military businesses, which do not publicity disclose the full scale of their activities, leading to accusations of corruption and nepotism. These business ventures, combined with the estimated 20-to 40-percent share of the government's yearly budget for defence spending and millions in yearly foreign military aid, make the military one of the largest economic players in the country.[49] Unfortunately, the top management of all these organisations, which mostly comprises retired officers, is not trained to manage corporate ventures resulting in wastage of resources. The profitability of most of these organisations is questionable. Out of 96 businesses run by the military, only 9 file public accounts. The Foundations have also caused indirect financial loss to the exchequer in the form of non-payment of taxes, wangling loans or through paying lower taxes.

2014 National Action Plan

Military intervention in politics has been an important feature in Pakistan's politics. For more than half of its existence since independence in 1947, Pakistan has been ruled directly or indirectly by the military. On December 16, 2014, terrorists attacked the Army Public School in Peshawar leading to the death of 153 people, including 132 school children. As the nation mourned the tragedy, the civil and military leadership vowed to act sternly against terrorism. In an All Parties Conference (APC) called by Prime Minister Nawaz Sharif on December 24, 2014, the government came up with a twenty-point National Action Plan (NAP) as a response to the Peshawar incident. The highlight of the NAP was the proposal to establish special courts headed by the military officers. The proposal was later followed by the adoption of the 21st Constitutional Amendment

Bill and the Pakistan Army (Amendment) Bill, 2015 by the Parliament on January 06, 2015. The establishment of the military courts was termed as an extraordinary solution to an extraordinary problem by the government.[50] In order to meet the challenges to country's demoralised civilian justice system', in December 2014 the Pakistan army has strengthened its legal department by creating a new post of Director General Lawfare Directorate (DG LD) headed by a Major General.[51]

The NAP has followed two earlier strategies of the Sharif government to counter terrorism in the country. First, a 64-point National Internal Security Policy (NISP), approved by the federal cabinet in February 2014; and second, the Protection of Pakistan Act (PoPA), 2014.[52] The NAP assigned a prominent role for the military and contains essential law enforcement objectives, including action against banned jihadi groups, regulating the *madrassas*[53] and curbing terror financing.

The NAP's 20-points[54] relate to implementing existing laws and preventing banned organisations from operating and regrouping under new names. It dictates terrorist funding; dismantling terrorist communication networks and prohibiting private militias The NAP also covers against spreading hatred, sectarianism, intolerance and the dissemination of hate literature.[55] The NAP speaks about regulating the *madrassa* sector, rehabilitating internally displaced persons, introducing administrative and development reforms in FATA, and empowering the Balochistan government to lead in political reconciliation with all stakeholders. A number of bodies have been formed to oversee NAP's implementation. Policy guidelines are provided by a Central Committee, which is chaired by the Prime Minister and nine Cabinet members, along with 15 subcommittees to oversee specific NAP components. However, very little information is in public domain about the functioning and deliberations of the sub-committees. There are serious concerns in Pakistan that the military would use the committees to marginalise elected governments in the centre and the provinces. It has been alleged that the military takes all decisions in the province's apex committee.[56]

Peshawar attacks led to passing of 21st Constitutional amendments in Pakistan and establishment of special military courts for a period of two years to try civilians accused of terrorism related offences.[57] It means that the special military courts will cease to function on January 7, 2017. The main aim of NAP and the lifting of the moratorium on the death penalty was to execute 'terrorists' swiftly and effectively and send a strong message to perpetrators. The civil society in Pakistan firmly believes that 21st Amendment was passed because the military wanted it, not the civilians.[58] The next chapter will discuss the existing military justice system of Pakistan and the trial procedure being followed in the special military courts i.e., Field General Court Martial (FGCM).

Notes

1. Muhammad Ali Jinnah was not a thinker or a philosopher. He was a politician. In the early period of his political career, he was the staunch Indian nationalist and anti-British. When he joined Muslim League, he changed his stance and championed the cause of the Muslim community of the subcontinent. He supported the two-nation theory and in a number of his speeches declared that the Hindus and Muslims are two separate nations with different culture, customs and traditions. The two-nation theory became a hallmark of the Pakistan movement. When Jinnah delivered his August 11, 1947 speech, declaring all religious communities equal in the soon-to-be-born Pakistan, it not only shocked but surprised the leadership of the Muslim League and the bureaucracy. That's why the speech was censored. In 1949, when the Objectives Resolution was passed by the Legislative Assembly, Muhammad Ali Jinnah became irrelevant to Pakistani politics. It was decided that Pakistan would be a religious country. All three Constitutions of Pakistan were drafted in light of the Objectives Resolution. As a result, the Pakistani state has become an Islamic state and the process of Islamisation is continuing unabated. Ali Mubarak, Jinnah's Pakistan, *The Express Tribune*, August 14, 2010.
2. Islamic law constitutes one of the major legal systems in the world today. In many Arab countries it still forms the basis of the legal system though in many instances it has been reformed and codified. Many countries with majority Muslim populations are officially Islamic states and their constitutions contain provisions to the effect that Islam is the state religion and that all laws should be in conformity with Islam. This applies to Pakistan as well as to Afghanistan, Iran and Tunisia. Lau Martin, The Independence of Judges under Islamic Law, International Law and the New Afghan Constitution, *ZaoRV*, Vol. 64, 2004, pp. 917-927.
3. Pakistan: Human Rights Violations and the decline of the rule of law, Amnesty International Report.
4. O'Sullivan Michael and Krithika Subramanian, *The End of Globalization or a more Multi-polar World?* Credit Suisse AG, Switzerland, September 2015, p. 41.
5. Pakistan has 643,800 active military personnel (Army 550,000, Air Force 70,000, Navy 23,800) and 304,000 paramilitary forces. *The Military Balance*, International Institute for Strategic Studies, (London: Routledge, 2014), p. 269. At the time of partition of the British India in 1947, the Pakistan got six armoured, eight artillery and eight infantry regiments. The Pakistan Army had only one Division (the 7th). The 8th and 9th Divisions were raised in 1947; the 10th, 12th and 14th Divisions were raised in 1948. The 15th Division was raised in 1950. At some point before 1954,

6th Division was raised and the 9th Division was disbanded. The 6th Division was disbanded at some point after 1954 as the US assistance was available only for one armoured and six infantry divisions. Pakistan has always alleged that the division of assets including those related to the military was unjust. Behuria Ashok and Sumita Kumar, 'The Army of Pakistan: Dominant by Default', in Vishal Chandra (ed.). *India's Neighbourhood: The Armies of South Asia*, (New Delhi: Pentagon Press, 2011), p. 122.

6. The Pakistani Army is commanded by the Chief of the Army Staff (COAS), who operates from the General Headquarters, Rawalpindi, close to Islamabad, the capital of Pakistan. He is assisted at the level of Lieutenant General by eight principal staff officers. They include the Chief of General Staff, who is responsible for the functioning of Military Operations and Intelligence Directorates; the Chief of Logistics Staff; the Adjutant General; the Quarter-Master General; the Inspector General of Training and Evaluation; and the Military Secretary. In 2008, the incumbent COAS, Pervez Kayani, added two more Principal Staff Officers, viz., the Inspector General of Arms, and the Inspector General of Communications and IT. Behuria Ashok K. and Sumita Kumar, 'The Army of Pakistan: Dominant by Default', in Chandra Vishal (ed.)., *India's Neighbourhood: The Armies of South Asia*, (New Delhi: Pentagon Press, 2013), p. 127.
7. Available at: http://www,un.org/en/peacekeeping/resources/statistics/contributors.shtml, accessed on April 19, 2016.
8. After the death of General Zia ul-Haq, the Vice Chief of Army Staff Lt. Gen. Mirza Aslam Beg invited Ishaq Khan (an elderly bureaucrat who had been late Zia's most trusted civilian associate) for a meeting being held in the military headquarters. Immediately after the meeting Ishaq Khan became the President and Beg took over as the Army Chief. Isha Khan announced the holding of parliamentary elections. The ISI assembled a coalition of Islamist and pro-military parties, named the Islami Jamhoori Ittehad (IJI—Islamic Democratic Alliance) to serve as the military's proxy in elections. The IJI's most resourceful leader was Nawaz Sharif, a young industrialist whom Zia ul-Haq had appointed Chief Minister of the Punjab. Haqqani Hussain. *Pakistan: Between Mosque and Military*, (Gurgaon, India: Penguin Books, 2016), pp. 222-224.
9. One organisation in Pakistan which had benefited most during the Afghan war years was the ISI. It became a clumsy, frequently blundering, hydra-headed monster of great influence. In the realm of domestic politics, the ISI remained busy in dislodging governments. The driving force behind the ISI continued to be the military hierarchy, but the agency has been increasingly operating independently as well. The ISI believes that it has inherent right to decide the national interest. Abbas Hasan, Pakistan Through the Lens of the "Triple A" Theory, *The Fletcher Forum of World Affairs*, Vol. 30, No. 1, Winter 2006, pp. 181-192.
10. *The Military Balance* , International Institute for Strategic Studies (London: Routledge, 2014) p. 218.
11. Behuria Ashok K. and Sumita Kumar, 'The Army of Pakistan: Dominant by Default', in Chandra Vishal (ed.). *India's Neighbourhood: The Armies of South Asia*,(New Delhi: Pentagon Press, 2013) p. 121.
12. An Introduction to Pakistan's Military, Belfer Centre for Science and International Affairs, 2011, available at:http://www.operationspaix.net/data/document/4025 ~ v ~ An_Introduction_to_Pakistan_s_Military.pdf, accessed on March 9, 2016.

13. Under the Martial Law regimes, the functions of government were carried on under Laws (Continuance in Force) Orders or Provisional Constitution Orders. Martial law was declared in Pakistan in 1958, 1969, 1977, 1999 and 2007.
14. President Iskander Mirza disbanded the Legislative Assembly on October 7, 1958, and declared Martial Law. General Mohammad Ayub Khan, Pakistan's first Army Commander in Chief, assisted Mirza in abrogating the constitution of 1956 and removing the politicians he believed were bringing Pakistan to the point of collapse.
15. Article 245 of the 1973 Constitution provides that the Armed Forces shall, under the direction of the Federal Government, defend Pakistan against external aggression or threat of war, and, subject to law, act in aid of civil power when called upon to do so. Article 148 states that it shall be the duty of the Federation to protect every Province against external aggression and internal disturbance and to ensure the Government of every Province is carried on in accordance with the provisions of the Constitution.
16. In his proclamation, President Mirza abrogated the Constitution, dismissed the central and provincial governments, dissolved the National Assembly and the provincial assemblies of the East and West Pakistan, banned all political parties and postponed the general elections indefinitely. Prime Minister and members of cabinet were put under house arrest.
17. *The State v. Dosso* PLD 1958 SC 533.
18. The preamble of the Constitution of 1962, stated as follows: "Now therefore, I, Field Marshal Mohammad Ayub Khan, Hilal-i-Pakistan, Hilal-i-Jura'at, President of Pakistan, in exercise of mandate given to me on the Fourteenth day of February, 1960, by the people of Pakistan, do hereby enact this Constitution."
19. Martial Law (Pending Proceedings and {Protection) Order 1962, President Order No. 26 of 1962.
20. Articles 4 to 8, Martial Law (Pending Proceedings and {Protection) Order 1962, President Order No. 26 of 1962.
21. The first amendment also made a significant change in the renaming of the Republic as the 'Islamic Republic of Pakistan'. Constitution (First Amendment) Act, 1963, Act I of 1964.
22. The Constitution provided that the Minister of Defence must be of rank of Lieutenant General (or equivalent in the Air Force and Navy); Article 238, the Constitution of Pakistan, 1962.
23. Article 245, the Constitution of Pakistan, 1973.
24. Article 6, the Constitution of Pakistan, 1973.
25. At one of the Formation Commanders' Meeting, various officers conveyed him (Zia) the 'shame that many officers feel in wearing their uniform in public', since masses had come to associate the army with dictatorship and harsh Islamic justice, many of these officers were sub-martial administrators, who had to deal with summary punishments meted out by military courts, which included public flogging and lashing. Nawaz Shuja. *Cross Swords: Pakistan, Its Army and the Wars Within*, (Oxford: Oxford University Press, 2008) p. 379.
26. *Sh Liaquat Hussain v. Federation of Pakistan* PLD1999 SC 504.
27. Provisional Constitutional Order PLD 1999 Central Statutes 448.
28. Ahmed Naveed and Syeda Mahpara Safder, Paradoxes of Judicial Independence in Pakistan: Some Reflections from the US, *South Asian Studies*, Vol. 29, No.2, July-December 2014, pp. 483-496.

29. See: Ahmed Naveed and Syeda Mahpara Safder, Paradoxes of Judicial Independence in Pakistan: Some Reflections from the US, *South Asian Studies*, Vol. 29, No.2, July-December 2014, pp. 483-496.
30. The Constitution of Pakistan contains specific provisions for the independence of the judiciary. The Preamble and Article 2–A of the Constitution state that the independence of the judiciary shall be fully secured. With a view to achieve this, Article 175 further provides that the judiciary shall be separated progressively from the executive. The Supreme Court in the cases of *Government of Sindh v. Sharaf Fafridi* PLD 1994 SC 1054; *Al-Jehad Trust v. Federation of Pakistan* PLD 1996 SC 324; *Malik Asad Ali v. Federation of Pakistan* PLD 1998 SC 1616; *Mehram Ali v. Federation of Pakistan* PLD 1998 SC 1445; and *Liaquat Hussain v. Federation of Pakistan* PLD 1999 SC 504 has clarified the constitutional provisions and strengthened the principle of judicial independence and the separation of the judiciary from the executive. In addition Article 209 of the Constitution provides for the constitution of a 'Supreme Judicial Council of Pakistan' to deal with the issues relating to higher judiciary.
31. The *Quran* does not contain any express provision on the independence of the judiciary, however, the Supreme Court of Pakistan in the case of *Al-Jehad Trust v. Federation of Pakistan* PLD 1996 SC 324 has observed: Upon the advent of Islam, judicial functions were separated from the executive functions at its very initial stage....The reason being that the foundation of Islam is justice. The concept of justice in Islam is different from the concept of the remedial justice of the Greeks, the natural justice of the Romans or the formal justice of the Anglo-Saxons. Justice in Islam seeks to attain a higher standard of what we may call 'absolute justice' or 'absolute fairness'.
32. *Zafar Ali Shah v General Pervez Musharraf* 2000 SCMR 1137: PLD 2000 SC 869.
33. *Al-Jehad Trust v. Federation of Pakistan* PLD 1996 SC 324.
34. Seventh United Nations Congress on the Prevention of Crime and the Treatment of offenders, 1985.
35. For instance during General Yahya's Martial Law government reacted by promulgating the Courts (Removal of Doubts) Order, 1969, to remind the judges the limitations of their powers. General Zia placed restriction on the superior courts in October 1979, by inserting a new Article 212-A in the Constitution. Through this amendment, the power of judicial review, reserved for the superior courts by the Supreme Court in *Begum Nusrat Bhutto's case*, was completely nullified. In May 1980, General Zia further curbed the powers of High Court (retrospectively) available under Article 199 of the constitution through Presidential order No.1 of 1980, promulgated on May 27, 1980. This order restricted the "writ jurisdiction" of the High Courts and barred them from making an order relating to the validity or effect of any Martial Law regulation or any Martial Law order. The order also prohibited the High Courts from reviewing the judgments or sentences passed by military courts or tribunals. By promulgating Provisional Constitution Order (PCO) 1981, General Zia extinguished the "necessity" regime as sanctioned by the Supreme Court in *Begum Nusrat Bhutto's case* [PLD 1977 SC 657].
36. Shah Amanullah, Impact of Army on the Judiciary in Pakistan, available at: http://www.gu.edu.pk/New/GUJR/PDF/Dec-2009/7%20Amanullah%20Shah-Impact%20of%20Army%20on%20the%20Judiciary.pdf, accessed on March 11, 2016.
37. On November 3, 2007, General Musharraf imposed fifth Martial Law under nomenclature of emergency, sacked the judges of the superior courts and kept them

under house arrest for more than two weeks. The deposed Chief Justice of Pakistan, Justice Iftikhar remained under house arrest for the period of more than five months.

38. Ashraf Sajjad, Pakistan Reinforces Resolve to Fight Terror, ISAS Insight, No. 288, August 28, 2015.
39. Besides security policy making, the militaries in Asia and elsewhere frequently engage in socioeconomic activities, including nation building. The military's economic activities span a wide spectrum, including the management of defence production, manufacturing of commercial goods, ownership of television and radio broadcasting networks and news papers, management of national airlines, shipping corporations and utilities, farming, and rural development. The military's social service activities include rural health, education and relief work during natural disaster. These activities may be undertaken in a nonpartisan manner as part of national development at the behest of national government, alternatively the military may engage in these roles on its own initiative in order to strengthen its power and influence vis-à-vis other state institutions. A number of Asian militaries also engage in illegal activities such as drug trafficking, smuggling and extortion. At times they collude with local militias, bosses, and thugs to carry out political intimidations while bolstering their own personal fortunes. Algappa Muthiah (ed.). *Coercion and Governance: The Declining Political Role of the Military in Asia* (California: Stanford University Press, 2001), pp. 36-37.
40. The economic empire of the Pakistan military is not limited to the Fauzi Foundation (FF), Shaheen Foundation (SF), and Army Welfare Trust (AWT). It extends beyond and includes National Logistic Cell (NLC), the Frontier Works Organisation and the Special Communications Organization (SCO) which are controlled by the army. Siddiqa Ayesha, *Military Inc: Inside Pakistan's Military Economy*, London: Pluto Press, pp. 112-113. The Pakistan Air Force has followed the army in establishing its own Foundation in 1977. Its activities are confined to the aviation but have also ventured into the real estate, IT and knitwear. Pakistan Navy followed suit in 1982 and established Bahria Foundation (BF). It started projects related to the harbour services, dredging, diving and salvaging. The navy's real estate and housing ventures have limited success. Bangash, L. Gen (Retd) Humayun Khan, Military's Commercial Interests, Issue Paper, Civil-Military Relations, Pakistan Institute of Legislative Development and Transparency-PILDAT, July 2014, p. 9.
41. The origins of business activities go back to the British period, when the British Indian army created a welfare fund as a share of the Post-war Services Reconstruction Fund that was bequeathed to the Pakistan army. It provided the initial funds for the establishment of the Fauji Foundation. The rest of the foundations were established during subsequent Martial Laws in the 1970s and 1980s. For more details see: Siddiqa Ayesha, *Military Inc.: Inside Pakistan's Military Economy* (London: Pluto Press, 2007).
42. The manipulation of the economic foundations for political and institutional purposes allegedly began during General Zia-ul-Haq's regime. Zia used the top positions in the Foundations as reward to officers after their retirement for exceptional obedience towards him and to sideline those who posed a threat. Officers serving in the top managerial positions enjoy all perks and privileges that they would in their military positions. The placement of military officials in key positions in the Ministry of Defence and in the Ministry of Finance by various military rulers has made these institutions subservient to military interests.

43. Book shines light on Pakistan military's '£10bn empire', *The Guardian*, available at: http://www.theguardian.com/world/2007/may/31/books.pakistan, accessed on December 10, 2016.
44. Land of impure, *The Economist*, June 17, 2010, available at: http://www.economist.com/node/16377259, accessed on March 11, 2016.
45. Parliament should watch over military's business activities: senator, Pakistan Today, May 19, 2014, http://www.pakistantoday.com.pk/2014/05/19/national/parliament-should-watch-over-militarys-business-activities-senator/, accessed on January 12, 2016.
46. After retirement, Lt. Gen. Humayun Khan Bangash was the CEO of World Call Tele-communication company for five years. As Adjutant General of Pakistan Army he was a member of Committee of Administration of Fauji Foundation and Chairman of Army Welfare Trust. He was the Founding Chairman of Askari Bank Limited, when it was setup in 1992.
47. See in general: Bangash, Lt. Gen. (Retd) Humayun Khan, Military's Commercial Interests, Issue Paper, Civil-Military Relations, Pakistan Institute of Legislative Development and Transparency-PILDAT, July 2014.
48. Bangash, Lt. Gen. (Retd) Humayun Khan, Military's Commercial Interests, Issue Paper, Civil-Military Relations, Pakistan Institute of Legislative Development and Transparency-PILDAT, July 2014, p. 10.
49. Pakistan Cultural Intelligence Studies: Pakistan Military Culture, Product Number: MCIA-2420-PAK-001-12, November 2011, available at: https://info.publicintelligence.net/MCIA-PakistanMilitaryCulture.pdf, accessed on May 10, 2015.
50. Peshawar Tragedy: Responses by the Civilian and Military Leadership in the Context of Civil-Military Relations, Pakistan Institute of Legislative Development and Transparency (PILDAT), PILDAT Monitor, December 2014.
51. For details, see: Army gears up for legal battles, *Dawn*, January 2, 2015 available at: http://www.dawn.com/news/1154555/armygears-up-for-legal-battles,accessed on March 12, 2015.
52. The NISP called for modernising all aspects of the criminal justice system, along with better oversight and regulation of mosques and madrassas, and a range of "soft" interventions. The PoPA empowered security agencies, including the military and paramilitary forces, to hold suspects in preventive detention for up to 90 days, detaining suspects without revealing their whereabouts except to the Supreme Court or a High Court, and concealing the reasons for detention. Military and paramilitary personnel and police officers were given broad discretion in exercising shoot-to-kill authority. The PoPA also called for creation of special courts to try cases in which the burden of proof would shift to the accused and proceedings would be held in-camera. Revisiting Counter-terrorism Strategies in Pakistan: Opportunities and Pitfalls, International Crisis Group, Asia Report No. 271, July 22, 2015.
53. Madrassas or seminary (plural madris) is school that imparts secondary and post-secondary religious education using a specialized curriculum, Dars-i-Nizami. Pakistan's madrassas have attracted the attention of policymakers in the United States and elsewhere since the 9/11 terrorist attacks. Even though none of the attackers studied in madaris in Pakistan or elsewhere, madaris are alleged to be incubators of militants in Pakistan and responsible for creating communities of support for militancy in the region. Fair C. Christine.. *The Madrassa Challenge: Militancy and Religious Education in Pakistan*, (Washington DC: United State Institute of Peace Press, 2006).

54. The list of 20-point National Action Plan is as follows: 1. To enforce executions for terrorists sentenced to death. 2. To avoid criminals evading punishment due to weaknesses in the legal system, special trial courts will be established under military officers so such elements can be dealt with without delay. These courts will exist for two years. Constitutional amendments will be made for these courts. 3. No armed militant group or organisation will be allowed to operate. 4. The anti-terrorism organisation, NACTA, will be strengthened and activated. 5. Censoring Literature, newspapers and magazines that are spreading hate, violence sectarianism, extremism and intolerance. 6. All funding for terrorists and terrorist organisations will be eliminated. 7. Banned organisations will not be allowed to re-establish themselves under another name. 8. A special anti-terrorism force of 10,000 soldiers will be created. 9. Action is being taken to stop religious extremism and protect minorities. 10. The government will register and regulate all madarssas. 11. Print and electronic media will be banned from glorifying the views of terrorists and terrorist organisations. 12. Reforms in FATA will be given priority to ensure the speedy return of internally displaced persons. 13. The communication networks of terrorists will be completely dismantled. 14. The government will take steps to stop the spread of terrorism on the Internet and social media. 15. There will be no space left for terrorism in any part of the country, including Punjab. 16. The ongoing operation in Karachi will continue until it accomplishes its goals. 17. For broader political consensus, stakeholders will work to empower the Balochistan government. 18. Decisive action will be taken against sectarian elements. 19. A comprehensive policy for the repatriation of Afghan refugees is being developed. 20. The government will focus on legislation to ensure provincial intelligence organisations get access to terrorists' communication networks and anti-terrorism organisations.
55. In Pakistan, the loudspeaker is used at mosques to deliver sermons and sometimes to incite violence and hatred against other groups. Some laws exist to limit the use of the loudspeaker, such as the Punjab Sound System (Regulations) Ordinance 2015, which allows only one speaker for Azan and restricts Arabic sermons to Friday. For violating the loudspeaker law, the police have arrested over 3900 people. In a landmark decision, Anti-Terrorism Court has sentenced a prayer leader in the city of Kasur to 5 years imprisonment for delivering a hate speech at a public gathering. While these are good steps and solid metrics, the assault on minorities has not let up, when compared to the overall decline of terror attacks.
56. Revisiting Counter-terrorism Strategies in Pakistan: Opportunities and Pitfalls, International Crisis Group, Asia Report No. 271, July 22, 2015, p. 7.
57. Malik Salma, *Pakistan in 2015: A Forecast*, Institute of Peace and Conflict Studies (IPCS) Special Report No. 171, January 2015, p. 24.
58. Mir Waqqas, Saying not what the Constitution is...but what it should be: Comment on the Judgment on the 18th and 21st Amendments to the Constitution, *LUMS Law Journal*, Vol. 2, 2015, pp. 64-76.

2

Military Legal System

Introduction

In most of the countries in the world, the armed forces are governed by a special code of conduct to ensure discipline amongst the military personnel and others who are associated with it. The British military legal system adopted for the mercenary forces in undivided India was followed by Pakistan, when it got independence in 1947. Laws relating to Pakistan Army, Air Force, and Navy are contained in three different sets of statutes, with include Acts, Ordinances and Rules. The Pakistan Army is governed by the Army Act, 1952, the Army Act Rules, 1954, the Regulations, and the Orders issued by the Chief Of the Army Staff. The basic law of the Pakistan Navy is contained in the Navy Ordinance, 1961, while the Air Force is governed by the Air Force Act, 1953. The nomenclature and composition of military courts vary slightly according to the service, but the procedures of military courts, type of offences, scale of punishments, jurisdictional authority, review and appeal are almost identical in the three services. In addition, certain provisions of the Pakistan Penal Code, 1860, the Civil Procedure Code, 1908 and the Criminal Procedure Code, 1898 also relate to functioning of the three wings of the military forces. Pakistan armed forces have tried to maintain an Islamic identity, and related amendments in military legal systems have been undertaken.

Institution of Court Martial is a primary tool in the hands of a Commander to enforce discipline amongst his troops. Commanding Officers and other senior officers in military also have power to discipline the troops by awarding minor punishments without intervention of Court Martial to those accused of not so serious offence. Such power of punishment depends upon the rank of the accused and the rank and appointment of the Military Commander. For instance a Commanding

Officer may award 28 days of detention, rigorous imprisonment, or field punishment to a person below the rank of non-commissioned officer.[1] In this study, for the sake of clarity, reference is made only to laws relating to the Pakistan Army; i.e., the Army Act, 1952, the Army Act Rules, 1954, and the Regulations for the Army.

Jurisdiction

The Army Act, 1952, gives Courts Martial jurisdiction over military personnel, civilians working in the military establishments, and other civilians who are accused of seducing any military person from his duty or allegiance to the government. Every person subject to the Army Act remains so, until duly retired, released, discharged, removed or dismissed from the service. A retired military person can also be tried by a Court Martial, if the alleged offence was committed while he was subject to the Army Act. He can be taken into and kept in military custody and tried and punished for such offence as if he had continued to be so subject to. However, it is necessary that his trial should commence within six months after he has ceased to be the subject to the Act. This period of six months would not be applicable in cases of offences of desertion, fraudulent enrolment, mutiny, insubordination, and frauds relating to property. If the military personnel is accused of aforesaid offences, he could be tried by a Court Martial or criminal court.[2] Jurisdiction of a Court Martial does not depend on where the offence was committed; a military accused can be tried in any place.[3]

Persons subject to the Army Act could be categorised into three categories. In the first category are Commissioned Officers, Junior Commissioned Officers, Warrant Officers and those enrolled under the Army Act on a regular basis and remain permanently subject to the Act until "duly retired, released, discharged, removed or dismissed from the service." These individuals form the bulk of the military. In addition, persons subject to the Air Force Act and the Navy Ordinance, when seconded for service with the army remain become subject to the Army Act during the period of their second spell.

The second category covers civilians who are employed within the military establishments, but become subject to the Army Act only on active service. Accordingly, it has been provided under section 2 (C) of the Army Act that the Act will be applicable to: Persons not otherwise subject to the Army Act who are on active service in camp, on the march, or at any frontier post specified by the Federal Government by notification in this behalf, are employed by, or are in the service of or are followers of, or accompany any portion of the army. The term "active service" means the time during which the military or a part of it is engaged in operations against an enemy or is engaged in a military operation.[4] The Federal Government may also place the army on active service even when they are no such operations.

The third category consists of civilians, who are not a part of the military but accused of (i) seducing or attempting to seduce any person subject to the Army Act from his duty or allegiance to the Government, or (ii) having committed in relation to the Pakistan Armed Forces any offence punishable under the Official Secrets Act, 1923.[5] In Pakistan, the Chiefs of Army Staff (COAS) while exercising powers as Chief Martial Law Administrators have amended the law to bring civilians and other criminals within the ambit of the Army Act for trial.[6] On January 6, 2015, less than a month after a terrorist attack on the Army Public School in Peshawar[7], Parliament voted to amend the Constitution of Pakistan,[8] and the Army Act, to allow military Court Martial to try civilians for offences related to terrorism committed by those who claim to, or are known to, belong to a terrorist organisation "using the name of religion or a sect".[9] For speedy trial of terrorists and other involved in waging war or insurrection against Pakistan, the Army Act was amended twice in 2015. The amendments have a sunset clause of two years, after which they will cease to be in effect, although there is always a possibility they could be reintroduced.

The amendments also bring certain offences included in Protection of Pakistan Act, 2014 within the jurisdiction of military courts. These offences include: crimes against minorities; killing, kidnapping, extortion, attacks or assaults on government officials, members of the judiciary, foreign officials, tourists, media personnel, social workers or "other important personalities"; destruction of or attacks on energy facilities, gas or oil pipelines, aircrafts and airports, national defence materials and institutions, and educational institutions; illegally crossing national boundaries "in connection with" any of the above-mentioned offences. The amendments extend the jurisdiction of military courts only to those who claim to or are alleged to both belong to organisations that use the name of "religion or a sect" and to have carried out the above listed offences. Those charged with committing acts of violence and terrorism, including those listed above, who are accused of being members of, for example, separatist or nationalist groups, do not come under the ambit of the amendments. After the amendments made in 1967, 1975, 2007 and 2015, section 2 of the Army Act reads as follows:

Persons subject to the Act:

The following persons are subject to the Pakistan Army Act, namely:

A. Officers, junior commissioned officers and warrant officers of the Pakistan Army and those enrolled under the Army Act;
B. Persons subject to the Pakistan Navy Ordinance, 1961 or the Pakistan Air Force Act, 1953 when seconded for service with the Pakistan Army as directed by the Federal Government;
C. Persons not otherwise subject to the Army Act, who, on active service, in camp, on the march or at any frontier post specified by the Federal Government by notification in this behalf, are employed by, or are in the service of, or are followers of, or accompany any portion of, the Pakistan Army;
D. Persons not otherwise subject to the Army Act, who are accused of:
    i. seducing or attempting to seduce any person subject to the Army Act from his duty or allegiance to the Government, or
    ii. having committed, in relation to any work of defence, arsenal, naval, military or air force establishment or station, ship or aircraft or otherwise in relation to the naval, military or air force affairs of Pakistan, an offence under the Official Secrets Act, 1923;
    iii. claiming or are known to belong to any terrorist group or organisation using the name of religion or a sect[10]; and (a) raise arms or wage war against Pakistan, or attack the Armed

Forces of Pakistan or law enforcement agencies or attack any civil or military installation in Pakistan; or (b) abduct any person for ransom, or cause death of any person or injury; or (c) possess, store, fabricate or transport the explosives, fire-arms, instruments, articles, suicide jackets; or (d) use or design vehicles for terrorist acts; or (e) provide or receive funding from any foreign or local source for the illegal activities under this provision; or (f) act or over-awe the state or any section of the public or sect or religious minority; or (g) create terror or insecurity in Pakistan or attempt to commit any of the said acts within or outside Pakistan; shall be punished under this Act; and

iv. claiming or are known to have belonged to any terrorist group or organisation using the name of religion or a sect and raise arms or wage war against Pakistan, commits an offence under certain provisions[11] of the Protection of Pakistan Act, 2014;

Provided that any person who is alleged to have abetted, aided or conspired in commission of any offence falling under sub-paragraph (iii) or (iv) above shall be tried under the Army Act, wherever he may have committed that offence;

Provided further that notwithstanding anything contained in this Act or any other law for the time being in force, any person arrested, detained or held in custody by the armed forces, civil armed forces or law enforcement agencies and kept under arrest, custody or detention before coming into force of the Pakistan Army (Amendment) Act, 2015, shall be deemed to have been arrested or detained pursuant to the provisions of this Act as amended by the Pakistan Army (Amendment) Act, 2015 if the offence in respect of which such arrest or detention was made also constitutes an offence referred to in sub-clause (iii) or sub-clause (iv);

Provided further that no person accused of an offence falling under sub-clause (iii) or (iv) shall be prosecuted without the prior sanction of the Federal Government.

- Every person subject to this Act under clause (A) shall remain so subject until duly retired, released, discharged, removed, or dismissed from the service.
- Every person subject to this Act under clause (B) shall remain so subject during the period of his secondment to the Pakistan Army.
- The Federal Government shall have the power to transfer any proceedings in respect of any person who is accused of any offence falling under sub-clause (iii) or (iv) above, pending in any court for trial under this Act.
- Any proceedings after transfer shall be deemed to have been instituted under this Act.
- Where a case has been transferred, it shall not be necessary to recall any witness or again record any evidence that may have been recorded.[12]

When a Notification has been issued by the Federal Government, declaring the whole of the army on active service, civilians working in the army on active service could be tried by Field General Court Martial.[13] The words, "persons not otherwise subject to this Act" used in clause (C) includes all those civilians or persons who are connected with the Army, but should be made subject to it in circumstances gravely affecting the maintenance of discipline in the Army. Therefore, even a retired military person can be brought within the ambit of the Act if accused of seducing certain members of the military forces in Pakistan.[14]

By an amendment in 1977, entire population of a district was made subject to the jurisdiction of Pakistan Army Act, 1952, rendering them liable for trial under the Act for a large number of offences under the Pakistan Penal Code, 1860 and other penal laws. An exclusive jurisdiction was conferred upon Court Martial to convict civilians of entire district for such offences, and ordinary criminal courts of the district were deprived of jurisdiction to try civilians of such district, unless the case was transferred to them by the authorised military officer. It was held by the Supreme Court that the Army Act was primarily meant for maintaining internal discipline of the military personnel and those civilians directly connected with the armed forces. Making sweeping amendments in the

Army Act and bringing entire civilian population of province, or any part thereof, within the ambit of the Act was totally against the object and reasons of the Act, hence a fraud upon the statue.[15]

Arrest and Custody

The Army Act, 1952 confers powers of arrest. The method of arresting a person subject to the Army Act is informal. The offences are not classified as cognisable and non-cognisable, and no warrant is issued or required to be issued for carrying out an arrest. The order for placing the person under arrest can be oral or written. The authorities competent to arrest a person subject to the Army Act are (a) any superior officer, when the person to be arrested is charged with an offence; (b) any officer, irrespective of rank, when the person, being an officer is engaged in a quarrel, affray or disorder; and (c) a provost marshal.[16] Civilians accused of offence punishable under sections 3 of the Official Secrets Act, 1923, in relation to military affairs of Pakistan can be arrested and detained by military authorities.[17] In military there are two types of arrests, the "open arrest" and the "closed arrest". The restraint imposed under each type is according to the usages of the service and the regulations. Under closed arrest, a person is usually confined to a room or barracks and remains under the escort of a person of equal rank. Under open arrest, he remains under a moral restraint not to go beyond a certain area, usually the camp. Unless justified, arrested persons cannot be kept in solitary confinement and cannot be blind-folded during air journey in custody from one place to another[18]. The Supreme Court has held that under Army Regulations (Instructions) No 269A blind-folding and handcuffing of offender was permissible during his transportation from unit to the place of trial for the offence of waging war against the government.[19]

The Commanding Officers have specific duty to take care that a person under his command when charged with an offence is not detained in custody for more than 48 hours after the committal of such person into custody is reported to him, without the charge being investigated, unless investigation within that period seems to him to be impracticable. The case of every person, being detained in custody beyond a period of 48 hours, and the reason thereof, to be reported by the Commanding

Officer[20] to superior officer and to whom application would be made to convene a General or District Court Martial for the trial of the person charged. In reckoning the period of 48 hours, all public holidays shall be excluded.[21] The Commanding Officer can try an accused by awarding summary punishment, if the offence charged with is not very serious and the accused is a non-commissioned officer or below in rank.

If the Commanding Officer remands the case for trial by Court Martial, the case is adjourned for recording a 'summary of evidence' against the accused. A 'summary of evidence' is a written statement of the evidence similar to depositions taken at a magistrate's court. Its chief purpose is to give particulars of evidence in respect of the charge or charges to the Commanding Officer, the convening officer and the accused. The accused is not entitled to be represented at the recording of the summary of evidence but he can cross-examine all witnesses who depose against him. After conclusion of summary of evidence, the Commanding Officer can still try the accused summarily if within his power, or he can make an application to a competent officer for trial by a Court Martial.

Kinds of Court Martial

Pakistan Army Act provides for four kinds of Court Martial, General Court Martial (GCM), District Court Martial (DCM), Field General Court Martial (FGCM), and Summary Court Martial (SCM). A GCM may be convened by the Chief of the Army Staff (COAS) or by an officer empowered on this behalf by the warrant of the COAS. A DCM may be convened by an authority having power to convene a GCM or by an officer empowered in this behalf by a warrant of any such authority. A warrant issued for the convening of GCM or DCM may contain restrictions, reservations or conditions, as the issuing authority may think fit. The FGCM may be convened by any of the following authorities: (i) an officer empowered in this behalf by an order of the Federal Government or the COAS; (ii) on active service,[22] an officer commanding a portion of the army, not below the rank of Brigadier, if in the opinion of such officer commanding, it is not practicable with due regard to the discipline and the exigencies of the service to try the alleged offender by GCM. The opinion of the officer to hold FGCM must be in writing and to be conclusive.[23] Depending on the rank of the accused and the severity of the alleged offence, the accused's Commanding Officer enjoys great discretion to try him summarily or by a Summary Court Martial or refer the case to a superior authority to assemble a FGCM, GCM or DCM. An accused has no right to choose any particular kind of Court Martial.

Composition of Court Martial

A GCM consists of minimum five officers, each of whom must have held commissioned service of three years and of whom not less than four would be of the rank of Captain. A DCM consists of minimum three officers, each of whom must have held commission for at least two years. A FGCM consists of minimum three officers. Unlike the GCM and DCM, the Army Act does make any stipulation about the seniority of the officers constituting a FGCM. A SCM is held by the Commanding Officer alone, however, it must be attended by two officers/ junior commissioned officers or one of the either. The officers/ junior commissioned do not take any part in the proceedings, however the Commanding Officer may consult them. In the trial of an accused who is a Muslim for an offence punishable under an Islamic Law, the Commanding Officer holding the trial by SCM, and the officers/ junior commissioned officers must be Muslim. In case, the Commanding Officer is a non-Muslim, a Muslim officer shall be appointed by the formation commander for holding a SCM. In case a Court Martial after the commencement of trial is reduced below the minimum number of required officers, it shall be dissolved.[24]

The Army Act of Pakistan covers three types of offence. The first type of offence is 'military' in character and concerns, for example, offences in relation to enemy, mutiny, desertion, assault, negligent performance of duty, malingering, destruction of service property and insubordinate conduct. The second type of offence is criminal in nature and relates to acts such as assault and the falsification of documents. The third type of offence is related to civilian criminal offences and concerns, specifically acts such as serious assault, murder of a service person and fraud.

A person subject the Army Act can be tried by a Court Martial for any offence committed by him which is listed in the Act or any other penal codes of the country. There is an exception that for the three serious civil offences if committed against a civilian, i.e., murder, culpable homicide not amounting to murder, or *Zina* or *Zina-bil-jabr*, a person subject the Army Act cannot be tried by a Court Martial.[25] However, for these serious offences also he could be tried by a Court Martial, if committed while on active service, at any place outside Pakistan, or at a frontier post notified by the Federal Government.[26]

If a person subject to the Army Act is arrested by the civil police and the offence for which he is accused can be tried by a Court Martial, the custody of such person and the investigation of the offence of which he is accused may be taken over by the Commanding Officer of such person under the said Act. Section 549 of the Pakistan Criminal Procedure Code provides that the Federal Government may make rules consistent with the Code and any similar law for the time being in force [Pakistan Army Act, 1952 the Pakistan Air Force Act, 1953 and the Pakistan Navy Ordinance, 1961] as to the cases in which person subject to military naval or air force law shall be tried by a court to which this Code applies, or by Court Martial. Further, when any person is brought before a Magistrate and charged with an offence for which he is liable to be tried either by a court to which this Code applies or by a Court Martial, such Magistrate shall deliver him together with a statement of the offence of which he is accused to the Commanding Officer of the military unit for trial by a Court Martial.

The Army Act provides [27] that when a criminal court and a Court Martial have each jurisdiction in respect of an offence, it shall be the discretion of the competent officer of the military[28] to decide before which court the proceedings shall be instituted. If that officer decides that the proceedings should be instituted before a Court Martial, he shall direct that the accused person shall be detained in military custody.

In a recent case, Major Zahid Raja of the Army was arrested by the civil police for killing Islamabad Electric Supply Company (IESCO) lineman Mehboob Ahmad, when the latter reached the house of the officer to disconnect electricity connection over non-payment of dues. The army officer later dumped the dead body near Gujjar Khan with help of his cousin. Based on a written request made by the Director General GHQ seeking the trial by a Court Martial; the civil judge on January 1, 2016 ordered the Islamabad police to hand over the arrested army officer to the military police. In effect, Pakistani civilian courts have no jurisdiction over military personnel (unless the military permits the civilian courts to exercise jurisdiction) whereas, under the 21st Constitutional Amendment, military courts have jurisdiction over civilians.[29]

Power of Punishment

Under the Army Act, a Court Martial has the power to award following sentences in the descending order of severity: stoning to death; death; amputation of hand, foot or both; imprisonment for life; imprisonment for any term not exceeding 25 years; whipping not exceeding 100 stripes; dismissal from the service;[30] detention up to six months for person other than officers, JCOs or WOs; field punishment; reduction in grade or rank for persons other than officers; forfeiture of pay and service; fine; and any other punishment provided for in any Islamic law or any other law for the time being in force.[31] However, a person shall not be sentenced to stoning to death, amputation, whipping or simple imprisonment except in respect of an offence for which he is convicted under an Islamic law.[32]

Field Punishments

The Army Act also provides for the award of field punishment to persons below the rank of warrant officer. Where an offender is sentenced to field punishment, he may be during the continuance of his sentence, unless the Court Martial or the officer may direct, be punished as follows:

- He may be kept in irons, that is to say, in fetters or hand cuffs or both fetters and hand-cuffs, and may be secured so as to prevent his escape.
- When in irons, he may be attached for a period or periods not exceeding two hours in any one day to a fixed object, but he must not be so attached during more than three out of any four consecutive days, not during more than twenty-one days in all.

The offender must be attached so as to be standing firmly on his feet which, if tied, must not be more than twelve inches apart, and it must be possible, for him to move each foot at least three inches. If he is tied around the body there must be no restriction of his breathing. If his arms or wrists are tied, there must be six inches of play between them and the fixed object. His arms must swing either by the side of his body or behind his back. For the purpose of this punishment, irons should be used when available, but straps or ropes may be used in lieu of them when necessary. Any straps or ropes used for the purpose must be of sufficient width to inflict no bodily harm and leave no permanent mark on the offender. He may be subjected to the like labour, employment and restraint and dealt with in like manner as if he were undergoing a sentence of rigorous imprisonment. The field punishment should not cause injury or leave any permanent mark on the offender; and a portion of a field punishment must be discontinued upon a report by a responsible Medical Officer that the continuance of that portion be prejudicial to the offender's health. The filed punishment is to be carried out within the unit to which offender belongs or is attached so long as that unit is actually on the move, but when the unit is halted at any place where there is a provost marshal the punishment shall be carried out under the orders of that officer.

A GCM or FGCM have the power to try any person subject to the Army Act for any offence made punishable under the Act and pass any sentence authorised by the Act. A DCM has the power to try any person subject to the Army Act, except an officer, junior commissioned officer or warrant officer. It can award any sentence authorised by the Act other than a sentence of stoning to death, or death or amputation of hand, foot or both or imprisonment for more than two years or whipping exceeding 45 stripes. The power of a SCM to award the sentence is similar to that of a DCM except that it cannot award imprisonment exceeding one year or whipping exceeding 25 stripes.

Trial Procedure in Brief

A convening order is issued by the officer empowered to convene a GCM, DCM or FGCM. It contains the list of court members, date of assembly and charges against the accused. SCM can be convened by the

Commanding Officer himself. Court Martial are *ad hoc* bodies and are assembled for each trial. The trial procedure followed in a GCM and DCM is elaborate, while in the case of FGCM and SCM it is very brief. The presence of judge advocate is must only in the case of a GCM.[33]

The trial procedure in the case of a GCM and DCM is as follows. The accused is supplied with a copy of convening order, charge sheet, and a copy of summary of evidence to prepare his defence. When the trial begins, the accused is asked whether he objects to any court members, present in the court. The Court Martial then considers the grounds of objection raised by the accused, in the absence of objected member. If satisfied with the plea of the accused, the objected member is replaced by a waiting member, otherwise the trial continues. The accused is then asked, whether he pleads guilty to charge(s).

If the accused pleads guilty to the charge, the judge advocate or the Presiding Officer explains to the accused the meaning of the charges to which he has pleaded guilty and the general effect of the plea. Thereafter, summary of evidence is then read in the court and the accused may make any statement in reference to the charges and in mitigation of punishment. In case, the accused does not plead guilty to the charge(s), the prosecution witness are called in the court, one by one, who may be cross-examined by the accused. The accused is then asked to produce his witnesses, or make a statement in his defence.

After recoding the statement of witnesses; or in case the accused has pleaded guilty, the reading of summary of evidence, the court members deliberate on the findings in the closed court. After the finding on every charge is recorded, it is announced in open court. If the accused is found guilty, the court deliberates on sentence in close court. The accused may make any statement in mitigation of his sentence. The sentence is pronounced in open court, subject to the confirmation by the convening authority. The convening officer may ask the Court for revision of the finding, or sentence, or both.

Revision of Court Martial

The findings of a Court Martial are not valid unless confirmed by the competent military authorities, who is generally the convening officer or his superior. The Army Act has unique provisions by which an officer assembling a Court Martial may ask the court members to review their decisions about the findings or/and sentence awarded by the court. If the confirming authority is dissatisfied with the findings of a GCM, DCM or FGCM, the findings and sentence may be revised once under his orders. On such revision, the court, if so directed by the confirming authority, may take additional evidence.[34] The court, on revision, consists of the same officers as were present when the original decision was arrived at, unless any of those officers are unavoidably absent. However, number of officer reviewing the decision in Court Martial, should not fall below the minimum number of officers required to constitute such courts (i.e., five in cases of GCM and three in the case of FGCM or DCM).

When the finding is sent back for revision, the court re-assembles in open court, the revision order is read and if the court is directed to take fresh evidence, the same is taken in open court. The court then deliberates on its finding in closed court. If it does not adhere to its earlier finding, it revokes the finding and sentence and records the new finding, and if necessary passes a fresh sentence. When the sentence alone is sent for revision the court cannot revise the finding. After revision, the proceedings are transmitted for confirmation. [35] The law does not require the confirming authority to give a hearing to the petitioner either before ordering revision under the Army Act or before confirming the revised sentence.

Remedy Against Finding and Sentence

The Army Act provides for a remedy against the finding and sentence awarded by the Court Martial. The accused, if considers himself aggrieved with the finding and sentence of GCM, DCM or FGCM; may submit petition (i) before confirmation, to the officer empowered to confirm it, and (ii) after confirmation to the Federal Government or the Chief of the Army Staff or an officer superior to one who has confirmed the proceedings.[36] The remedy under sections 131 is not a remedy available to the accused person in the real sense. It is merely power granted to various specified authorities. Thus, in reality, there is no right of appeal against the order of the Court Martial. It has been held that the remedy of review provided to aggrieved person should not be equated with remedy of appeal, wherein an affected person has the right to appear before the appellate court and can be heard in support of his appeal.[37]

The Federal Government, COAS or any prescribed officer may annul the proceedings of any Court Martial on the grounds of being illegal or unjust.[38] Once the finding and sentence are confirmed, it is promulgated to the accused by his Commanding Officer.

Appeals Against the Court Martial

In Pakistan there have been several occasions when the Chief of the Army Staff has also functioned as Chief Martial Law Administrator or the President exercising the power over mercy petitions under Article 45 of the Constitution. It has been held that the Chief Martial Law Administrator has the power under Article 45 to consider mercy petitions and grant pardon to a military convict.[39]

Pakistan does not have any civilian appellate forum where persons convicted by a Court Martial could appeal against its order, findings or sentence. For a longtime the Pakistan Army as well as the government was of the view that rights to appeal against finding and sentence of Court Martial, if provided within the military legal system, would adversely affect discipline.[40] However, in 1992 the Army Act was amended to create an appellate forum within the military. These Courts of Appeal became effective since December 22, 1992 and had no retrospective powers to decide an appeal.[41]

Court of Appeal for Hadd Cases

The Court of Appeal for *hadd* cases are constituted under section 133A of the Army Act. The Court of Appeal consists of the Chief of the Army Staff (COAS) and another Muslim officer, designated by the COAS. A sentence awarded by a Court Martial as *hadd* under an Islamic law cannot be executed unless it is confirmed by the Court of Appeals for *hadd* cases. Any person to whom a Court Martial has awarded a sentence of *hadd* under an Islamic law may, within 60 days from the date of award of sentence can prefer an appeal against the finding and sentence of Court Martial. The Court of Appeal has the power to confirm the finding or/

and sentence; substitute a valid finding or sentence; call a witness for recoding additional evidence; annul the proceedings of Court Martial on the grounds of illegality of being unjust; or order retrial of the accused.

Court of Appeals for Other Cases

Accused persons convicted by military courts and sentenced to stoning to death, death, amputation, imprisonment for life, imprisonment exceeding three months, or dismissal from service have the right to appeal against the verdicts and sentences to a military Court of Appeal constituted under section 133B of the Army Act. A Court of Appeal is presided over by the COAS or an officer not below the rank of Brigadier and one or more officers designated by the COAS. In case of Court Martial proceedings have been confirmed by an officer of the rank of Brigadier, the Court of Appeal shall not be presided over by an officer below the rank of Major General. Where the sentence is awarded by the Court Martial under an Islamic law, the officers so designated shall be Muslim. A Court of Appeal may be attended by a judge advocate. The law provides that every appellate court hearing “may be attended by a judge advocate” who shall be an officer belonging to the Judge Advocate General’s Department of the Pakistan Army. If such an officer is not available, a person may be appointed by the COAS in lieu.

The Court of Appeal has the power to accept or reject the appeal in whole or part; substitute a valid finding or sentence; call a witness for recoding additional evidence; annul the proceedings of Court Martial on the grounds of illegality of being unjust; order retrial of the accused; or remit the whole, or part of the punishment, or reduce, or commute the punishment for any lesser punishment mentioned in the Army Act, or enhance the punishment. The verdict of a military court that is upheld by a military Court of Appeal is final and cannot be appealed before a civilian court, even the High Court or the Supreme Court of Pakistan.

The Pakistan Army Act Rules originally afforded a person sentenced the right to get a copy of the Court Martial proceedings. But through an amendment introduced in 1985 the Army Chief gave himself the authority to refuse copy of the proceedings if deemed "prejudicial to the safety or interests of the state". This makes the right to appeal meaningless as the convict has no way of knowing what exactly has been held against him and why. In addition, the army headquarters have ordered (through an administrative instruction) that once the Chief or Vice Chief confirms a sentence; the Court of Appeals cannot change the verdict without first obtaining permission from the Chief of the Army Staff or the Vice Chief. The Army Act Rules also provide that the high command can award censure to members of a Court Martial. No prudent person in military chain of command would risk career progression and give different verdict than that desired by his superiors.[42]

Judge Advocate General

The Judge Advocate General (JAG) branch of the Pakistan's armed forces is composed of military officers and civilians and comes under the Adjutant-General of the army. The JAG's legal service includes judge advocates, warrant officers, paralegal non-commissioned officers and junior enlisted personnel, and civilian employees who provide legal services to the army, air force and the navy. The JAG is a Brigadier rank officer, who oversees all the military-related litigation within the army and in the civilian courts. The Pakistan army has strengthened its legal department and created a new post of Director General Lawfare Directorate,[43] held by an officer of the rank of Major General since December 2014.[44]

The JAG officers provide legal help to the military in all aspects, in particular advising the Presiding Officers of Court Martial on military law. In practice, a military commander receives legal advice from a judge advocate prior to assembling a Court Martial (pre-trial advice) and after the trial (post-trial advice) before confirming a punishment awarded by the court. However, a commander is not bound to follow such advices. The guiding rules for commanders' military justice decisions are virtually non-existing, and even if they exist, they are based on military culture and are arbitrary. According to the military legal system of Pakistan, the JAG's decision cannot be challenged in civilian courts.

Review of Punishment by High Court and Supreme Court

The Army Act bars civilian courts from exercising their appellate jurisdiction over decisions of Courts Martial. Section 133 of the Army Act explicitly provides: "No remedy shall lie against any decision of a Court Martial and no appeal or application shall lie in respect of any proceedings or decision of a Court Martial to any court exercising any jurisdiction whatsoever." The 1992 amendment to the Army Act, which established military court of appeal for *hadd* and other cases, may be illusory to provide relief to those aggrieved by the finding and sentence of a Court Martial. The proceedings in these courts of appeal cases are taken up after they are confirmed by the COAS, and no officer in military chain of command constituting 'court of appeal' would dare to set aside the verdict of a court martial confirmed by the COAS.

In the past, senior army officers have been able to deter the higher judiciary into submission. In one case, the Army Chief himself tried to influence the Supreme Court and, when a case was brought against him for offering contempt, compelled the Court to back off. In another case of "lifting" of a senior journalist by the ISI, a Lahore High Court judge claimed lack of jurisdiction "because the ISI contained serving army officers" despite the fact that the ISI was created by an Act of Parliament and worked under the Prime Minister.[45]

The High Court and the Supreme Court in Pakistan have, however, held they may use their extraordinary writ jurisdiction to hear cases related to military courts where any action or order of any authority relating to the Armed Forces of Pakistan is either *coram non judice*, *mala fide*, or without jurisdiction.[46] In a case where the military accused was convicted and sentenced by FGCM for committing sodomy, the Lahore High Court declined to interfere on the grounds that the case did not fall in the category of *corum non judice*, mala fide, or without jurisdiction.[47] The Supreme Court, responding to petitions challenging the 21st amendment, reiterated this power of judicial review in cases decided by military courts.

On January 12, 2009, the Lahore High Court has set aside a sentence of the FGCM against an army officer, who was found guilty of filing fake income tax returns, apart from other instances of fraud. The decision was considered "revolutionary" because the court has not been under pressure to ignore the legal lacuna in the case.[48]

The Supreme Court has considered a case wherein seven individuals[49] were accused of seducing and attempting to seduce persons in the military forces of Pakistan from their allegiance to the Government of Pakistan, under section 31(d) and 59 of the Pakistan Army Act. They were arrested and tried by the FGCM and were found guilty for the offences charged with. On July 21, 2005, the FGCM sentenced the accused to imprisonment for life. The sentence was confirmed by the confirming authority. In the appeals filed by them, under section 133-B of the Army Act, the Appellate Court dismissed their appeals and also enhanced their sentences from life imprisonment to death. The accused had approached the High Court by filing Writ Petitions, but the same was dismissed as being not maintainable under Article 199 (3) of the Constitution of Pakistan.

The Supreme Court examined the appellate provision contained in section 133-B of the Army Act.

Section 133B-Court of Appeals for other cases

- Any person to whom a Court Martial has awarded a sentence of death, imprisonment for life, imprisonment exceeding three months, or dismissal from the service after the commencement of the Pakistan Army (Amendment) Act, 1992, may, within forty days from the date of announcement of finding or sentence or promulgation thereof, whichever is earlier, prefer an appeal against the finding or sentence to a Court of Appeals consisting of the Chief of the Army Staff or one or more officers designated by him in this behalf, presided by an officer not below the rank of Brigadier in the case of General Court Martial or Field General Court Martial or District Court Martial or Summary Court Martial convened or confirmed or counter signed by an officer of the rank of Brigadier or below as the case may be, and one or more officers, presided by an officer not below the rank of Major General in other cases, hereinafter referred to as the Court of Appeals:

  Provided that where the sentence is awarded by the Court Martial under an Islamic law, the officer or officers so designated shall be Muslims:

Provided further that every Court of Appeals may be attended by a judge advocate who shall be an officer belonging to the Judge Advocate General's Department, Pakistan Army, or if no such officer is available, a person appointed by the Chief of the Army Staff.

- A Court of Appeals shall have power to:
  a. accept
  b. or reject the appeal in whole or in part; or
  c. substitute a valid finding or sentence for an invalid finding or sentence; or
  d. call any witness, in its discretion for the purpose of recording additional evidence in the presence of the parties, who shall be afforded an opportunity to put any question to the witness; or
  e. annul the proceedings of the Court Martial on the ground that they are illegal or unjust; or
  f. order retrial of the accused by a fresh court; or
  g. remit the whole or any part of the punishment or reduce or enhance the punishment or commute the punishment for any less punishment or punishments mentioned in this Act.

- The decision of Court of Appeals shall be final and shall not be called in question before any court or other authority whatsoever.

In terms of section 133-B, the Appeal Court has the power to annul the proceedings, remit the whole or any part of sentence or reduce or enhance the punishment when an appeal against conviction and sentence has been filed before it within 40 days from the date of announcement of finding, sentence or promulgation thereof. The period of limitation would run from the date of announcement of finding, sentence or promulgation, whichever is earlier.

The Supreme Court observed that the accused had filed the appeal before the Appeal Court in two batches on September 2,2005 and November 26, 2005, which was beyond the permissible period of 40 days stipulated under section 133-B. The convicts were not given any opportunity to show cause as to why their sentence should not be enhanced. The Supreme Court found that the appeals before the

Appeal Court were barred by time. There were thus no appeals before the Appeal Court in terms of section 133-B. Enhancement of sentence could not have been made in a vacuum. The Court pronounced that the enhancement of punishment from imprisonment for life to death by the Appeal Court was essentially against the principle of natural justice enshrined in the maxim *audi alteram partem* and Articles 4 and 9 of the Constitution.

The Supreme Court referring to its earlier decisions[50] declared that Article 199(3) of the Constitution prohibits the High Court from making an order in relation to a person who is a member of Armed Forces of Pakistan or who is for the time being subject to any law relating to any of those forces or in respect of any action taken in relation to him as a member of the Armed Forces of Pakistan or as a person subject to such law but not when acts, actions or proceedings which suffer from defect of jurisdiction and are thus *coram non judice*. [51]

Execution of Sentence

In awarding a sentence of stoning to death, a Court Martial is to direct that the sentence shall be executed in the manner provided for the Offence of *Zina* (Enforcement of *Hudood*) Ordinance, 1979. In awarding a sentence of death a Court Martial, has the discretion to direct that offender should suffer death by being hanged by the neck, or being shot to death. In awarding a sentence of amputation of hand, foot or both the Court Martial is to direct that sentence shall be executed in the manner provided in the Offences Against Property (Enforcement of *Hudood*) Ordinance, 1979. The regulation number 18 contained in the Army Regulations Volume II (Instructions) 1991 states:

> In case of stoning to death of a male convict, he shall be firmly secured to an object, whereas for a female convict a hole or excavation should be dug to receive her as deep as her waist. As regards amputation of hand, foot or both, it will be, after medically examining the convict, at the discretion of the authorised medical officer to decide as to the manner in which the sentence will be executed.[52]

A person sentenced to death may, pending confirmation or execution, be committed to a civil prison for safe custody. The sentence of imprisonment for a period not exceeding three months, if the confirming officer so directs, can be carried out in military custody. In other cases of imprisonment, the Commanding Officer of the convicted person forwards a warrant to the officer-in-charge of the civil prison along with the convicted person. The sentence of detention is carried out in military custody/ detention barracks. Recently, the Lahore High Court (Rawalpindi Bench) in *Ex-Brigadier Ali Khan v. Government of Punjab*[53] examined the provisions relating to remission under the Pakistan Prison Rules, 1978. In this case Brigadier Khan was convicted by a FGCM on three charges, namely: (i) under section 59 of the Army Act read with section 11-F(2) of Anti-Terrorism Act, 1997 for professing to belong a proscribed organisation; (ii) under section 31(d) of the Army Act, for attempting to seduce a person in the military forces of Pakistan from his allegiance to the Government of Pakistan; and (iii) under section 59 of the Army Act for being party to a criminal conspiracy to commit an offence punishable with death under section 120-B read with section 302 of the Pakistan Penal Code. He was sentenced by a FGCM to suffer rigorous imprisonment for five years and dismissal from service. For serving the sentence, a warrant of commitment dated August 3, 2012 was issued and the convict was handed over initially to the Superintendent, District Jail, Sialkot and later shifted to Central Jail, Rawalpindi. On behalf of the petitioner, his wife made a representation to the Home Department, Government of the Punjab, seeking remissions and other facilities admissible under Prison Rules, 1978. The government refused to grant any relief and intimated that since the petitioner was sentenced under Section 11(F)(2) of the Anti-Terrorism Act, 1997, he was not entitled to any kind of remission in view of the provisions of Section 21-F of the said Act.

The Court analysed chapter 8 of Prison Rules, which deals with remission.[54] The Court held that refusal to grant remission to the petitioner is a violation of the Pakistan Prison Rules, 1978 for the period of conviction of the petitioner to the extent of four years and six months after exclusion of the period of maximum six months conviction under section 11-F(2) of the Anti-Terrorism Act, 1997. The court thus allowed the remission and the jail authorities are directed accordingly.

The Federal Government as well as the higher military authorities are empowered to pardon a convicted person under the Army Act. They can also mitigate the punishment awarded or commute such punishment for any less punishment mentioned in the Act. Any punishment awarded as *hadd* under an Islamic law, can only be pardoned, mitigated or commuted in accordance with such law. [55] A civil servant convicted by a Court Martial could be pardoned by the Chief Martial Law Administrator (CMLA) and reinstated in public office;[56] whereas those convicted by a criminal court could not be reinstated in the service, even if pardoned by the CMLA.[57]

The Constitutional 21st Amendment authorising the military Court Martial to try terrorist and other civilians accused of serious crimes was passed in the Pakistan National Assembly on January 6, 2015. With this the government created parallel systems within the justice system. The trial procedure in FGCM, which have been constituted after the 21st Amendment, is different from the one followed in GCM or DCM.

Field General Court Martial

Military courts, i.e., the Field General Court Martial (FGCM) constituted for trial of civilians and terrorists by the Pakistan Army are exceptional kind of military tribunals.[58] They have no parallel in the Australian, British or American military justice system. The FGCM existed in the British military justice system till 2006 but was rarely convened after 1980. As the name suggest, such Court Martial are to be convened in the field or active areas only, when it is not possible without serious detriment to public service for the offence to be tried by a GCM or DCM. The scheme of the FGCM clearly suggests that such a type of court is essentially meant for combat situations. The Manual of Pakistan Military Law provides some guidance in this respect: "A court of this character is not suited during peace conditions, but it may sometimes be necessary to convene such a court at a remote station where a sufficient number of officers to constitute a GCM are not available.[59]

Convening of FGCM

A FGCM can be convened by an officer who has been issued necessary warrant for this by the Federal Government or the Chief of the Army Staff. On active service, an Officer Commanding a part of the Army, not below the rank of Brigadier, can convene a FGCM, if in his opinion it is not practicable with due regards to discipline and the exigencies of the service to try the alleged offender by a GCM.[60] Such opinion is required to be recorded in the convening order. Therefore, in Pakistan, FGCM can be convened during active service as well as during peacetime.[61] A FGCM is essentially suited for active service, where suitable number of officer may not be available to constitute a GCM. During peace time, it may be sometimes necessary to convene a SGCM at a military station where sufficient number of officers to constitute a GCM may not be available. The Federal Government or the Chief of the Army Staff may empower any officer to convene a FGCM at any station during the peacetime.[62]

Composition

A FGCM, as discussed in the last chapter, consists of only three officers. Unlike the GCM, for which each officer to be appointed as members is required to have held a commission for not less than three years, no minimum specific length of commissioned service is laid down as requirement for a member of a FGCM. In fact FGCM was envisaged by the British government in an era when its forces were deployed in remote locations, had no communication with the headquarters; and in the interest of discipline it was necessary to try military offenders urgently. Therefore, no officer is disqualified or ineligibe for appointment as member in FGCM, unless he a member of military police or prosecutor or a witness. The appointment of judge advocate for a FGCM is not a legal necessity, but his presence is not a legal necessity and he has no decision-making authority. During the Martial Law, a civilian magistrate, despite not being an army officer, could be appointed as member of FGCM.[63]

Procedure at Trial

The law provides for an abbreviated procedure to be followed at a trial by FGCM. However, the Supreme Court of Pakistan has held that as far as feasible, if held during peacetime, FGCM should follow the procedure as laid down in GCM.[64] The rules relating to the procedure to be adopted at a trial by FGCM forms a separate section in the Army Act Rules, 1954, and is as follows.

The proceedings in FGCM may be recorded in accordance with the prescribed form, with such variations as the circumstances of each case may require. In place of a detailed charge-sheet as required for a GCM or DCM; for trial by FGCM, the statement of an offence may be made briefly in any language sufficient to describe or disclose an offence under the Army Act.[65] A list of charges and statement of witnesses recorded by the civil police would be sufficient to meet the requirement of FGCM.[66] The court may be sworn at the same time to try any number of accused persons then present before it for an offence committed collectively. The names of the Presiding Officer and members of the court are to be read over to the accused and he is asked if he has objection to be tried by any of these officers. An objection raised by the accused is to be decided by the remaining members, as in the case of GCM; and the vacancies being filled from among the waiting members, or by fresh members being appointed by the convening officer.

After the court is sworn or affirmed, the President of FGCM, or judge-advocate (if appointed) is to inform the accused about the offence with which he is charged with and shall ask the accused whether he is guilty or not guilty of the offence. If the accused pleads "guilty" the summary of evidence, may be read and attached to the proceedings. It is not necessary for the court to hear witnesses for the prosecution, respecting matters contained in the summary of evidence so read.

In case accused does not plead guilty, the witnesses for the prosecution are called and the accused is allowed to cross-examine them and to call any available witnesses for his defence. Before a witness gives his evidence, an oath or affirmation is administered to him. The judge advocate or the Presiding Officer is required to make a brief record of the evidence of the witnesses at the trial and of the defence of the accused; which is attached to the proceedings. If it appears to the Convening Officer that military exigencies or other circumstances prevent compliance the recoding of evidence, he may direct that the trial to be carried on without any such brief record being taken down. The court is then closed to consider its finding. If the finding on any charge is "guilty", the court may receive any available evidence as to previous convictions and character of the accused. The court then deliberates on the sentence in closed court.

Upon the court arriving at a finding of "not guilty", or awarding the sentence in case of having arrived at a finding of "guilty", the, Presiding Officer signs the finding or sentence, as the case may be. The proceedings are then transmitted to the confirming officer, for confirmation. Every finding and sentence of a SGCM is subject to confirmation. The provisions relating to revision, remedy against findings and sentence, and appeals as applicable in the cases of GCM/DCM is also applicable to a person convicted by FGCM. The Supreme Court has held that "rules of procedure applicable for trial of a person in a criminal case before a military court do not violate any accepted judicial principle governing trial of an accused person. Procedure prescribed for trial before military courts is in no way contrary to the concept of a fair trial in a criminal case.[67] Procedure adopted in the FGCM was challenged before Supreme Court in a petition under Article 184 (3) of the Constitution which was dismissed on the ground that no question of public importance was conferred by Article 9, 10 and 14 of the Constitution was involved.[68]

The Supreme Court refused to interfere in a case of trials held by FGCM, where two military personnel were awarded death sentence by FGCM. In the first case, Ex-Gunner Muhammad Mushtaq of Pakistan Army was awarded death sentence for committing murder of his colleague on February 28, 2004 while posted at Siachin Glacier.[69] In second case, Lance Naik Mukarram Hussain was awarded the death sentence by a FGCM for killing Havildar Noor Muhammad and Lance Hawaldar Bashir Ahmed in 2001. Their sentences were confirmed by the Chief of Army Staff and writ petitions were dismissed by the Peshawar and Lahore High Court. On appeal, the Supreme Court held that Article 199 (3) of the Constitution of Islamic Republic of Pakistan clearly prohibits the High Courts from making an order in relation to a person who is member of the Armed Forces of Pakistan, or who is for the time being subject to any law relating to any of such forces, or in respect of any action taken in relation to such person as a member of the Armed Forces, or a person subject to such law. Under Article 199, the jurisdiction of the High Court is barred with regard to the conviction recorded and sentences awarded by the FGCM. As the appellant was member of armed forces, therefore, writ could not have been issued by the High Court against the FGCM or against the Appellate Authority which confirmed the conviction and sentences. In view of Article 199(5) of the Constitution, the FGCM is excluded from the definition of 'person' in Article 199(1)(i) of the Constitution. The Supreme Court did not find any *mala fide* on the part of the military authorities in a trial by FGCM as there was sufficient evidence to prove the guilt of the appellants. The Court held that in absence of any *mala fide* on the part of the prosecution, the conviction and sentences awarded to the appellants by the FGCM cannot be stamped to be *coram non judice*.[70]

The 2015 amendments to the Army Act allow the Federal Government to transfer proceedings pending in any other court against any person accused of committing prescribed offences under the amended law to a military court. Where cases are transferred from other courts, an FGCM may admit as evidence and base a verdict on previously recorded statements. It means that witnesses who have already testified before a civilian court are not required to testify again before the military court after the case has been transferred. The amendment to the Army Act also allows an FGCM to hold *in camera* trials, and keep the identities of individuals associated with the cases secret.[71] Under the Army Act, there is no requirement that trials in a Court Martial or appeals in the Court of Appeal be heard in public. Further, an accused person may be tried and punished for offences under the Act "in any place whatever".[72]

During the British rule, FGCM (extra-ordinary court martial) [73] was presided over by a British commissioned officer with two native officers as members and could award the sentence up to the death. In case the sentence did not exceed the power of a DCM; it was carried out forthwith, or else after confirmation by the convening authority.[74] In field areas, the convening authority was also a British officer. An interpreter was required to be appointed for every Court Martial; however, if no qualified or competent person was available, the President of the court preformed the duty of interpreter.[75]

Functioning of Military Courts for Trial of Civilians

In Pakistan, provincial apex committees comprising civilian and military officials are responsible for selecting the cases of individuals charged with terrorism related offices to be referred to the military courts for trial and forwarding them to the Ministry of the Interior for final approval. What criterion is used by the committee for the selection of such cases is not known. The Ministry of the Interior vets the list submitted by the provincial committees, and sends a final list of cases to the military for trial. Since the 21st amendments of the Constitution in January 2015, the Pakistan Government has constituted 11 military courts to hear "terrorism" cases under the amended Army Act, 1952. These military courts have been set up in Khyber Pakhtunkhwa, Punjab, Sindh, and Balochistan.[76]

It has been reported that the military courts, set up after the December 16, 2014 carnage at the Army Public School in Peshawar, have so far convicted 81 militants, of which 76 have been awarded death sentences and four life terms.[77] The Pakistan Army has not provided any information about the fate of the people not found guilty by military courts. It is unknown whether they have been acquitted and set at liberty; still being detained for other charges; or if their cases have been transferred to other courts.[78] It is believed that around 100 cases are still pending before the various military courts in the country.[79]

The families of few individuals convicted by military courts have challenged the convictions before the Supreme CourtHC on the grounds that suspects were denied the right to a fair trial, including the right to engage counsel for defence, the right to cross-examine witnesses, and the right to be free from torture or other ill-treatment.[80] The Supreme Court is seized with 17 different appeals instituted against convictions by the FGCM. This includes two cases, where families claim that the convicts were children when they were arrested by the law enforcement agencies.[81]

According to the International Commission of Jurists, a Geneva based think-tank, proceedings before Pakistani military courts have serious shortcomings when examined in the light of international standards requiring fair trials before independent and impartial courts. For instance, in a FGCM, military officers performing the task of judges are part of the executive branch of the State and continue to be subjected to military command; the right to appeal to civilian courts is not available; the right to a public hearing is not guaranteed; and a duly reasoned, written judgment, including the essential findings, evidence and legal reasoning, is denied. In addition, the procedures of military courts, the selection of cases to be referred to them, the location and timing of trial and details about the alleged offences are not made public.[82] The convicted persons are also denied the proceedings of Court Martial, thus unable to appeal in the higher courts.[83] The Special Rapporteur on extrajudicial, summary or arbitrary executions has stated that the International Covenant on Civil and Political Rights (Article 14) addresses not only the rights of accused persons but also the public's right to information on the use of the death penalty. States have a duty to make information on the death penalty publicly available.[84]

The UN Human Rights Committee has emphasised that in trials leading to the imposition of the death penalty, "scrupulous respect of the guarantees of fair trial is particularly important" and "imposition of a sentence of death upon conclusion of a trial, in which the provisions of Article 14 of the Covenant have not been respected, constitutes a violation of the right to life....The death penalty is of particular concern when imposed by military courts and tribunals, especially on civilians." [85] The Working Group on Arbitrary Detention has concluded that military justice systems should be prohibited from imposing the death penalty under all circumstances.[86]

The military officers constituting a Court Martial are generally not trained in law and remain unaware of the nuances of rational criteria to punish an individual for criminal offences. Sentencing is a complex exercise and consistency of approach is essential to maintain public confidence. Those who sentence have discretion to reflect the gravity of the offence, the effect on the victim, the circumstances of the offender, and the public interest. Whether the military officers in Pakistan have been issued with any guidelines for sentencing in a military court is not known. The FGCM set up under the Army Act are hardly capable of dispensing justice to members of the armed forces, let alone suspects in a war that the army is waging against citizens-turned-terrorists. The military courts are not meant to try those who don't belong to the military and the FGCM established under the Army Act are not truly independent in the judicial sense. These courts have been set up in haste by giving judicial power to military officers to execute civilians. The approach of the Pakistan Government to amend criminal justice post-Peshawar could be logical but would always be morally, legally or logically incorrect. The military legal system has been designed to maintain discipline in the armed forces. It can never be used to mete out justice to those who wrong society. [87] Even if the law needed to be amended, the Pakistan Government should have incorporated the safeguards suggested by the Supreme Court, which allowed an appeal procedure to the higher courts. The amendment violated basic human rights and such laws had been in force under dictators in Pakistan and democratic governments should avoid them. According to Ahmer Bilal Soofi, an expert in international law and conflict resolution, this amendment should be viewed as a 'law of war' rather than a 'law of peacetime'.[88] The United Nations human rights bodies have expressed their grave concern over the establishment of FGCM, which lack independence and impartiality and are not in line with Pakistan's international human rights obligations.[89]

The next two chapters will discuss whether the trial in military courts adheres to the right to fair trial; and whether the military court established under 21st Amendment are against the basic foundation/ structures of the Constitution of Pakistan and international human rights treaty obligations.

Notes

1. The Federal Government may on recommendations of the Chief of the Army Staff prescribe the minor punishments to which the persons subject to in the Army Act shall be liable without intervention of a Court Martial, and the officer by whom, and the extent to which, such minor punishments may be awarded; see: Section 23, Army Act, 1952.
2. Section 92, Army Act.
3. Section 93, Army Act.
4. Section 8 (a), Army Act.
5. Section 2(d), Army Act.

6. On November 10, 2007, an Ordinance (No LXVI) issued by Musharraf amended the Army Act, 1952, and increased the competence of military courts to try civilians. Under this Ordinance, section 2 of the Army Act was amended by which the civilians could be prosecuted, after an investigation conducted by the military and rules of evidence and procedures prescribed by law and the constitution for civilian trials did not apply. The Ordinance gave wide powers to the military courts to try civilians for any offence punishable under the Explosive Substances Act, 1908; prejudicial conduct under the Security of Pakistan Act, 1952; the Pakistan Arms Ordinance, 1965; the Prevention of Anti-National Activities Act, 1974; the Anti-terrorism Act, 1997; and several sections of the Pakistan Penal Code [Sections 109, 117, 120B, 121, 121-A, 122, 123, 123-A, 124, 124-A, 148, 302, 353 and 505 of the Pakistan Penal Code or attempt to commit any of the said offences]. Thus, under the amended Army Act civilians could be tried in military courts for acts of treason, sedition and less specific offences such as "giving statements conducive to public mischief.
7. On December 16, 2014, seven gunmen affiliated with the *Tehrik-i-Taliban (TTP)* conducted a terrorist attack on the Army Public School in Peshawar. The terrorists entered the school and opened fire on school staff and children, killing 141 people, including 132 schoolchildren, ranging between eight and eighteen years of age. A rescue operation was launched by the Pakistan Army's Special Forces, who killed all seven terrorists. On December 2, 2015, Pakistan hanged four terrorists involved in the Peshawar massacre.
8. The 21st amendment to the Constitution also provides for entering the Pakistan Army Act 1952, the Pakistan Army Act 1953, the Pakistan Navy Ordinance 1961 and the Protection of Pakistan Act, 2014 in the first schedule of the Constitution. The first schedule of the Constitution contains laws which are exempted from the application of Article 8 (1) and (2) of the Constitution. These articles are part of Chapter 1 of the Constitution relating to the Fundamental Rights. The 21st Amendment Act provides for the creation of military speed trial courts (STCs) for offences relating to terrorism, waging war against Pakistan and prevention of acts threatening the security of the country. The Act shall remain in force for two years starting January 7, 2015 after the President signed the Act.
9. On January 6, 2015, the National Assembly and the Senate approved the 21st Constitutional Amendment Bill and Pakistan Army Act (Amendment) Bill 2015 unopposed. These laws provided constitutional cover for extending the jurisdiction to Military Courts for the trial of terrorism suspects. The amendments apply to all persons who claim to, or are known to, belong to "any terrorist group or organisation using the name of religion or a sect" and carrying out acts of violence and terrorism, including: attacking military officers or installations; kidnapping for ransom; possessing, storing or transporting explosives, firearms, suicide jackets or other articles; using or designing vehicles for terrorist attacks; causing death or injury; possessing firearms designed for terrorist acts; acting in any way to "over-awe the state" or the general public; creating terror or insecurity in Pakistan; attempting to commit any of the above listed acts within or outside of Pakistan; providing or receiving funding for any of the above-listed acts; and waging war against the state.
10. The term 'sect' means a sect of religion and does not include any religious or political party regulated under the Political Parties Order, 2002.
11. Offences mentioned at serial Nos. (i), (ii), (iii), (v), (vii), (viii), (ix), (x), (xi), (xii), (xiii), (xv), (xvi), (xvii) and (xx) in the Schedule to the Protection of Pakistan Act, 2014. These relate to crimes against ethnic, religious and political

groups or minorities; use of arson, bombs, biological or chemical weapons; killing, kidnapping, extortion or attack on officers and employees of Pakistan government, members of armed forces, social or welfare workers; destruction of communication systems, gas or oil pipelines; attack on defence installations, prisons, educational institutions; attacking transport systems; violence against nuclear arms and sites; and illegally crossing national boundaries in connection with scheduled offence; etc.

12. Section 2, The Pakistan Army Act after its amendment in 2015.
13. *Federation of Pakistan v. Khursheed Ahmed*, 1999 SCMR 664 (a).
14. Sections 2, clauses (C) and (D) of Army Act and sections 3 of the Official Secrets Act, 1923 taken together, See: *F. B. Ali v. State* PLD 1975 SC 506.
15. *Darwesh M. Arbey v. Federation of Pakistan*, PLD 1977 Lah 846.
16. Sections 73 and 79, the Army Act, 1952.
17. Section 3 of the Official Secrets Act, 1923 and sections 2, 73, 74 and 75 of the Army Act, 1952.
18. *Begum Shamin Afridi v. Province of Punjab*, PLD 1974 Lah 120.
19. *Shahida Zahir Abbasi v. President of Pakistan*, PLD 1966 SC 632 (k) and (j).
20. When an officer was arrested on the orders of the Chief of the Army Staff, production of such officer before his commanding officer was not necessary. *Shahida Zahir Abbasi v. President of Pakistan*, PLD 1966 SC 632 (i).
21. Sections 74, the Army Act, 1952.
22. The term "active service" has been defined under the Army Act section 8 (1): Active Service as applied to as applied to a person subject to the Army Act, means the time during which such person is attached to, or forms part of a force which is engaged in operations against an enemy, or is engaged in military operations in, or is on the line of march to, a country or place wholly partly occupied by an enemy, or is attached to or forms part a force which is in military occupation of a foreign country. The power to declare a person to be on active service is contained in section 7 of the Act. It provides that the Federal Government may, by notification, direct that any person or class of persons subject to the Army Act shall, with reference to any area in which they may be serving or with reference to all or any of the provision of the Army Act or of any other law for the time being in force, be deemed to be on active service within the meaning of the Army Act.
23. Sections 80-84, the Pakistan Army Act.
24. Sections 85-89, Pakistan Army Act.
25. Offence of *Zina* by person subject to the Army Act against a civilian shall be triable exclusively by a court of session and a question of reference to prescribed officer under section 549 of Pakistan Criminal Code would not arise. The trial of such person by a court of session would not suffer from any infirmity for non-compliance of section 94 of the Army Act; see: *Abdur Rashid v. State*, PLD 1986 FSC 290.
26. Section 59, Pakistan Army Act.
27. Section 94, Pakistan Army Act.
28. Section 94 of the Army Act read with Rule 168 of the Pakistan Army Act Rules, 1954 states that Brigade Commander shall be the competent officer under the Army Act section 94 to take decision regarding the trial of a military person accused of civil offence. Also see: *Allah Ditta v. State*, PLD 1976 Lah 823.
29. Javaid Zeeshan, Civil Court Hands over Military Officer to Military Police, *Pakistan Observer*, available at: http://pakobserver.net/detailnews.asp?id=284116, accessed on January 5, 2016.

30. The authorities under Section 16 of the Pakistan Army Act, 1952, can dismiss any military person by Court Martial or on administrative grounds. An administrative dismissal is simple; the COAS in the light of inquiry can recommend dismissal of the accused person, which is required to be confirmed by the Federal Government. Federal Government could dismiss or remove from service any army officer, if the government is of the opinion that the officer by reasons of misconduct has become unworthy of holding of commission in the Pakistan army. *Iftikhar Ahmed v. Federal Government*, 2001, YLR, 2679.
31. Amended by the Army Act (Amendment) Act 2015. Amendment of section 60, Army Act, 1952: In the said Act, in section 60, in clause (k), after the word "law" occurring at the end, the words "and any other law for the time being in force", shall be added.
32. Section 60, Army Act.
33. In the military, trial by Court Martial is conducted in a just and fair manner. The accused is given full opportunity to put forward his point of view in a series of forums progressively. First of all, a court of inquiry is conducted and, if found guilty, a decision is taken by the competent authority to record a summary of evidence in which, again, the accused gets the full opportunity to put across his point of view. In normal circumstances, the accused during his trial can hire a civilian defence counsel. A provision for appeal also exists even if the accused is found guilty and convicted. The aim is to bring truth to the fore and to provide speedy justice in the Army. Khan Lt. Col. Khalid Masood, *The Nation*, 29 April 2016, available at: http://nation.com.pk/columns/29-Apr-2016/accountability-syndrome, accessed on May 1, 2016.
34. Section 126, Army Act.
35. The Constitution of Pakistan and most criminal justice systems bar repeat trials for the same offence. In case of Court Martial under the Army Act, the findings and sentence remain invalid unless confirmed by the convening authority. The convening authority can refuse to confirm the sentence or annul the court martial proceedings on various grounds. He can also order retrial of the accused to obtain desired result. Sattar Babar, Militarised justice, *The International News*, December 5, 2015, available at: http://www.thenews.com.pk/Todays-News-9-355146-Militarised-justice, accessed on January 12, 2016.
36. Section 131, Army Act.
37. *Muhammad Riaz v. The Federal Government*, PLD 1980 FSC 1.
38. Section 132, Army Act, 1952.
39. *Nazir Beg v. Government of the Punjab* PLD 1982 Lah 40.
40. In re: *The Pakistan Armed Forces Nursing Services Act, 1952*, PLD 1985 FSC 365.
41. In the case of *Farmanullah Hashmi v Government of Pakistan*, 1998 MLD 1883 (b), the accused was sentence to death on December 5, 1991, when the right to appeal was not available. It was held that the right to appeal available under section 133A of the Army Act, 1952 had no retrospective applicability. In *Muhammad Parvez v. Federation of Pakistan* 1998 SCMR 1270, where a military officer was sentenced to death by a FGCM, it was held that he has no right to appeal under section 133B of the Army Act as the provision has no retrospective effect. Subsequent availability of right of appeal as provided through Pakistan Army (Amendment) Act 1992 would not create right of appeal in favour of petitioner who sustained conviction before the provision of appeal was introduced in the relevant law; see: *The Government of Pakistan through Secretary, Ministry of Defence v. The General Public*, PLD 1989 SC 6.

42. Sattar Babar, Militarised justice, The International News, December 5, 2015, available at: http://www.thenews.com.pk/Todays-News-9-355146-Militarised-justice, accessed on January 12, 2016.
43. The term 'lawfare' is of recent origin. The term appeared in a military strategy book *Unrestricted Warfare*, written by two officers of the People's Liberation Army in 1999, who used it to denote to a nation's use of legalised international institutions to achieve strategic ends. In contemporary counterterrorism operations, in which Pakistan army is involved, the term can be used for construction of legal institutions as a tool to defeat terrorism.
44. Asad Malik, Army gears up for legal battle, Dawn, January 2, 2015, available at: http://www.dawn.com/news/1154555, accessed on March 10, 2016.
45. National Institute of Military Justice (NIMJ) News: January 15, 2009, available at: http://www.nimj.com/home.aspx, accessed on January 16, 2009.
46. When any action of the army authorities regarding a serving officer of the armed forces or any other person subject to the Army Act, 1952, was established to be either *mala fide*, *quorum non judice* or without jurisdiction then the same could be assailed through a constitutional petition by the aggrieved person, and the bar of jurisdiction under Article 199(3) of the Constitution would have no applicability. See: 2014 SCMR 1530.
47. *Ghulam Abbas v. Federation of Pakistan* 2014 SCMR 849.
48. National Institute of Military Justice (NIMJ) News: January 15, 2009, available at: http://www.nimj.com/home.aspx, accessed 16 January 2009.
49. CRP 229/06 in CA 802/06: Zubair Ahmed, Rashid Qureshi, Ghulam Sarwar Bhatti, Ikhlas Ahmed, Naik Arshad Memood (Ex-Number 7351783), Rana Muhammad Naveed, and Ameer Sohail, decided by the Supreme Court on February 28, 2013. For judgment see: *Rana Muhammad Naveed v. Federation of Pakistan*, 2013 SCMR 596.
50. *Federation of Pakistan v. Malik Ghulam Mustafa Khar* (PLD 1989 SC 26), *Secretary, Ministry of Religious Affairs and Minorities v. Syed Abdul Majid* (1993 SCMR 1171), and *Ghulam Abbas Niazi v. Federation of Pakistan* (PLD 2009 SC 866).
51. *Rana Muhammad Naveed v. Federation of Pakistan*, 2013 SCMR 596. Also see: *Federation of Pakistan v. Malik Ghulam Mustafa Khar*, PLD 1989 SC 26; *Secretary, Ministry of Religious Affairs and Minorities v. Syed Abdul Majid*, 1993 SCMR 1171; and *Ghulam Abbas Niazi. v. Federation of Pakistan*, PLD 2009 SC 866.
52. As quoted in Ahmed Ishtiaq. *The Pakistan Military in Politics: Origin, Evolution, Consequences* (New Delhi: Amaryllis,2013), p. 298.
53. Writ Petition No 2983 of 2015, decided on December 21, 2015, decision available at: http://sys.lhc.gov.pk/appjudgments/2016LHC222.pdf.,accessed on December 25, 2015.
54. In view of Rule 199 of Pakistan Prison Rules, 1978, a prisoner sentenced to imprisonment, whether by one sentence or by consecutive sentences, for a period of four months or more may by good conduct and industry, become eligible for release when a portion of his sentence ordinarily not exceeding one-third of the whole sentence has yet to run. Such provision contains a prohibition under Rule 214-A, which provides that no person, who is convicted for espionage or anti-state activities shall be entitled to ordinary or special remission, unless otherwise directed by the Provincial Government. The Court observed that the petitioner was never convicted and sentenced for any such offence resulting into refusal of remission

under Pakistan Prison Rules, 1978, and therefore Rule 214-A of Prison Rules would not be applicable in his case.

55. Section 143, Army Act.
56. *Muhammad Idrees v. Chief Director, Central Directorate of National Savings*, 1988 PLC (CS) 1.
57. *Tehsin Miran Gillani v. Central Board of Revenue, Government of Pakistan*, 1989 PLC (SC) 558, 1596.
58. The Pakistan Army on January 9, 2015 announced establishment of military courts in all the four provinces: Punjab, Khyber Pakhtunkhwa, Sindh and Balochistan....., would be headed mainly by Brigadier ranked officers and comprise of the officers of Lieutenant Colonel and Colonel ranks. The special trial courts would be working under the administrative ambit of Field General Court Martial (FGCM) and work in close coordination between the AG and JAG branches and the working of these courts would directly supervised by the GHQ. The sentences handed to the terrorists would come into effect only after the Chief of the Army Staff signs the related warrants. 9 military courts being set up across country in first phase, *Daily Times*, Islamabad, January 10, 2015.
59. Manual of Pakistan Military Law, Paragraph 106.
60. Section 84, Army Act.
61. Manual of Pakistan Military Law, Volume I, Part I, Chapter IV, Paragraphs 106 and 107.
62. Section 84, Army Act, 1952.
63. By virtue of the Chief Martial Law Administrator's Order No. 4, paragraph 5, a civilian magistrate could be appointed as a member of FGCM and there would be no illegality in the constitution of such courts; see: *Ghulam Mustafa Khar v. Pakistan*, PLD 1988 Lah 49.
64. *Shahida Zahir Abbasi v. President of Pakistan*, PLD 1996 SC 632 (I).
65. *Muhammad Khan v. State*, 1979 P.Cr. LJ Note 21.
66. Rules 23 and 24, the Army Act Rules, 1954; *Mohammad Afraaq Ahmed v. Raunaq*, PLJ 1978 Lah 331.
67. *Shahida Zahir Abbas v. President of Pakistan*, 1996 PLD 632.
68. *Al-Jehad Trust v. President of Pakistan*, PLD 2000 SC 84(d), case referred: *Mrs Shahida Zahir Abbasi v. President of Pakistan*, PLD 1996 SC 632.
69. Civil Appeal No. 718 and 1366 of 2007, decided by the Supreme Court on April 1, 2015.
70. Decision available at: http://www.supremecourt.gov.pk/web/user_files/File/C.A._718_2007.pdf., accessed on January 12, 2016.
71. The 2015 Amendment has inserted a new provision, 'Section 2(C)', in the Army Act, 1952, and is as follows: "Protection to Witnesses, President, Members of the Court, Defending Officers, Prosecutors and persons concerned with court proceedings: The convening authority or the court constituted under this Act may make such orders or take such measures, like sitting *in camera*, not publishing the names of the court officials etc, as it deems fit, within available resources, for the protection of witnesses, President, members, prosecutors, defending officers and other persons concerned in court proceedings for an offence under this Act, as may be prescribed."
72. Section 93, Army Act.
73. Article 72, (The British) Indian Article of War 1869.
74. Article 92, (The British) Indian Article of War 1869.
75. Article 102, (The British) Indian Article of War 1869.

76. Pakistan: The trial of civilians by military courts, Briefing Paper, January 2016, International Commission of Jurists, Geneva,(Name of the author, Place, publisher) p.1.
77. Iqbal Nasir, SC stays execution of three convicted by military courts, *Dawn*, May 11, 2016, available at: https://www.dawn.com/news/1257599, accessed May 12, 2016.
78. Press statement by the ISPR, December 12, 2015, available at: http://m.ispr.gov.pk/front/main.asp?o=t-press_release&latest=1, accessed December 15, 2015.
79. Pakistan: The trial of civilians by military courts, Briefing Paper, January 2016, International Commission of Jurists, Geneva, ,(Name of the author, Place, publisher) p. 3.
80. Since their establishment, military courts (FGCM) have tried a number of alleged terrorists and awarded death sentence. The findings and sentences of these FGCM have been confirmed by Chief of Army Staff General Raheel Sharif. The families of a few convicts had filed the writ petitions in the Peshawar High Court against the military courts judgment. These petitions were dismissed for lack of sufficient material. In appeal to the Supreme Court, the relatives of the convicts claimed that they came to know about the death sentences of their relatives through newspapers or internet and the military courts have not supplied the copies of the judgement. The appellants alleged that the convicts were not present during the trial conducted by military courts. They were not given any opportunity to cross-examine witnesses. A few have alleged that the army personnel produced the convicts duly hand cuffed and blindfolded in the military courts therefore they could not witness the court proceedings. Further, the convicts were asked to put thumb impression on papers, without informing them about the contents thereof. The Supreme Court is yet to give its verdict in the case. SC to hear military execution cases from March 7, *The Nation*, February 25, 2016, available at: http://nation.com.pk/editors-picks/25-Feb-2016/sc-to-hear-mily-courts-execution-cases-from-march-7, accessed on March 01, 2016.
81. A five-member bench of the Supreme Court, headed by Chief Justice Anwar Zaheer Jamali, has stayed execution of 17 civilian convicts sentenced to death by Field General Court Martial. The military courts have so far convicted 81 people, 77 of whom were sentenced to death, and there have been no acquittals. Of the cases that have come before the Supreme Court, the legal arguments have concluded in nine. The court has been hearing the cases for the remaining appellants, and is expected to give a verdict on all the cases together, possibly in the coming weeks. Hashim Asad, Pakistan Supreme Court to decide on validity of Army-run Tribunals, *The Wire*, June 28, 2016, available at: http://thewire.in/46597/pakistan-supreme-court-to-decide-on-validity-of-army-run-tribunals/, accessed July 01, 2016.
82. Pakistan: ICJ denounces hangings following secret trials by military courts, available at: http://www.icj.org/pakistan-icj-denounces-hangings-following-secret-trials-by-military-courts/, accessed on December 15, 2015.
83. The Pakistan Army Act Rules, 1954, originally afforded a person sentenced the right to get a copy of the trial proceedings. However, after an amendment introduced in 1985, the Army Chief can refuse copy of proceedings if deemed "prejudicial to the safety or interests of the state". This makes the right to appeal meaningless as the convict has no way of knowing what exactly has been held against him and on what grounds.
84. UN Doc. E/CN.4/2006/53/Add.3, paragraph 12.

85. Human Rights Council doc A/HRC/30/18 dated July 16, 2015.
86. UN Doc. E/CN.4/1999/63, paragraph 80.
87. Sattar Babar, Militarised justice, *The International News*, December 5, 2015, available at: http://www.thenews.com.pk/Todays-News-9-355146-Militarised-justice, accessed December 7, 2015.
88. NA Amends Pakistan Army Act, *Dawn,* November 12, 2015.
89. Tahir Niazi, UN bodies voice objection to military courts, available at: http://nation.com.pk/islamabad/07-Dec-2015/un-bodies-voice-objection-to-military-courts, accessed on January 10, 2016.

3

Anti-Terrorism Laws

Pakistan has traditionally relied on special laws and courts to deal with internal security and terrorism. In the last four decades various legislations dealing with the issue of terrorism have been passed by the military rulers as well as democratically elected governments. These include the Suppression of Terrorist Activities (Special Courts) Act, 1975; Special Courts for Speedy Trial Ordinance, 1987; Terrorist-Affected Areas (Special Courts) Ordinance, 1990; Terrorist-Affected Areas (Special Courts) Act, 1992; Anti-Terrorist Act, 1997; Pakistan Armed Forces (Acting in Aid of Civil Power) Ordinance, 1998; The Investigation for Fair Trial Act, 2013; and The Pakistan Protection Act, 2014. The main focus in these laws has been to create 'catch all' categories that make it easier for the state to convict an individual. These laws have given greater role to the military and intelligence services in internal security matters; for instance in the arrest, interrogation and investigation. Two of the above laws, i.e., the Anti-Terrorist Act, 1997, the 1998 Ordinance and the Pakistan Protection Act, 2014, are discussed in greater detail.

The Anti-Terrorist Act, 1997

Before December 2014 attack on the Army Public School in Peshawar, the provisions of Anti-Terrorism Act, 1997[1] (ATA) were applied for the trial of individuals involved in terrorism in Pakistan. The Government while taking up 21st Amendment claimed that anti-terrorism law was deficient in countering terrorism and there was a need for robust legal regime for the trial of such cases. In fact a US State Department report of 2010 had termed the anti-terror legal system of Pakistan as almost incapable of prosecuting suspected terrorists.[2]

The ATA was enacted by Parliament in 1997; however, as on March 2016, the law has been amended as many as 20 times to adapt to the changing nature of the terrorist threat. Other special laws have supplemented the ATA, such as the Investigation for Fair Trial Act, 2013, and Protection of Pakistan Act, 2014, to respond to some of the other areas of the terrorist threat not covered by the ATA. The ATA not only deals with terrorism and sectarian violence but also deals with various other heinous offences, for example kidnapping for ransom etc. The ATA, however, lays down the basic legal framework by defining offences of terrorism and terrorist acts.

What is Terrorism?

The ATA section 6 (1) defines terrorism as:

The use or threat of action where:

- The action falls within the meaning of section 6 (2), and
- The use or threat is designed to coerce and intimidate or overawe the Government or the public or a section of the public or community or sect or a foreign government or population or an international organisation or create a sense of fear or insecurity in society, or
- The use or threat is made for the purpose of advancing a religious, sectarian or ethnic cause or intimidating and terrorising the public, social sectors, media persons, business community or attacking the civilians, including damaging property by ransacking, looting, arson or by any other means, government officials, installations, security forces or law enforcement agencies,

Provided that nothing herein contained shall apply to a democratic and religious rally or a peaceful demonstration in accordance with law.

Section 6 (2) further lays out 17 types of actions, or threat of actions, covered under the above definition, including those causing death, grievous violence or damage to property, kidnapping, extortion, intimidation, and barring public servants from their duties, etc. Section 6 (3) further qualifies this by defining any of these types of actions that involve the use of firearms, explosives, or any other weapon as terrorism, whether or not subsection 6 (1) (c) is satisfied. Additionally, subsection 6 (3) (a) states that any violation of international conventions on terrorism signed by Pakistan are also considered acts of terrorism under the ATA.

Further, section 34 of the ATA grants the government the authority to amend the list of all offences punishable under the law (Third Schedule of the ATA) through a notification, without any changes to the law. Following a 2004 amendment, this was broadened to give Anti-Terrorism Courts (ATCs) exclusive authority to try cases of (i) abduction or kidnapping for ransom; (ii) use of firearms or explosives by any device, including bomb blast in a mosque, *imambargah*, church, temple or any other place or worship, whether or not any hurt or damage is caused thereby; and (iii) firing or use of explosives by any device including bomb blast in the court premises.

The basic flaw in the ATA is that it provides extremely broad definition of terrorist acts, resulting in overburdening the police, prosecution, and courts. This has caused delay in disposal of real cases of terrorism and large-scale acquittals. The preamble of the ATA describes the rationale of the law as providing for the prevention of terrorism, sectarian violence and for speedy trial of 'heinous offences' and for matters connected there with and incidental there to. The addition of the words 'heinous offences', which are not defined in the legislation, has widened the application of the ATA to include cases other than terrorism.[3] Though the ATA lays down comprehensive prohibitions on the activities of members of banned terrorists' organisations, but in reality there is no ban on the illegal activities of financial institution, issue of arms licences and passports, and travel abroad.

Anti-Terrorism Courts

Special anti-terrorism courts (ATCs) have been established under the ATA to hear the cases in which the ATA is applied. The anti-terrorism courts follow the same procedural law as is followed under the ordinary criminal law i.e. the Criminal Procedure Code and the Qanoon-e-Shahadat Order, 1984, (law of evidence). There are some departures from the ordinary criminal law; for instance, the ATA makes confession before a senior police officer admissible and prescribes a shorter timeline for trials. However, in practice these differences in legal provisions are not observed strictly due to superior courts' adverse observations about confessions before police officers. Similar to general criminal law, the burden of proof remains on the prosecution.

Low Conviction Rate

According to the Punjab Prosecutor General, during 2014, anti-terrorism courts heard 785 cases of terrorism in the province, resulting in 589 acquittals or mere 25 percent convictions. One of the major reasons for the low rate of conviction under the ATA has been the legal requirements contained in the law of evidence mandating an excessive dependence on eye witness accounts for proving any offence and the absence of a witness protection programme. In addition, the legal requirements developed by judges over the years for ensuring the rights of defendants under the ordinary criminal law hamper convictions under the ATA. For instance, the process for the identification parade is very cumbersome and risky. Witnesses are required to go to the prison for the identification parade in the presence of a magistrate. They have to go in front of the criminal and actually tell the magistrate by touching the shoulder or arm of the criminal. Thus the identity of the witness is revealed to the person accused of terrorism. This has a chilling effect on the witnesses, who often refuse to identify an alleged accused, retract their statements or fail to appear because of threats against them and their families.[4] Another reason for the low conviction is the disproportionate dependence on listing of names and events in the First Information Report (FIR) of the case. In Pakistan, the FIR is a necessary element for conviction. In more than half cases, the accused have not been convicted because their names were not mentioned in the FIR.[5]

In Pakistan anti-terrorism courts are choked with cases not related to terrorism, such as murder, drug trafficking and even kidnapping for ransom. At present, there are about 17,000 cases pending for trial in these courts, though 85 percent of these cases are not even terrorism-related. According to the Supreme Court, anti-terrorism court and judges are insufficient in number and the prosecution has been toothless and politically corrupted. [6] On a number of instances, the civilian courts' judges were openly threatened by Islamic militant groups such as the *Taliban* and the *Lashkar-e-Taiba*. A number of lawyers have been killed for prosecuting the extremists. Many judges have fled the country after receiving death threats. In Pakistan, it is not easy to go against Islamists. In the past, liberal politicians were killed for speaking against controversial blasphemy laws and in favour of secular legislation. The perpetrators of these crimes have still not been brought to justice.[7] Anti-terrorism trial system in Pakistan is unnecessarily long, corrupt and incompetent to deal with the menace of terrorism.

The Supreme Court in *Mehram Ali's* case[8] struck down many provisions of the ATA for being in conflict with the Fundamental Rights guaranteed by the Constitution and thus *ultra vires*. The Court held:

- Section 5(2)(i) of the ATA was invalid to the extent it authorises the officer of police, armed forces and civil armed forces to open fire or order for opening of fire against person who in his opinion in all probability is likely to commit a terrorist act or any scheduled offence, without being fired upon.
- Section 10 of the ATA to be amended as to provide that before entering upon premises which is suspected to have material or a recording in contravention of section 8 of the Act, the concerned officer of police, armed forces or civil armed forces shall record in writing his reasons for such belief and serve on the person or premises concerned a copy of such reasons before conducting such search.
- Section 19(10)(b) of the ATA, which provides for trial of an accused *in absentia* on account of his misbehaviour in the court, is violative of Article 10 of the Constitution and, therefore, invalid.
- Sections 24, 25, 27, 28, 30 and 37 of the ATA are also not valid in their present form as they militate against the concept of independence of judiciary and Articles 175 and 203 of the Constitution. They need to be amended as to vest the appellate power in a High Court instead of Appellate Tribunal.
- Section 26 of the ATA is not valid in its present form as it makes admissible the confession recorded by a police officer not below the rank of a Deputy Superintendent. The provision violates Articles 13(b) and 25 of the Constitution.
- Section 35 of the ATA in its present form is not valid as it militates against the concept of the independence of judiciary and also violates Articles 175 and 203 of the Constitution.

According to Justice Maqbool Baqar of Sindh High Court, the main reason for pendency in the anti-terrorist courts was the non appointment of judges to these courts. Further, the main reason for low conviction rate under ATA was due to the defective investigation conducted by the investigation officer, who either failed to collect any convincing evidence or collected inadmissible evidence. On September 20, 2008, a suicide bomber in a vehicle laden with approximately 800kg of explosives blew himself up at the entrance of the Marriott Hotel Islamabad, killing 54 people, including 15 foreigners and maiming 250. A police investigation led to the arrest of four people accused of involvement in the attack. On May 5, 2010, however, the anti-terrorist court hearing the case acquitted all four accused for lack of admissible evidence. Out of the 42 anti-terrorism cases which came up in appeal before the Supreme Court during a period of four years from 2008-2011, there were 21 acquittals.[9] In practice, the ATA has been deficient in countering terrorism in Pakistan. In terms of substantive law, the ATA is not up to date with the latest trends in terrorism. It does not cover suicide bombing, planning for terrorist attacks beyond areas to which ATA extends, for instance the FATA or transportation and possession of large quantities of explosives.[10]

The Pakistan Armed Forces (Acting in Aid of Civil Power) Ordinance, 1998

In 1998, the Government of Pakistan imposed emergency in the Sindh province.[11] This led to an invitation to the military, acting in its capacity of "aid to civil power," to take over law and order duties in the Sindh province under the Pakistan Armed Forces (Acting in Aid of Civil Power) Ordinance, 1998. The purpose of the ordinance was to empower the governor to take all necessary actions "to create a peaceful environment in which ordinary citizens can conduct their day-to-day affairs in accordance with their constitutional rights and entitlement within the province."

The Ordinance, which had application only to the Sindh province, extended broad judicial powers to the military. The Ordinance granted military officers of the rank of Brigadier and above the right to "convene as many courts as may be deemed necessary to try offenders". Such courts could try civilians. Appeals against conviction by such courts would lie only with such AppellateTribunals as the military authorities deemed necessary to establish. Moreover, cases pending before other courts (regular courts and anti-terrorism courts) could be transferred to such newly established military courts. The courts would have jurisdiction to award sentences, including the death penalty, for specified crimes. The Ordinance also created a "new crime" punishable with a penalty of up to seven years of rigorous imprisonment—the crime of "civil commotion".[12]

The jurisdiction of the Ordinance was later extended to the whole of Pakistan. In addition, the Ordinance was amended so that accused "absconders" from justice could be tried *in absentia* by any military court established in Pakistan.[13] The definition of the crime of "civil commotion", particularly subject to implementation by military courts, was very troublesome—many of the activities defined as "crimes" could also be interpreted as "normal" political behaviour. Numerous constitutional petitions were filed before the superior courts challenging the validity of the Ordinance. The Supreme Court consolidated such petitions and heard the petitioners. The Supreme Court, in *Liaquat Hussain v. Federation of Pakistan,* delivered one of the most unequivocal decisions ever rendered by the Supreme Court of Pakistan.[14] It declared the Pakistan Armed Forces (Aid to Civil) Ordinance "unconstitutional, without legal authority, and with no legal effect." Furthermore, the court, as per the unanimous decision of the nine-member full bench, rejected the duration the Act's validity only to the Sindh province. The court also rejected the government's contention that the Ordinance was expedient and defensible under the so-called "doctrine of necessity".

The Supreme Court also found the Ordinance to be unconstitutional in that: (i) civilians cannot be tried by military courts; (ii) the special courts cannot perform parallel functions to those assigned to regular courts; and (iii) the military's powers with regard to "aid to civil authority" do not extend to the creation of courts or the exercise of judicial functions. The Ordinance was repealed in April 1999; however, "civil commotion" was made a crime under the Anti-Terrorism Act.

The Protection of Pakistan Act, 2014

The Protection of Pakistan Act, 2014, (PoPA) was enacted in July 2014 in the wake of terrorism incidents and army operations in SWAT and Waziristan.[15] The 21st Amendment has brought certain offences included in PoPA within the jurisdiction of military courts, when the offences are alleged to have been committed by those claiming to, or known to, belong to any terrorist group or organisation using the name of religion or a sect.[16] The amendments extend the jurisdiction of military courts only to those who claim to or are alleged to both belong to organisations that use the name of "religion or a sect" and to have carried out the above listed offences.[17] Where PoPA is applied, it will take precedence over the ATA.

The PoPA allows the government to suppress peaceful political opposition and freedoms of speech, privacy, peaceful assembly, and violate due process protections embodied in international law. The Act also provides that person arrested under the law shall be presumed to be engaged in waging war or insurrection against Pakistan unless he establishes his non-involvement in the offence.[18] This violates the right to presumption of innocence. Section 3(2)(a) of the PoPA authorises an officer of the police not below BS-15 or member of the armed forces or civil armed forces with the right to shoot any person "who is committing or in all probability is likely to commit a scheduled offence" and makes it lawful for any such officer "after forming reasonable apprehension that death or grievous hurt may be caused by such act" to fire or order the firing upon any such person.

The PoPA provides for preventive detention of enemy aliens and persons involved in actions against the security, integrity, public order and defence of Pakistan for a period of up to 90 days subject to the protections provided in Article 10 of the Constitution through oversight by the High Court. The law also provides a larger role to the armed forces in that, where the armed forces have been called in aid of civil powers, they can perform the functions of an investigation agency and hold persons in detention under PoPA. The minimum punishment under any of the scheduled offences under PoPA is 20 years but death penalty can also be awarded under other relevant laws. PoPA also empowers the special court to exclude the public from the proceedings of a trial if the prosecution submits an application stating such exclusion is considered necessary on the grounds of public safety.[19] When PoPA was made effective, the anti-terrorism courts constituted under the ATA were already in operation to try terrorism related offences. Therefore, the establishment of new special courts under the PoPA with similar jurisdiction had no justification.[20]

The United Nations human rights bodies have expressed their grave concern over the establishment of military courts in Pakistan and provisions of PoPA. It has been observed that certain provisions of the legislation are not in line with Pakistan's international human rights obligations and other international human rights and humanitarian standards. The UN bodies have particularly objected to section 3 (2) (b) relating to "arrest and search without warrant," section 22 which defines "scheduled offences," section 6 which deals with "preventive detention," section 9 (I), section 9 (2) (a), section 9 (2) (b) which relate to "withholding information and secret detention," section 15 which deals with "presumption of guilt," section 8 which relates to "special courts and secret hearings," section 6 (5) which relates to "retrospective authorisation" and section 20 which deals with "immunity and impunity" of the PoPA. Section 22 of the PoPA allows the government to amend the list of "scheduled offences" by adding, modifying or omitting any entry. According to UN human rights bodies such vaguely defined offences may be in contravention of Article 9 of the ICCPR which establishes the right of any person not to be arbitrarily deprived of his liberty except on grounds established by law. The human rights committee while interpreting Article 9 of the ICCPR established that any substantive grounds for arrest or detention must be prescribed by law and should be defined with sufficient precision to avoid overly broad or arbitrary interpretation or application.[21]

While the Protection of Pakistan Bill, 2014, duly passed by the National Assembly on April 7, 2014 was sent to Senate for approval, the International Commission of Jurists (ICJ) had urged the Pakistan Senate to reject the same. The ICJ was of the opinion that the Bill granted the military and law enforcement authorities wide powers to preventively detain individuals in violation of international safeguards; to search and seize property without warrant; and to withhold information about the location, fact of detention, and for some people, even grounds for detention. Further, the provisions of the Bill were inconsistent with respect for the principle of separation of powers and the independence of the judiciary. The ICJ felt that if adopted, the law would permit secret and otherwise unfair proceedings before Special Courts and facilitate human rights violations including arbitrary detention, incommunicado detention, enforced disappearance, and torture and other ill-treatment.[22]

By promulgating the Investigation for Fair Trial Act, 2013, the Pakistan Protection Act, 2014, and introducing amendments to the Anti-Terrorism Act, 1997, the Government in Pakistan has given prominent role to the military and intelligence agencies to curb the terrorism. In view of the serious involvement of the army and intelligence services of Pakistan in enforced disappearances, and the inability of the higher courts to discover the whereabouts of missing citizens suspected of being held by security agencies, it is feared that unless the right of the state to order preventive detention is strictly scrutinised the provisions of PoPA are liable to be misused. In Pakistan, the anti-terror laws have not been able to achieve their aims and objectives. According to Fayyaz, at times, charges have been framed against a particular organisation or person, but action has been delayed on account of unexplained reasons.[23]

Notes

1. The Anti-Terrorism Act, 1997, of Pakistan does not comprehensively cover all terrorism related activity and therefore several other statutes are also used in such cases. These are: The Protection of Pakistan Act, 2014; The Investigation for Fair Trial Act, 2013; Explosives Act, 1884; Explosive Substances Act, 1908; The Arms Ordinance, 1965; The Pakistan Penal Code, 1860; The Criminal Procedure Code, 1898; and The *Qanun-e-Shahadat* Order, 1984. These laws cover criminal behaviour not covered under the Anti-Terrorism Act, 1997 (ATA). For instance, the use of any explosives during the commission of a crime is declared an offence under the Explosives Act 1884 and the Explosive Substances Act 1908 while the use of illegal firearms is covered under the Arms Ordinance 1965. Similarly, some offences not covered by the ATA are instead proscribed under the general law i.e. Pakistan Penal Code. The general principle used in cases of terrorism is that all relevant sections from all relevant laws are applied in the First Information Report (FIR) which becomes the basis for subsequent prosecution of these cases. The FIR forms the basis for all police investigations. However, wherever the ATA is applied, even when other offences are also applied from other statutes, the case is taken up under the provisions of the ATA. A Joint Investigation Team (JIT) under the ATA investigates the case and the trial begins in the special court established

under the ATA. See: Hameed Zulfiqar, *Changes in Pakistan's Counter-terrorism Legal Regime: Challenges, Prospects, and Recommendations* (Washington: New America, 2015).

2. The US State Department, Office of the Coordinator for Counterterrorism, Country Reports on Terrorism 2010, August 2011, p. 122, available at: www.state.gov/documents/organization/170479.pdf., accessed on January 29, 2016.
3. For instance section 34 of the ATA has extended its scope beyond cases of terrorism. Kidnapping for ransom and abduction may be heinous offences, but they cannot be considered terrorist acts unless militant organisations carry them out to further their respective ideologies or political goals. In Pakistan, the practice of Kidnapping for ransom and abduction is widespread. There were 2,092 cases of kidnapping for ransom and 79,863 abduction cases in Pakistan reported to the police between 2008 and 2013. Classifying these all as terrorist acts has overburdened the already overstretched criminal justice system, slowing down disposal of cases. Tariq Parvez and Mehwish Rani, An Appraisal of Pakistan's Anti-Terrorism Act, United States Institute of Peace, Special Report 377, August 2015.
4. A study conducted by the Counter-Terrorism department of the Punjab province on the reasons cited by ATA courts for acquittal of terrorism accused, found that in 35 percent of cases lack of identification parade was given as a reason for acquittal.
5. In many cases in anti-terrorist courts, the judges have mentioned in their judgments that, since the accused has not been mentioned in the FIR, this goes in his favour. NasirIqbal, Judge Wants Anti-Terror Law Examined, Dawn, January 25, 2015, available at: www.dawn.com/news/1159335/judge-wants-anti-terror-law-examined, accessed on November 21, 2015.
6. Kaiser Fawad, Military jurisdiction over non-military persons, *Daily Times*, February 16, 2016, available a: http://www.dailytimes.com.pk/opinion/16-Feb-2015/military-jurisdiction-over-non-military-persons, accessed on February 23, 2016.
7. Pakistan's military courts -a solution or a problem? *Dawn*, available at: http://www.dw.com/en/pakistans-military-courts-a-solution-or-a-problem/a-18633959, accessed on January 10, 2016.
8. *Mehram Ali v. Federation of Pakistan*, PLP 1998 SC 1445.
9. Baqar, Justice Maqbool, Improving the Criminal Justice System - Response to Terrorism, available at: http://pgil.pk/wp-content/uploads/2014/04/Improving-the-criminal-Justice-System.pdf, accessed on January 10, 2016.
10. Hameed Zulfiqar, Changes in Pakistan's Counter-terrorism Legal Regime: Challenges, Prospects, and Recommendations, Washington: New America, June 11, 2015, p. 2.
11. On October 17, 1998, Hakim Muhammad Said, one of Karachi's most well-known citizens, a former Governor of Sindh and founder of the Hamdard Foundation and Hamdard University, was murdered. Under increasing political pressure and most likely from the military to do something to curb such lawlessness and violence, Nawaz Sharif chose to impose Article 232 and declare a state of emergency (Governor's Rule) in Sindh Province.
12. According to Section 6 of the Pakistan Armed Forces (Acting in Aid of Civil Power) Ordinance, 1998, "Civil commotion" means creation of internal disturbances in violation of law or intended to violate law, commencement or continuation of illegal strikes, go-slows, lock-outs, vehicle snatching/lifting, damage to or destruction of State or private property, random firing to create panic, charging protection money/

extortion, acts of criminal trespass, distributing, publishing or pasting of a handbill or making graffiti or wall-chalking intended to create unrest or fear or create a threat to the security of law and order.

13. Pakistan Armed Forces (Acting in Aid of Civil Power) (Amendment) Ordinance, 1999, dated January 30, 1999.
14. *Liaquat Hussain v. Federation of Pakistan* PLD 1999 SC 504.
15. In 2014, the PoPA was the latest in a series of laws to strengthen Pakistan's efforts to fight insurgencies, terrorism and other unspecified threats faced by the country. The PoPA incorporated many provisions of the Protection of Pakistan Ordinance, 2013 (2013 PPO), and the Protection of Pakistan (amendment) Ordinance, 2014 (2014 PPO), both of which were Presidential promulgations, passed without any debate in Parliament. The 2013 PPO was promulgated by President Mamnoon Hussain in October 2013. It created special courts for trying offences set out in the Ordinance and gave law enforcement agencies wide powers to preventively detain individuals suspected of being involved in the Scheduled Offences. The 2013 PPO was later amended through 2014 PPO to circumvent the Supreme Court's judgment in the *Muhabat Shah* case. The case involved allegations related to the unauthorised removal of 35 persons from a Malakand internment centre by the armed forces. Despite multiple orders of the Court, the army authorities only produced seven persons before the Court and the remaining 28 persons remain unaccounted for. The Supreme Court held that the unauthorised removal of detainees from an internment centre amounted to enforced disappearance. Protection of Pakistan Bill, 2014: An affront to Human Rights, International Commission of Jurists, South Asia, Rule of Law Programme, May 2014. If not extended, the PoPA would lapse on July 15, 2016.
16. The list of offences under the PoPA has twenty entries and is quite comprehensive. These offences include: crimes against minorities; killing, kidnapping, extortion, attacks or assaults on government officials, members of the judiciary, foreign officials, tourists, media personnel, social workers or other important personalities; destruction of or attacks on energy facilities, gas or oil pipelines, aircrafts and airports, national defence materials and institutions, and educational institutions; illegally crossing national boundaries "in connection with" any of the above-mentioned offences.
17. The term "sect" has been defined as a group of people with somewhat different religious beliefs (typically regarded as heretical) from those of a larger group to which they belong. The New Oxford Dictionary of English, 2000, p. 1680.
18. The PoPA empowers police and security agencies to arrest anybody on the basis of "credible" information that he/she is involved in anti-state activities, terrorism and treason. Several of its provisions contravene international human rights standards, for example by allowing security forces to conceal the location of detained persons, and their handing over to security forces without legal oversight.' Pakistan: Background information, including actors of protection, and internal relocation, Country Information and Guidance, UK, Home office, October 6, 2014, available at: https://www.gov.uk/government/publications/pakistan-country-information-and-guidance, accessed on January 24, 2016.
19. Hameed Zulfiqar, Changes in Pakistan's Counter-terrorism Legal Regime: Challenges, Prospects, and Recommendations, Washington: New America, June 11, 2015.
20. According to ICJ, the Government of Pakistan has failed to provide any "objective

and serious reasons" to justify the creation of special courts under the PoPA and to justify the distinction between offences to be tried by the special courts to be established by the PoPA, the anti-terrorism courts constituted under the ATA and ordinary courts, which try offences under the Pakistan Penal Code, 1860. Thus, the provisions of section 8 of the PoPA that authorises the establishment of special courts and grant them jurisdiction over the offences that appear in the Schedule annexed to the Act, do not appear to be consistent with Pakistan's obligation to safeguard the independence and impartiality of the administration of justice to ensure that trials by special courts are limited to "exceptional" cases where it is "necessary and justified by objective and serious reasons". Protection of Pakistan Bill, 2014: An affront to Human Rights, International Commission of Jurists, South Asia, Rule of Law Programme, May 2014.

21. Niazi Tahir, UN Bodies voice objections to military courts, The Nations, December 7, 2015, available at: http://nation.com.pk/islamabad/07-Dec-2015/un-bodies-voice-objection-to-military-courts, accessed on January 12, 2016.
22. Protection of Pakistan Bill, 2014: An affront to Human Rights, International Commission of Jurists, South Asia, Rule of Law Programme, May 2014.
23. Fayyaz, Shabana, Responding to Terrorism: Pakistan's Anti-Terrorism Laws, *Perspectives on Terrorism*, Vol. II, issue 6, March 2008, pp. 10-19.

4

The Right to a Fair Trial

Introduction

Since their inception in January 2015, the military courts (FGCM) established under the Army Act, 1952 have concluded trials of nearly 80 individuals. Almost every accused has been found guilty; while most have been awarded the death sentences, a few have been sentenced to life imprisonment. The information about the execution of those awarded the deaths is not in public domain. The families of a few individuals convicted by the military court have challenged the verdict before the constitutional courts on the grounds that suspects were denied the right to a fair trial by FGCM. In at least two cases, families claim the convicts were children when they were arrested by the law enforcement agencies. A few of these petitions are pending in the Supreme Court of Pakistan.[1]

The right to a fair trial is a norm of international human rights law. It is designed to protect individuals from the unlawful and arbitrary curtailment or deprivation of their basic rights and freedoms, the most prominent of which are the rights to life and liberty. The chapter will examine whether the military courts, in particular trial under FGCM meet the international standards of a right to fair trial.

The Right to a Fair Trial

The right to a fair trial as enshrined in Article 10 of the Universal Declaration of Human Rights (UDHR) declares: "Everyone is entitled in full liberty to a fair and public hearing by an independent and impartial tribunal, in determination of his rights and obligations and of any criminal charges against him." Article 11 (1) of the UDHR further states: "Everyone charged with a penal offence has the right to be presumed innocent until proved guilty according to law in a public trial at which he has had all the guarantees necessary for his defence." These two rights are further elaborated under Article 14 of the International Covenant on Civil and Political Rights (ICCPR),[2] which provides that "everyone shall be entitled to a fair and public hearing by a competent, independent and impartial tribunal established by law." The Human Rights Committee in their General Comment No. 32 on Article 14 of the ICCPR has stated, "The right to equality before the courts and tribunals and to a fair trial is a key element of human rights protection and serves as a procedural means to safeguard the rule of law."[3]

The UN General Assembly has adopted the Basic Principles on the Independence of the Judiciary, in 1985, which provides that "everyone shall have the right to be tried by ordinary courts or tribunals using established legal procedures."[4] In addition the Commission on Human Rights has also reiterated that "everyone has the right to be tried by ordinary courts or tribunals using duly established legal procedures and that tribunals that do not use such procedures should not be created to displace the jurisdiction belonging to the ordinary courts or judicial tribunals." The provisions on the right to a fair trial and judicial guarantees are also contained in regional human rights instruments like the American Convention on Human Rights (Article 8), the European Convention on Human Rights (Article 6) and the African Charter on Human and Peoples' Rights (Article 7).

The right to a fair trial is applicable both to the determination of an individual's rights and duties in a suit at law and with respect to the determination of any criminal charge against him or her. The term "suit at law" refers to proceedings in various types of courts, including military and administrative courts. The standards against which a trial is to be assessed in terms of fairness are numerous, complex and constantly evolving.[5] They may constitute binding obligations that are included in human rights treaties to which the State is a party. They may also be found in documents which, though not formally binding, can be taken to express the direction in which the law is evolving.[6]

The Human Rights Committee did not consider initially that the trial of civilians by military courts was, *per se*, incompatible with the ICCPR, provided that the jurisdiction of such courts was in keeping with the provisions of Article 14 of the Covenant. However, the Committee gradually came to criticise such tribunals during its consideration of periodic reports.[7] The Committee subsequently made it increasingly clear that it was in favour of limiting the jurisdiction of military tribunals for the trial of civilians by military tribunals was incompatible with the administration of fair, impartial and independent justice.[8]

The Basic Principles on the Independence of the Judiciary, adopted in September 1985, provides that "everyone shall have the right to be tried by ordinary courts or tribunals using established legal procedures". The Commission on Human Rights in its resolution of April 22, 2002,[9] entitled "Integrity of the judicial system", had declared that every person is entitled: (i) to a fair and public hearing by a competent, independent and impartial tribunal, in the determination of his/her rights and obligations and of any criminal charge against him/her; (ii) has the right to be tried by ordinary courts or tribunals using duly established legal procedures and that tribunals that do not use such procedures should not be created to displace the jurisdiction belonging to the ordinary courts or judicial tribunals; (iii) any court trying a person charged with a criminal offence must be based on the principles of independence and impartiality; and (iv) the states that have military courts for trying criminal offenders to ensure that such courts are an integral part of the general judicial system and use the duly established legal proceedings.

The World Conference on the Independence of Justice, held in Canada, in June 1983, adopted the Universal Declaration on the Independence of Justice.[10] It provides: "The jurisdiction of military tribunals shall be confined to military offences committed by military personnel. There shall always be a right of appeal from such tribunals to a legally qualified appellate court."

The issue of the administration of justice through military tribunals is, also explicitly addressed by certain standards of a non-treaty nature. Article 5 of the draft declaration on the independence and impartiality of the judiciary, jurors and assessors and the independence of lawyers, referred to as the "Singhvi declaration",[11] provides that the jurisdiction of military tribunals should be confined exclusively to "military offences". Article 5 reads as follows: (i) no ad hoc tribunals shall be established to displace jurisdiction properly vested in the courts; (ii) in times of emergency, the State shall endeavour to provide that civilians charged with criminal offences of any kind shall be tried by ordinary civilian courts...; and (iii) the jurisdiction of military tribunals shall be confined to military offences. There shall always be a right of appeal from such tribunals to a legally qualified appellate court or tribunal or a remedy by way of an application for annulment.

Constitution of Pakistan and the Right to a Fair Trial

Article 10A of the Constitution of Pakistan provides for the right to fair trial in the following terms: "For the determination of his civil rights and obligations or in any criminal charge against him a person shall be entitled to a fair trial and due process." Article 10-A is largely inspired by Article 6 of the European Convention on Human Rights as the legislators in Pakistan have introduced two fundamental concepts i.e. of due process and fair trial. The scope of these two concepts has much wider meaning than fair trial,[12] however, while incorporating Article 10A in the Constitution the legislature did not define or describe the requisites of a 'fair trial'.

According to Pakistan Supreme Court[13] the basic requirements of the doctrine "due process of law", is enshrined in Article 4 of the Constitution. It is intrinsically linked with the right to have access to justice, which is a Fundamental Right. This right *inter alia* includes the right to have a fair and proper trial and a right to have an impartial court or tribunal. A person cannot be said to have been given a fair and proper trial unless he is provided a reasonable opportunity to defend the allegation made against him. Further, the right of due process envisages the right to have a fair and proper trial and right to have impartial court or tribunal. The right to a fair trial has been elaborately defined under Article 14 of the ICCCPR.

FGCM and Fair Trial

The military courts established in Pakistan while trying military offenders have jurisdiction to both, exclusive military offences as well as civil offences committed by military personnel. They also have the jurisdiction to try civilians (for examples, terrorists or others suspected of involved in terrorism) for offences under the Army Act, 1952 as amended in 2015 or any other law.

Pre-Trial Rights

The Prohibition of Arbitrary Arrest and Detention

The Protection of Pakistan Act (PoPA), 2014, empowers the members of the armed forces (Army, Navy, Air Force and their reserves), civil armed forces (Police, Frontier Constabulary, Frontier Corps, Pakistan Coast Guards, Rangers and any other civil armed forces as notified) to arrest without warrant and detain any suspect for 90 days.[14] The aforesaid members of the armed forces may on reasonable apprehension of commission of a scheduled offence use necessary force to prevent the commission of offence and can exercise all powers of a police officer under the Pakistan Code of Criminal Procedure, 1898. They can use lethal force against any suspect. In the event of the death or grievous hurt of a suspect in firing, the matter will be investigated by the concerned law enforcement agency. In case the firing has resulted in the death, the matter will be investigated by a person appointed by the Federal Government. The members of the law enforcement agencies can register more than one FIR against any suspect. Arrest can be made on charges of corruption, money laundering and financial embezzlement. For example, if a person is facing money laundering charges related to terror financing, military personnel can detain such an individual under PoPA despite the fact that money laundering is a scheduled offence under Federal Investigation Agency Act, 1974.

The PoPA also empower security forces involved in the fight against terrorism in Pakistan, to order preventive detention without adequate safeguards, and in some cases, to even detain individuals secretly, and to retroactively apply the law to legitimise illegal detentions. The POPA also grants immunity to the law-enforcement officers who might be responsible for serious human rights violations such as arbitrary detention and enforced disappearance. These provisions are incompatible with a number of international human rights norms and standards, including the ICCPR, which Pakistan ratified on June 23,

2010 and the UN declaration on the protection of all persons from enforced disappearance.

The liberty of a person has been interpreted narrowly, to mean freedom of bodily movement, which is interfered with when an individual is confined to a specific space, such as a prison or a detention facility. The prohibition of arbitrariness mentioned in Article 9 (1) of ICCPR serves to ensure that the law is not arbitrary, i.e., that the deprivation of liberty permitted by law is not manifestly disproportional, unjust or unpredictable, and the specific manner in which an arrest is made must not be discriminatory and must be able to be deemed appropriate and proportional in view of the circumstances of the case.

The Right to Know the Reasons for Arrest

Article 9(2) of the ICCPR provides that "anyone who is arrested shall be informed, at the time of arrest, of the reasons for his arrest and shall be promptly informed of any charges against him". These provisions have been interpreted to mean that anyone who is arrested must be informed of the general reasons for the arrest "at the time of arrest", while subsequent information, to be furnished "promptly", must contain accusations in the legal sense. Section 22 of the PoPA allows the government to amend the list of "scheduled offences" by adding, modifying or omitting any entry. Such vaguely defined offences contravene Article 9 of the ICCPR which establishes the right of any person not to be arbitrarily deprived of his liberty except on grounds established by law.[15] The Human Rights Committee while interpreting Article 9 of the ICCPR has amplified that any substantive grounds for arrest or detention must be prescribed by law and should be defined with sufficient precision to avoid overly broad or arbitrary interpretation or application.

The Right to Legal Counsel

On November 7, 2015, a woman approached the Pakistan Supreme Court against the death sentence awarded to her cleric son by a military court for terrorism, after her plea was dismissed by Peshawar High Court. The petitioner alleged that while the High Court dismissed her plea over the unavailability of record of the convict, military authorities did not allow her son to engage a counsel. It was claimed by the petitioner that the High Court's judgment was not in accordance with the directions and observations made by the Apex Court in its judgment on the 18th and 21st Constitutional Amendments case.[16] Section 6 of the PoPA empowers the government of Pakistan and law-enforcing agencies to preventively detain individuals suspected of being involved in "scheduled offences" for 90 days. As far as the right to a counsel in a trial by FGCM, no such right exists under the Army Act, 1952. He may be allowed to have any person to assist him during the trial.

The right to be provided and communicate with counsel is the most scrutinised specific guarantee of a fair trial, because it has been demonstrated to be the one that is violated most often. Principle 1 of the Basic Principles on Lawyers states that "all persons are entitled to call upon the assistance of a lawyer of their choice to protect and establish their rights and to defend them in all stages of criminal proceedings". This right is particularly relevant in the case of pre-trial detention. Principle 5 of the Basic Principles on Lawyers specifically provides that when a person is arrested, charged or detained, he or she must be promptly informed of the right to legal assistance of his or her choice. Article 7 of the Basic Principles on Lawyers requires governments to ensure that all persons arrested or detained should have access to a lawyer within 48 hours of arrest or detention. [17]

The Right to a Prompt Appearance Before a Judge to Challenge the Lawfulness of Arrest and Detention

Article 9(3) of the ICCPR refers specifically to the rights of a person arrested or detained on a criminal charge to "be brought promptly before a judge or other officer authorised by law to exercise judicial power and ......shall be entitled to trial within a reasonable time or to release". Article 9(4) of the ICCPR provides for the right to *habeas corpus*, that is, the right of anyone deprived of liberty by arrest or detention to "take proceedings before a court, in order that that court may decide without delay on the lawfulness of his detention and order his release if the detention is not lawful". In this context, the term "court" signifies not only a regular court, but a special court, including an administrative, constitutional or military court.[18] Lastly, Article 9(5) of the ICCPR provides that "anyone who has been the victim of unlawful arrest or detention shall have an enforceable right to compensation". Such a claim arises when the arrest or detention has contravened the provisions of Article 9(1) to (4) and/or a provision of domestic law. All these human rights provisions are violated when an individual is detained under PoPA as a suspect and could be detained secretively up to 90 days.

The Prohibition of Torture and the Right to Humane Conditions During Pre-Trial Detention

Article 7 of the ICCPR prohibits torture or cruel, inhuman or degrading treatment or punishment and is a norm of customary international law that also belongs to the category of *jus cogens*. The definition of torture,[19] which is prohibited by the ICC Statute as a crime against humanity when committed on a widespread or systematic basis, is slightly broader in that Statute than in the 1984 Convention against Torture. The incommunicado detention, authorised under PoPA for up to 90 days, may violate Article 7 of the ICCPR which prohibits torture, as well as inhuman, cruel and degrading treatment.

Principle 19 of the Body of Principles states that a "detained or imprisoned person shall have the right to be visited by and to correspond with, in particular, members of his family and shall be given adequate opportunity to communicate with the outside world, subject to reasonable conditions and restrictions as specified by law or lawful regulations". At a minimum, the right to communicate with "the outside world" includes the right to communicate with one's family, a lawyer and a doctor.

Rights during Hearing

Equal Access to, and Equality before, the Courts

The first sentence of Article 14(1) of the ICCPR provides that "all persons shall be equal before the courts and tribunals", and has been interpreted to signify that all persons must be granted, without discrimination, the right of equal access to a court.[20] This, on the one hand, means that establishing separate courts for different groups of people on the basis of their race, colour, sex, language, religion, political or other opinion, national or social origin, property, birth or other status would be a contravention of Article 14(1). On the other hand, the establishment of certain types of special courts with jurisdiction over all persons belonging to the same category, such as military personnel, remains a thorny issue. The second sentence of Article 14(1) relates to the right to a fair and public hearing by a competent, independent and impartial tribunal established by law. It includes the basic components of due process of law which is, in criminal cases, further supplemented by the other provisions of Articles 14 and 15. During the trial by FGCM, an accused is not entitled to engage a civilian counsel. Instead, he is provided with a military officer to act as "defending officer" for the defence of the accused. The military officer remains in the chain of command of the convening officer who has assembled the Court Martial. The expectation that the military "defending officer" would provide an effective defence to an accused is imprudent and absurd.

The Right to a Fair and Public Hearing

The right to a fair hearing as provided for in Article 14(1) of the ICCPR encompasses the procedural and other guarantees laid down in paragraphs 2 to 7 of Article 14 and Article 15. However, the right is wider in scope, as can be deduced from the wording of Article 14(3) which refers to the concrete rights enumerated as "minimum guarantees". The single most important criterion in evaluating the fairness of a trial is the observance of the principle of equality of arms between the defence and the prosecution.

Article 14(1) of the ICCPR also guarantees the right to a public hearing as one of the essential elements of the concept of a fair trial. However, it also permits several exceptions to this general rule under specified circumstances. The publicity of a trial includes both the public nature of the hearings in all the stages of the proceedings, as well as the publicity of the judgement eventually rendered in a case. It is a right belonging to the parties, but also to the general public in a democratic society. The right to a public hearing means that the hearing should as a rule be conducted orally and publicly, without a specific request by the parties to that effect. The court or tribunal is, *inter alia*, obliged to make information about the time and venue of the public hearing available and to provide adequate facilities for attendance by interested members of the public, within reasonable limits. The public, including the press, may be excluded from all or part of a trial for the reasons specified in Article 14(1), but such exclusion must be based on a decision of the court rendered in keeping with the respective rules of procedure. Article 14(1) is violated in cases where the hearing has taken place in camera when the State party has failed to justify this measure in accordance with the terms of the ICCPR.[21]

A public hearing is an essential feature of the right to a fair trial. However, the Army Act, 1952 does not require that trials in Court Martial should take place in public. The Army Act, 1952, after its amendment in November 2015, allows judges of military courts to hold *in camera* trials, and keep the identities of individuals associated with the case secret.[22] Since in a trial by FGCM, public is completely excluded; its fairness always remains doubtful. By rendering the administration of justice visible, publicity contributes to the achievement of a fair trial, the guarantee of which is one of the fundamental principles of any democratic society. Transparency is fundamental to the administration of justice. A transparency safeguard is contained in Article 14 (1) of the International Covenant on Civil and Political Rights. The Human Rights Committee observed that transparency "is a duty upon the State that is not dependent on any request by the interested party".[23]

The Right to a Competent, Independent and Impartial Tribunal Established by Law

The military courts in general and FGCM in particular cannot be called a competent, independent and impartial tribunal. The court members, judge advocate, if detailed, and defending officer always remain under full command of the convening authority. The latter exercises command and control over court functionaries in all areas of their service carrier, including assessment in their annual reports, future promotions, training course for their career progression, postings and appointment. The members of the court, though empowered to award the death sentence after a brief trial, have no training in law. They determine both guilt and punishment of an accused. The presence of judge advocate is not a legal requirement for a FGCM. Even if a judge advocate is present in the court, the members are not bound by his advice.

Under the ICCPR, the right to be tried by an independent and impartial tribunal must be applied at all times and is contained in Article 14(1), which provides that "in the determination of any criminal charge against him, or of his rights and obligations in a suit at law, everyone shall be entitled to a fair and public hearing by a competent, independent and impartial tribunal established by law." The rationale of this provision is to avoid the arbitrariness and/or bias that would potentially arise if criminal charges were to be decided on by a political body or an administrative agency. The general aim of this provision is to ensure that criminal charges are heard by a court set up in advance and independently of a particular case and not prior to and specifically for the offence involved. The establishment of special military courts to try certain groups of individuals in Pakistan violates this provision.

The Right to a Presumption of Innocence

According to Article 14(2) of the ICCPR, "everyone charged with a criminal offence shall have the right to be presumed innocent until proved guilty according to law". As a basic component of the right to a fair trial, the presumption of innocence, *inter alia*, means that the burden of proof in a criminal trial lies on the prosecution and that the accused has the benefit of doubt. The presumption of innocence must, in addition, be maintained not only during a criminal trial *vis a vis* the defendant, but also in relation to a suspect or accused throughout the pre-trial phase. It is the duty both of the officials involved in a case as well as all public authorities to maintain the presumption of innocence by "refraining from prejudging the outcome of a trial".

The Right to Prompt Notice of the Nature and Cause of Criminal Charges

Everyone against whom any criminal charge is brought shall be entitled, in full equality, "to be informed promptly and in detail in a language which he understands of the nature and cause of the charge against him".

This duty to inform relates to an exact legal description of the offence ("nature") and of the facts underlying it ("cause"), and is thus broader than the corresponding rights granted under Article 9(2) of the ICCPR applicable to arrest. The rationale is that the information provided must be sufficient to allow the preparation of a defence.

The Right to Adequate Time and Facilities for the Preparation of a Defence

Article 14(3)(b) of the ICCPR provides that everyone is entitled in the determination of any criminal charge against him or her "to have adequate time and facilities for the preparation of his defence and to communicate with counsel of his own choosing". The right to adequate time and facilities for the preparation of a defence applies not only to the defendant, but to his or her defence counsel as well and is to be observed in all stages of the proceedings. What constitutes "adequate" time will depend on the nature of the proceedings and the factual circumstances of a case. The factors to be taken into account include the complexity of the case, the defendant's access to evidence, and the time limits provided for in domestic law for certain actions in the proceedings.

The Right to a Trial Without Undue Delay

Everyone shall be entitled in the determination of any criminal charge against him/her, "to be tried without undue delay".[24] This provision has been interpreted to signify the right to a trial that produces a final judgement and, if appropriate, a sentence without undue delay. The time limit "begins to run when the suspect (accused, defendant) is informed that the authorities are taking specific steps to prosecute him". The assessment of what may be considered undue delay will depend on the circumstances of a case, i.e., its complexity, the conduct of the parties, whether the accused is in detention, etc. The right is not contingent on a request by the accused to be tried without undue delay. Under the provisions of PoPA, persons arrested and detained under 'preventive detention' are denied their right to be brought promptly before a court, and not to be detained beyond the initial legal period without the authority of a magistrate, as provided by Article 10 of the Constitution of Pakistan."

The provisions relating to preventive detention are not compatible with international standards.

The Right to Defend Oneself in Person or Through Legal Counsel

Article 14(3)(d) of the ICCPR guarantee the right of anyone charged with a criminal offence to defend himself in person or through legal assistance of his own choice. The right of access to legal assistance must be effectively available, and the accused or his lawyer must have the right to act diligently and fearlessly in pursuing all available defences and the right to challenge the conduct of the case if they believe it to be unfair. In cases where the court is empowered to award the death sentence, the legal assistance to the accused must be provided in ways that adequately and effectively ensure justice.

The right to counsel in the pre-trial stages of a criminal trial is clearly linked to the right to a defence during trial, as set out in Article 14(3)(d) of the ICCPR. The provision includes the following specific rights: (i) the right to be tried in one's presence, which means that the trial would not be *in absentia*; (ii) the right to defend oneself in person; (iii) the right to choose one's own counsel; (iv) the right to be informed of the right to counsel; and (v) the right to receive free legal assistance. Article 14(3)(d) of the ICCPR provides that in the determination of any criminal charge, everyone shall be entitled "to have legal assistance assigned to him, in any case where the interests of justice so require, and without payment by him in any such case if he does not have sufficient means to pay for it".

According to the Human Rights Committee's jurisprudence under Article 14(3)(d): "The court should ensure that the conduct of a case by a lawyer is not incompatible with the interests of justice. .... in a capital case, when counsel for the accused concedes that there is no merit in the appeal, the Court should ascertain whether counsel has consulted with the accused and informed him accordingly. If not, the Court must ensure that the accused is so informed and given an opportunity to engage other counsel."[25] Unfortunately, in a trial by FGCM, the convening authority has the right to deny a counsel to an accused. Instead, he may detail a military officer to defend the accused, thereby making entire provision meaningless.

The Right to Examine Witnesses

Article 14(3)(e) of the International Covenant provides that, in the determination of any criminal charge against him, everyone shall be entitled to "examine, or have examined, the witnesses against him and to obtain the attendance and examination of witnesses on his behalf under the same conditions as witnesses against him". This right is an essential element of the principle of equality of arms. The terms "to examine" and "have examined" should be read as recognition of the two main systems of criminal justice, the inquisitorial and accusatorial one. However, the defence does not have an unlimited right to obtain the compulsory attendance of witnesses on the defendant's behalf, but only "under the same conditions" as witnesses against him/her.

In addition, Article 14(3)(e) has been concretely interpreted to mean that the prosecution must inform the defence of the witnesses it intends to call at trial within a reasonable time prior to the trial, so that the defendant may have sufficient time to prepare his/her defence. The defendant also has the right to be present during the testimony of a witness and may be restricted in doing so only in exceptional circumstances, such as when the witness reasonably fears reprisal by the defendant. A military officer detailed by the convening authority works under the command influence. To expect him to defend an accused against the interest of convening authority would be absurd.

The Right to an Interpreter

According to Article 14(3)(f) of the Covenant everyone shall be entitled to "have the free assistance of an interpreter if he cannot understand or speak the language used in court". The Army Act Rules provide for the detailing of an interpreter in military courts, or else the Presiding Officer of the court can perform the task of an interpreter.

The Prohibition on Self-incrimination

In the determination of any criminal charge against him/her, everyone is entitled "not to be compelled to testify against himself or to confess guilt".[26] This provision aims to prohibit any form of coercion, whether direct or indirect, physical or mental, and whether before or during the trial, that could be used to force the accused to testify against him/herself or to confess guilt. The judge must have the authority to consider an allegation of coercion or torture at any stage of the proceedings. In addition, silence by the accused may not be used as evidence to prove guilt and no adverse consequences may be drawn from an accused's exercise of the right to remain silent.

The amendments to the Pakistan Army Act allow the Federal Government to transfer proceedings pending in any other court against any person accused of committing prescribed offences under the amended law to a military court. Where cases are transferred from other courts, military courts may admit as evidence and base a verdict on previously recorded statements which means that witnesses who have already testified before a civilian court are not required to testify again before the military court after the case has been transferred. Even a previously recorded self-incriminating statement may be used against them in FGCM.

The Prohibition on Retroactive Application of Criminal Laws

Article 15(1) of the ICCPR, which embodies the principle *nullum crimen sine lege* (a crime must be provided for by law), can, in fact, be taken as a point of departure in any consideration of the fairness of a trial. In the broad sense, it expresses the principle of legality, according to which "no one shall be held guilty of any criminal offence on account of any act or omission which did not constitute a criminal offence, under national or international law, at the time when it was committed".[27] In the narrow sense, it is aimed at prohibiting the retroactive application of substantive criminal law and thus chronologically precedes a determination of the procedural fairness of a trial pursuant to Article 14.[28] It is one of the few inalienable rights provided for in Article 4(2) of the ICCPR.

The Prohibition on Double Jeopardy

The ICCPR contains the prohibition of double jeopardy or the principle of *ne bis in idem*, according to which "no one shall be liable to be tried or punished again for an offence for which he has already been finally convicted or acquitted in accordance with the law and penal procedure of each country".[29] Article 8(4) of the American Convention guarantees this principle in the following words: "An accused person acquitted by a non-appealable judgement shall not be subjected to a new trial for the same cause". Protocol No. 7 to the European Convention provides in its Article 4(1) that "no one shall be liable to be tried or punished again in criminal proceedings under the jurisdiction of the same State for an offence for which he has already been finally acquitted or convicted in accordance with the law and penal procedure of that State". However, according to Article 4(2) of the Protocol, these provisions "shall not prevent the re-opening of the case … if there is evidence of new or newly discovered facts, or if there has been a fundamental defect in the previous proceedings, which would affect the outcome of the case". The principle of *ne bis in idem* is non-derogable under the ECHR (Article. 4(3) of Protocol No. 7).

The Right to a Reasoned Judgement

The right to a reasoned judgement, inherent in the provision regarding a "fair trial", is not applicable in a trial by military courts. The Pakistan Army Act and Rules make no such provisions. In the absence of a reasoned decision the convicted persons cannot effectively approach higher courts for the review of his conviction and sentence.

Post-Trial Rights

The Right to Appeal

The ICCPR provides that "everyone convicted of a crime shall have the right to his conviction and sentence being reviewed by a higher tribunal according to law".[30] The existence of a right to appeal is a right guaranteed by the Covenant itself and its existence is thus not in theory dependent on domestic law; the reference to "according to law" refers here exclusively to "the modalities by which the review by a higher tribunal is to be carried out".

The Pakistan Army Act, 1952, was amended in 1992 to establish military Courts of Appeal. However, military officers constituting Appeal Courts are detailed by the same convening authority, which has assembled FGCM. The officers constituting Court of Appeal as well as Judge Advocate function under command influence. The most apprehensible forms of influence occur when the commander intervenes directly by suggesting the result he desires in a particular case. Any difference of opinion on the issue of conviction or sentence with the convening authority could affect the future careers of the court members/ judge advocate. The feasibility of evaluation of the evidence and the conduct of the trial in Court of Appeals can be ruled out. The decision of Court of Appeals remains final and could not be questioned before any court or authority.[31] In Pakistan, the High Courts and the Supreme Court may review decisions of military courts.

The Right to Compensation for Miscarriage of Justice

"When a person has by a final decision been convicted of a criminal offence and when subsequently his conviction has been reversed or he has been pardoned on the ground that a new or newly discovered fact shows conclusively that there has been a miscarriage of justice, the person who has suffered punishment as a result of such conviction shall be compensated according to law, unless it is proved that the non-disclosure of the unknown fact in time is wholly or partly attributable to him."[32] The compensation for miscarriage of justice may be granted only after a conviction has become final, and the claim may be brought regardless of the severity of the offence involved. There are three additional conditions that must be cumulatively met: (i) a miscarriage of justice must have been subsequently officially acknowledged by a reversal of the conviction or by pardon; (ii) the delayed disclosure of the pertinent fact(s) must not be attributable to the convicted person; and (iii) the convicted person must have suffered punishment as a result of the miscarriage of justice. The military legal system in Pakistan has no such provisions.

The Right to a Fair Trial and Military Tribunals

The Commission on Human Rights in its Sixty-second session has considered the report submitted by the Special Rapporteur on the issue of the administration of justice through military tribunals.[33] The report contains an updated version of "draft principles governing the administration of justice through military tribunals". These principles emphasise that the military justice must be an integral part of the general judicial system, and should have minimum level of universally applicable rules, leaving scope for stricter standards to be defined under domestic law.

A list of 20 principles contained in the document dictate that the military tribunals must be established by the Constitution or the law, respecting the principle of the separation of powers. They must be an integral part of the general judicial system. The tribunals must in all circumstances apply standards and procedures internationally recognised as guarantees of a fair trial, including the rules of international humanitarian law. In times of crisis, recourse to Martial Law or special regimes should not compromise the guarantees of a fair trial. Military tribunals should not be substituted for ordinary courts, in derogation from ordinary law. Further, the military courts should, in principle, have no jurisdiction to try civilians. In all circumstances, the state should ensure that civilians accused of a criminal offence of any nature are tried by civilian courts. Strict respect for the guarantees provided in the Convention on the Rights of the Child and the United Nations Standard Minimum Rules for the Administration of Juvenile Justice (Beijing Rules) should govern the prosecution and punishment of minors, who fall within the category of vulnerable persons. In no case, therefore, should minors be placed under the jurisdiction of military courts.

These principles also provide that the jurisdiction of military courts should be limited to offences of a strictly military nature committed by military personnel. In all circumstances, the jurisdiction of military courts should be set aside in favour of the jurisdiction of the ordinary courts to conduct inquiries into serious human rights violations such as extrajudicial executions, enforced disappearances and torture, and to prosecute and try persons accused of such crimes. Military secrecy may be invoked, under the supervision of independent monitoring bodies, when it is strictly necessary to protect information concerning national defence.[34] The organisation and operation of military courts should fully ensure the right of everyone to a competent, independent and impartial tribunal at every stage of legal proceedings from initial investigation to trial. The persons selected to perform the functions of judges in military courts must display integrity and competence and show proof of the necessary legal training and qualifications. Military judges should have a status guaranteeing their independence and impartiality. As in matters of ordinary law, public hearings must be the rule, and the holding of sessions in camera should be altogether exceptional and be authorised by a specific, well-grounded decision the legality of which is subject to review. The exercise of the rights of the defence must be fully guaranteed in military courts under all circumstances. In all cases where military tribunals exist, their authority should be limited to ruling in first instance. Consequently, recourse procedures, particularly appeals, should be brought before the civil courts. In all situations, disputes concerning legality should be settled by the highest civil court. Conflicts of authority and jurisdiction between military tribunals and ordinary courts must be resolved by a higher judicial body, such as a Supreme Court, composed of independent, impartial and competent judges. Codes of military justice should reflect the international trend towards the gradual abolition of the death penalty, in both peacetime and wartime. Lastly, the codes of military justice should be subject to periodic systematic review, conducted in an independent and transparent manner, so as to ensure that the authority of military tribunals corresponds to strict functional necessity, without encroaching on the jurisdiction that can and should belong to ordinary civil courts.

The European Court of Human Rights (ECtHR) has found a number of violations in respect of military tribunals constituted under the British military justice system. In *Findlay v. United Kingdom*, it was held that a Court Martial convened pursuant to the Army Act, 1955 did not meet requirements of independence and impartiality set by the European Convention [Article 6 (1)], in particular, the central role played in the prosecution by the "Convening officer": he was responsible for convening the Court Martial and for appointing its members and the Prosecuting Officer, but was closely linked to the Prosecuting Authorities (he had the final decision on the nature and detail of the charges to be brought) and was superior in rank to the members of the Court Martial. In *Grieves v. the United Kingdom* the ECtHR found that British naval court martial systems violated Article 6 because of the *ad hoc* appointments of Presidents for each Court Martial and the fact that Judge Advocates were serving military officers.[35] In pursuant to the decisions of the ECtHR, extensive reforms were made in the British military justice system.

International human rights instruments specify how justice is to be administered and under what conditions. The notions of an independent and impartial tribunal, due process of law and the existence of judicial guarantees are essential components. The United Nations General Assembly is of the opinion that an independent and impartial judiciary and an independent legal profession are essential pre-requisites for the protection of human rights and to ensure that there is no discrimination in the administration of justice. Unfortunately, the military courts established in Pakistan post-January 2015 lack almost all the guarantees of independent and impartial tribunals. Pakistan, or for that matter any other country in the world, has a duty to protect its people against terrorists. In case of attack on its people, the states have a duty to investigate and prosecute those responsible for unlawful acts. For the counter-terrorism measures to be effective in the long term, they must be legitimate. It has been alleged by the International Commission of Jurists that the laws authorising the trial of civilians in military courts for terrorism-related offences in Pakistan are incompatible with international standards, which require that those accused of any criminal offence- no matter how heinous- are guaranteed a fair trial by an independent, impartial and competent tribunal.[36] International standards require that military courts, like all other courts, must be independent, impartial and competent, and in criminal cases must respect minimum guarantees of fairness, including those contained in Article 14 of the ICCPR. FGCM constituted by Pakistani army for trial of civilians are not independent and the proceedings before them fall far short of the guarantees enshrined in Article 10A of the Constitution as well as international fair trial standards.

Notes

1. Appearing before the Supreme Court on behalf of one of the appellant Haider Ali in the matter, senior lawyer Asma Jahangir contended that Baloch Regiment nabbed Ali on September 21, 2009 under the Action in Aid of Civil Power Regulation,

2011 while he was juvenile. Asma Jahangir alleged that under Article 10-A of the Constitution due process of law was not observed in the trial, saying that her client was not familiar with English language but Pashto; while trial was conducted in English which was against the due process of law. Mohla Khudayar, Convictions by military court: SC reserves judgment on five judicial reviews, *Business Recorder*, June 14, 2016, available at: http://www.brecorder.com/general-news/172/56429/, accessed June 14, 2016.

2. International Covenant on Civil and Political Rights, UN General Assembly resolution 2200A (XXI), December 16, 1966, entered into force on March 23, 1976.
3. Human Rights Committee, General Comment No. 32, Article 14: Right to equality before courts and tribunals and to a fair trial, UN Doc. CCPR/C/GC/32 (2007).
4. Basic Principles on the Independence of the Judiciary, UN General Assembly resolution 40/32, November 29, 1985 and resolution 40/146, December 13, 1985.
5. Dominic McGoldrick. *The Human Rights Committee, Its Role in the Development of the International Covenant on Civil and Political Rights,* (Oxford: Clarendon Press, 1994) p. 415.
6. Non-binding documents of relevance to the conduct of criminal proceedings and to ascertaining fair trial standards include: the Basic Principles for the Treatment of Prisoners, UN General Assembly resolution 45/111, December 14, 1990; Standard Minimum Rules for the Treatment of Prisoners, UN Economic and Social Council resolution 663 C (XXIV), July 31, 1957 and resolution 2076 (LXII), May 13, 1977; Body of Principles for the Protection of All Persons under Any Form of Detention or Imprisonment, UN General Assembly resolution 43/173, December 9, 1988; Basic Principles on the Role of Lawyers, adopted by the Eighth United Nations Congress on the Prevention of Crime and the Treatment of Offenders, Havana, Cuba, August 27-September 7, 1990; UN Standard Minimum Rules for the Administration of Juvenile Justice, UN General Assembly resolution 40/33, November 29, 1985; Code of Conduct for Law Enforcement Officials, UN General Assembly resolution 34/169, December 17, 1979; Guidelines on the Role of Prosecutors, adopted by the Eighth United Nations Congress on the Prevention of Crime and the Treatment of Offenders, Havana, Cuba, August 27-September 7, 1990; Principles on the Effective Prevention and Investigation of Extralegal, Arbitrary and Summary Executions, UN Economic and Social Council recommended resolution 1989/65, May 24, 1989; Basic Principles on the Use of Force and Firearms by Law Enforcement Officials, adopted by the Eighth United Nations Congress on the Prevention of Crime and the Treatment of Offenders, Havana, Cuba, August 27-September 7, 1990.
7. Periodic Reports concerning Algeria, Colombia, Morocco, the Republic of Korea and Venezuela. See UN ECOSOC E/CN.4/Sub.2/2002/4 dated July 9, 2002.
8. In the cases of Cameroon, Chile, Egypt, Kuwait, Lebanon, Poland, the Russian Federation, Slovakia, the Syrian Arab Republic and Uzbekistan. See UN ECOSOC E/CN.4/Sub.2/2002/4 dated July 9, 2002.
9. Resolution 2002/37 adopted April 22, 2002, paragraphs 1, 2, 5 and 8.
10. E/CN.4/Sub.2/1985/18/Add.6, annex IV), paragraph 2.06 (e).
11. E/CN.4/Sub.2/1988/20/Add.1 and Add.1/Corr.1.
12. Shamshad Ahmad, The Tale of Democracy in Pakistan, September 16, 2013, available at: http://www.criterion-quarterly.com/the-tale-of-democracy-in-pakistan/, accessed December 22, 2015.
13. As held in *Sharaf Faridi v Islamic Republic of Pakistan*, PLD 1989 Karachi 404.

14. Section 6 of the PoPA empowers the government of Pakistan and law-enforcing agencies to preventively detain individuals suspected of being involved in "scheduled offences" for 90 days. Persons arrested and detained under 'preventive detention' are denied their rights to be informed of the grounds for arrest, to a lawyer of free choice, to be brought promptly before a court, and not to be detained beyond the initial legal period without the authority of a magistrate, as provided by Article 10 of the Constitution of Pakistan."
15. Article 9 (1) and (2) of the ICCPR provide: Everyone has the right to liberty and security of person. No one shall be subjected to arbitrary arrest or detention. No one shall be deprived of his liberty except on such grounds and in accordance with such procedure as are established by law. Anyone who is arrested shall be informed, at the time of arrest, of the reasons for his arrest and shall be promptly informed of any charges against him.
16. Hasnaat Malik, Women approaches supreme Court against military court's death sentence for cleric son, *The Express Tribune*, November 7, 2015, Available at: http://tribune.com.pk/story/986915/woman-approaches-sc-against-military-courts-death-sentence-for-cleric-son/, accessed on January 12, 2016.
17. The Human Rights Committee has stated that "all persons who are arrested must immediately have access to counsel." (Concluding Observations of the Human Rights Committee, Georgia, UN Doc. CCPR/C/79 Add.75, April 1, 1997 para 27).
18. The review by a superior military officer, government official or advisory panel would be insufficient. Regarding superior military officers, *Vuolanne v Finland* (Communication 265/1987, April 7, 1989, 1989 Report of the Human Rights Committee, UN Doc.A/44/40, at 265-257) stating that review of detention of a soldier by a superior military officer does not satisfy Article 9(4) of the ICCPR. As to government officials, the Human Rights Committee in *Torres v Finland* (Communication 291/1988, April 2, 1990, 1990 Report of the Human Rights Committee, Vol II, UN Doc.A/45/40, at 99-100), which states that the opportunity of an asylum-seeker to appeal to the Ministry of the Interior does not satisfy Article 9(4) of the ICCPR. Regarding advisory panels, see the European Court in *Chahal v United Kingdom* 70/1995/576/662, November 15, 1996, paras 130-133) which decided that an advisory panel which did not disclose its reasons for decision, had no binding decision-making power and which did not permit legal representation did not satisfy Article 5(4) of the European Convention.
19. The definition of and protection against torture was elaborated in the 1984 Convention against Torture: Art 1(1): ... the term "torture" means any act by which severe pain or suffering, whether physical or mental, is intentionally inflicted on a person for such purposes as obtaining from him or a third person information or a confession, punishing him for an act he or a third person has committed or is suspected of having committed, or intimidating or coercing him or a third person, or for any reason based on discrimination of any kind, when such pain or suffering is inflicted by or at the instigation of or with the consent or acquiescence of a public official or other person acting in an official capacity. It does not include pain or suffering arising only from, inherent in or incidental to lawful sanctions.
20. The right to equality before the law and equal treatment by the law, or, in other words, the principle of non-discrimination, conditions the interpretation and application not only of human rights law in strict sense, but also of international humanitarian law. For example Articles 1, 2 and 7 of the Universal Declaration of Human Rights; Articles 2(1), (3), 4(1) and 26 of the International Covenant on

Civil and Political Rights; Article 2(2) of the International Covenant on Economic, Social and Cultural Rights; Articles 2, 3, 18(3) and 28 of the African Charter on Human and Peoples' Rights; Articles 1, 24 and 27(1) of the American Convention on Human Rights; Article 14 of the European Convention on Human Rights; Articles 2 and 15 of the 1979 Convention on the Elimination of All Forms of Discrimination against Women; Article 2 of the 1989 Convention on the Rights of the Child; and the 1966 International Convention on the Elimination of All Forms of Racial Discrimination. Of the four 1949 Geneva Conventions, see e.g. Articles 3 and 27 of the Geneva Convention relative to the Protection of Civilian Persons in Time of War; Articles 9(1) and 75(1) of the 1977 Protocol Additional to the Geneva Conventions of August 12, 1949, and relating to the Protection of Victims of International Armed Conflicts (Protocol I); and Articles 2(1) and 4(1) of the 1977 Protocol Additional to the Geneva Conventions of August 12, 1949, and relating to the Protection of Victims of Non-International Armed Conflicts (Protocol II).

21. Human Rights Committee, Communication No. 74/1980, *M. A. Estrella v. Uruguay* (Views adopted on March 29, 1983), in UN doc. *GAOR*, A/38/40, p. 159, para. 10.
22. Section 2C, Army Act, 1952.
23. Communication No. 215/1986, *Van Meurs v. the Netherlands*, views adopted on July 13, 1990, para. 6.1.
24. Article 14(3)(c) of the ICCPR.
25. Communication No 663/1995, *M Morrison v. Jamaica*, November 3, 1998, in UN doc. *GAOR*, A/54/40.
26. Article 14(3)(g) of the ICCPR.
27. Article 15 (1) of the ICCPR.
28. The one exception to the prohibition of retroactive domestic criminal legislation is contained in Article 15(2) of the ICCPR: "Nothing in this Article shall prejudice the trial and punishment of any person for any act or omission which, at the time when it was committed, was criminal according to the general principles of law recognised by the community of nations." This provision has been interpreted to mean that certain violations of customary international law, such as war crimes, torture, slavery, etc. may be punished by states applying retroactive domestic criminal laws. However, in effect, this provision simply restates the position that persons may be held accountable for violations of international customary law: it merely facilitates the ability of States to legislate to this effect.
29. Article 14(7) of the ICCPR.
30. Article 14(5) of the ICCPR.
31. Section 133A and 133B, Army Act, 1952.
32. Article 14(6) of the ICCPR.
33. Report submitted by the Special Rapporteur of the Sub-Commission on the Promotion and Protection of Human Rights, Emmanuel Decaux, UN Doc E/CN.4/2006/58, January 13, 2006.
34. Principle 10 states that military secrecy may not be invoked: (a) Where measures involving deprivation of liberty are concerned, which should not, under any circumstances, be kept secret, whether this involves the identity or the whereabouts of persons deprived of their liberty; (b) In order to obstruct the initiation or conduct of inquiries, proceedings or trials, whether they are of a criminal or a disciplinary nature, or to ignore them; (c) To deny judges and authorities delegated by law to exercise judicial activities access to documents and areas classified or restricted for

reasons of national security; (d) To obstruct the publication of court sentences; and (e) To obstruct the effective exercise of *habeas corpus* and other similar judicial remedies.

35. *Grieves v. the United Kingdom*, December 16, 2003.
36. Pakistan: The trial of civilians by military courts, Briefing Paper, International Commission of Jurists, January 2016, pp. 7-9.

5

The Twenty First Constitutional Amendment

Introduction

The current Constitution of the Islamic Republic of Pakistan came into effect on August 14, 1973. Since then, the Constitution has frequently been amended by military coup leaders and 20 amendments have been adopted, many of them substantially affecting the balance of power between the different institutions of the State.[1] The 18th Amendment adopted on April 8, 2010 deleted the amendments to the Constitution by the country's previous military rulers and introduced fundamental changes in the process of appointment of the judges in superior judiciary.[2] On January 6, 2015, the National Assembly of Pakistan and the Senate approved the 21st Constitutional Amendment Bill and Pakistan Army Act 1952 (Amendment) Bill 2015 unopposed. Two religious parties i.e. Jamaat-e-Islami and the Maulana Fazl-ur-Rahman's Jamiat Ulema-e-Islam abstained on the grounds that religious parties were being targeted through this Amendment.[3] The Constitution's 21st Amendment was challenged in the Supreme Court in a number of petitions, mostly filed by Bar Associations. One of the arguments raised in the petition was that the classification given in the constitutional amendment conflicts with Article 4 and 25 of the Constitution as only terrorists "raising arms and insurgency using the name of religion or a sect" have been included and other terrorist organisations with other motives but still posing threat to the peace and security of Pakistan have been excluded.

Constitution and Fundamental Rights

In the Constitution of Pakistan, Fundamental Rights occupy prominent place. Chapter I of the Constitution containing Article 8 to 28 is devoted to the Fundamental Rights. Article 8 states: "Any law, or any custom or usage having the force of law, in so far as it is inconsistent with the rights conferred by this Chapter, shall, to the extent of such inconsistency, be void". The Constitution specifies, however, that this does not apply to "any law relating to members of the Armed Forces, or of the police or of such other forces as are charged with the maintenance of public order, for the purpose of ensuring the proper discharge of their duties or the maintenance of discipline among them". Further, the provision of Article 8 shall not apply to any of the "laws specified in the First Schedule or other laws specified in Part I of the First Schedule." Article 9 of the Constitution states: "No person shall be deprived of life or liberty saves in accordance with law."

Article 10 deals with the safeguards relating to arrest and detention. Clause 1 of Article 10 specifies, "No person who is arrested shall be detained in custody without being informed, as soon as may be, of the grounds of such arrest, shall not be denied the right to consult and be defended by a legal practitioner of his choice." Clause 2 of Article 10 provides for the right of any person arrested and detained in custody "to be produced before a magistrate before a period of twenty four hours of such arrest, excluding the time necessary for the journey from the place of arrest to the court of the nearest magistrate, and no such person shall be detained in custody beyond the said period without the authority of a magistrate." However, paragraph 3 of the same Article 10 provides that clauses 1 and 2 do not apply to "any person who is arrested or detained under any law providing for preventive detention."

Clauses 4 to 9 of Article 10 describe a system of "preventive detention" applicable to "persons acting in a manner prejudicial to the integrity, security or defence of Pakistan or any part thereof, or external affairs of Pakistan, or public order, or the maintenance of supplies or services", under which such persons may be detained for "a period exceeding three months" under the supervision of a Review Board. The provisions relating to preventive detention are not compatible with international standards, including with the Declaration on the Protection of All Persons from Enforced Disappearance.

Article 10A of the Constitution, results from the 18th Amendment and provides for the right to fair trial: "For the determination of his civil rights and obligations or in any criminal charge against him a person shall be entitled to a fair trial and due process."[4]

The Constitution prohibits slavery and forced labour (Article 11);[5] provides protection against retrospective punishment (Article 12); protects against double punishment and self incrimination (Article 13); deals with the inviolability of dignity of man (Article 14); provides freedom of movement (Article 15), assembly (Article 16) and association (Article 17); freedom of trade, business and profession (Article 18); free speech (Article 19); and the right to information (Article 19A).[6] The religious rights are protected under Article 20. The Constitution provides safeguard against taxation for purposes of any particular religion (Article 21); safeguards as to educational institutions in respect of religion (Article 22); makes provision as to the protection of property (Article 23) and property rights (Article 24); equality of citizens (Article 25); the right to education (Article 25A); nondiscrimination in respect of access to public places (Article 26); and safeguards against discrimination in services (Article 27); and deals with the preservation of language, script and culture (Article 28).

Constitutional remedy has been provided for the enforcement of Fundamental Rights. Under Article 199 of the Constitution, the High Courts or the Supreme Court can be moved by any person to enforce them even against the state. The courts in Pakistan in general and superior courts in particular are main operational source of protection of Fundamental Rights of people.

21st Amendment

The preamble of the 21st Constitutional amendments states that "Whereas extraordinary situation and circumstances exist which demand special measure for speedy trial of certain offences relating to terrorism, waging of war or insurrection against Pakistan", the National Assembly 2015, allowed to make changes in four laws, the Pakistan Army Act 1952, The Pakistan Air Force Act 1953, The Pakistan Navy Ordinance 1961, The Protection of Pakistan Act, 2014, enabling military courts to try civilians by compromising the Fundamental Rights of the citizens including 'right to fair trial'. The 21st Amendment made a very important change in the Constitution of Pakistan.[7]

It amended the Article 175 and the First Schedule of the Constitution to provide constitutional cover for extending the jurisdiction to military courts for the trial of civilians suspected to be involved in terrorism. The 21st Amendment also provides for inclusion of the Pakistan Army Act, 1952; the Pakistan Air Force Act, 1953; the Pakistan Navy Ordfinance, 1961; and the Protection of Pakistan Act, 2014 in the first schedule of the Constitution. The first schedule of the Constitution contains laws which are exempted from the application of Article 8 (1) and (2) of the Constitution. These articles are part of Chapter 1 of the Constitution relating to the Fundamental Rights. The 21st Amendment Act provides for the creation of military speed trial courts for offences relating to terrorism, waging war against Pakistan and prevention of acts threatening the security of the country.[8] The Act shall remain in force for two years starting January 7, 2015 after the President signed the Act.

An amendment to the Army Act in February 2015 through a Presidential Ordinance expressly gave military courts retrospective powers, i.e. they could try persons for conduct that occurred prior to the amendments. The Ordinance also provided all those associated with military courts complete indemnity from prosecution for actions taken in "good faith" and gives military courts broad powers to take measures such as like holding *in camera* proceedings and keeping the identities of individuals associated with the cases secret, "for the protection of witnesses, President and members of Court Martial, prosecutors, defending officers and other persons concerned in court proceedings". The Ordinance was enacted as law in November 2015.[9]

The Supreme Court Verdict

The petitions challenging 21st and 18th [10] Amendments to the Constitution were clubbed and heard together as the two sets of cases involving a common constitutional question as to whether there are any limitations on the powers of the Parliament to amend the Constitution and whether the Courts possess jurisdiction to strike down a Constitutional Amendment. To put briefly, the Supreme Court considered challenges to the new judicial appointments mechanism, the powers of leaders of political parties over parliamentarians and electorates for religious minorities under the 18th Amendment, as well as the Constitutional cover granted, under the 21st Amendment, to military courts to try civilians accused of specified offences.[11]

The 902-page judgment and the dissenting notes on various issues demonstrate a deep divide over the questions ranging from defining terrorists to how they should be dealt with by the state and the legality of steps which the government should take in tackling the menace.[12] In upholding that the 18th and 21st Amendments did not violate the basic structure of the Constitution; the Pakistan Supreme Court relied heavily on case law in Pakistan itself and in many other countries. In the following part of the chapter discussions is confined to 21st Amendment only. Some of the highlights of the majority judgment are as follows.

- At various points of time, control of the State on certain territories like SWAT, parts of North Waziristan, Khyber and other Tribal Agencies has been lost, which were in total control of the armed enemies of the State where the flag of Pakistan no longer flew nor its institutions functioned.
- The nerve centre of the armed enemies of Pakistan may be located in the territory held by them but their tentacles are spread all over the country in the garb of abettors and facilitators. The persons involved in the armed conflict against the State not only included foreigners but there were indications of foreign funding and instigation.
- Since the year 2002, more than 56,000 Pakistanis have been killed or wounded, including both civilians and the members of the law enforcement agencies.
- The armed persons waging war against Pakistan were well organised and well trained with declared foreign affiliations and the coordination and intensity of their aggression has created a situation, the gravity whereof cannot be squeezed into the narrow confines of a state of affairs where mere acting "in aid of civil power" by the armed forces would suffice.
- To counter the situation, large scale military operations are being conducted involving not only the Pakistan Army but also the Pakistan Air Force.
- Pakistan is currently confronted with a warlike situation and consequently the Federation is duty bound by the Constitution to defend the State. In these circumstances, the Federation must act in

accordance with the first part of Article 245(1), by categorising the current situation as a threat of war requiring extraordinary measures in terms of use of the armed forces in accordance with Article 245.

- On the basis of the information available to it, a value judgment has been made in this behalf by the Federal Government i.e. the Executive by directing the armed forces in terms of Article 245 to deal with the terrorists. The Parliament has also taken necessary action by enacting the 21st Constitutional Amendment and the Pakistan Army (Amendment) Act, 2015.
- Such legislative measures are in accordance with the Constitution in view of the law laid down by the Supreme Court in the cases of *Brig. (Retd) F B Ali* and *Sh. Liaquat Hussain*.[13] It was held in Ali's case that equal protection of the laws does not mean that every citizen, no matter what his condition, must be treated in the same manner. In criminal justice system, a classification may well be made on the basis of the heinousness of the crime committed or the necessity of preventing certain anti-social effects of a particular crime. Changes in procedure may equally well be effected on the ground of the security of the State, maintenance of public order, removal of corruption from amongst public servants, or for meeting an emergency.
- On the powers of judicial review by the constitutional courts, the Supreme Court relied on its earlier decision in *Federation of Pakistan v. Raja Muhammad Ishaque Qamar*,[14] and held that the bar to judicial review contained in Article 199(3) of the Constitution on the powers of the High Court is not absolute in nature. In respect of three categories of cases, namely, where the authority involved has acted without jurisdiction, *mala fide*, or *coram non judice*, the bar of Article 199(3) is not applicable.
- The executive discretion in selecting or transferring a case for trial before a Court Martial must be exercised reasonably, fairly, justly and for the advancement of the purpose of the enactment, as provided by Section 24A of the General Clauses Act, 1897.[15]
- The 21st Constitutional Amendment and the Pakistan Army (Amendment) Act, 2015 accumulatively provide, a temporary measure for the trial of terrorists accused of offences including

waging war against Pakistan by a forum already constituted under the law and consistent with a recognised procedure already available for and applicable to personnel of the Pakistan Army. The enlargement of the jurisdiction of such forum is subject to due compliance with an ascertainable criteria constituting a valid classification having nexus with the defence of Pakistan and does not abrogate, repeal, or substantively alter the salient features of the Constitution.

This judgement was perhaps the most important Constitutional law decision in the history of Pakistan. [16] The Supreme Court held that the provisions of the 21st Constitutional Amendment as such are *intra vires* the Constitution and the provisions of the Pakistan Army (Amendment) Act, 2015, are not *ultra vires* the Constitution. Further, the decision to select, refer or transfer the case of any accused person for trial under the Pakistan Army Act, 1952, shall be subject to judicial review both by the High Courts and the Supreme Court on the grounds of *coram-non-judice*, being without jurisdiction or suffering from *malafides* including malice in law. Any order passed, decision taken or sentence awarded under the Pakistan Army Act, 1952, as amended by the Pakistan Army (Amendment) Act, 2015, are also subject to judicial review by the High Courts and the Supreme Court on the above stated grounds.

In principle, five in the minority and eight justices in the majority agreed that the Supreme Court can strike down an amendment to the Constitution if it violates 'salient features' of the Constitution. The only difference was whether to let the Amendments under review stand. The power was announced in unequivocal terms, with five judges in favour of striking down one or more parts of the Amendments under review, while eight assumed the power but chose to let the Amendments stand.[17] Those in the government hailed the decision, calling "another strike against terror", adding, "it's a success for the nation and the military courts can crush terrorists."[18]

Critic to the Amendments and the Court's Verdict

There was a widespread criticism of the 21st Constitutional Amendment. There has been perception that situation in which Pakistan finds it today is largely of its own making. Pakistan army has been accused for creating terrorists and has been instrumental in supplying arms and equipment to state-sponsored terrorists in Khyber Pakhtunkhwa, Southern Punjab, Balochistan and some of the neighbouring countries. In these circumstances, the establishment of military courts would mean allowing the sponsors of terrorism to become both the judge and the jury in punishing only those terrorists who do not obey the military instructions.[19]

The six dissenting judges, in their notes, held the view that the 21st Amendment was incompatible with the right of fair trial and the independence of the judiciary. According to Justice Jawwad S Khawaja, who is now the Chief Justice of the Pakistan Supreme Court, the 21st Amendment in relation to the setting up of military courts "is liable to be struck down", and "was an infringement of the rights of the people." Further, the powers to make laws and Amendments to the Constitution are not absolute and untrammeled and are subject to the limitations imposed by the Constitution itself. Justice Khwaja observed that "the Parliament is not supreme", and "the Constitution itself places limits on Parliament's ability to pass laws and make amendments.[20] Justice Qazi Faez Isa was of the opinion that the categorisation of terrorists by using the name of religion or sect was not reasonable.

The judges in the dissenting opinion held,

> Every prudent person would agree that a person who kills and maims innocents must be prosecuted and punished. But this must be done in accordance with the law and the Constitution. If we rush to convict terrorists through unconstitutional means we stoop to their level. The Constitution does not permit the trial of civilians by the military as it would contravene Fundamental Rights, which cannot be excluded by invoking clause (3) of Article 8 and placing the Army Act, the Air Force Act, the Navy Ordinance and the Protection of Pakistan Act in the First Schedule to the Constitution. Moreover, Article 4 of the Constitution is a standalone Article and neither can it be excluded (by invoking Article 8 of the Constitution) nor can the rights encapsulated therein be infringed.

The International Commission of Jurists (ICJ) was of the view that the Supreme Court has missed an opportunity to reverse the militarisation of justice under the guise of combating terrorism and also failed to reinforce independence of the judiciary in the country. The judgment squarely puts Pakistan at odds with its international obligations and weakens the Supreme Court's hard won reputation as the last resort for protecting the rights of Pakistani people. The trial of civilians in military courts for terrorism-related offences is incompatible with international standards, which require that those accused of any criminal offence are guaranteed a fair trial by an independent, impartial and competent tribunal. International law is clear, all organs of the State, including the judiciary, must respect international human rights commitments, which include the right to a fair trial. According to ICJ, the majority judgment also goes against previous Supreme Court rulings on military courts. In the past, the Court had reasoned that military courts do not meet the requirements of independence and impartiality; the establishment of military courts for trial of civilians' amounts to creating a parallel judicial system; and that impeding the right to a fair trial cannot be justified on the basis of the public emergency or the doctrine of necessity.[21] The creation of military courts under the amendment violates Article 25(A) of the Constitution by giving discretionary powers to the government to choose certain accused to be tried by the military courts while others by the ordinary courts, as all citizens require equal treatment and are presumed to be innocent unless they are proven guilty.

According Siegfried, the 21st Amendments resemble a well-planned, gradual strategy intended to build up a formal role of the military in the country's political landscape. These Amendments are worrisome on the following grounds.[22]

- It transfers significant power to the military authorities in Pakistan. The fact that civilians can be subjected to military jurisdiction is a major cause of concern. After the 21st Amendment, the Chief of the Army Staff's has absolute discretion at every stage of a military proceeding; he can use his power and influence in such a way as to thwart the fairness, impartiality, and integrity of disciplinary proceedings against a civilian.[23]

- The discretion of the Federal Government to transfer any case pending in any trial court to military courts is fretful as it has given dominance to military in judicial affairs of the country. Besides, it has significantly reduced the importance of Higher Courts. This has distorted the separation of powers and undermined the basic structure of the Constitution of Pakistan. The power vesting in the Federal Government to pick and choose cases for trial by military courts violates the equality requirement stipulated in Article 25 of the Constitution.
- The Government of Pakistan, instead of correcting its counter-terrorism strategies, has placed reliance on a failed and blunt instrument of coercion and military force. The Amendment has created a fear that the trials by military courts will not only be used against terrorism but also against political opposition, critical media, or separatist groups, especially in the FATA region.
- Since the term "terrorism" has not been defined in international law, how the government will determine that the accusation is related to terrorism? There is a fear amongst the members of the civil society that the trials will not only be used against terrorism but also against political opposition, critical media, or separatist groups especially in Balochistan.[24]

According to Shah, the religion has been the main instrument at the hands of Pakistan military. The army has used the occasion to play an important role in shaping country's foreign policy in Post-Musharraf era[25] and strengthen its position in the country. The 21st Amendment has undermined the role of civil authorities and judiciary in the country. With the doubled edged sword, the military has cut both the government as well as the judiciary to size.[26] The inherent weaknesses of the police and the criminal justice system combined with the use of the death penalty carry a very high risk of irreversible miscarriages of justice. The decision to carry out executions could, therefore, result in arbitrary deprivation of life and be in breach of Pakistan's international obligations. Keeping in view the genesis of terrorism and Islamic fundamentalism in Pakistan, it would be imprudent to expect that public safety will improve or be guaranteed after the military trials and executions. While Pakistan needs a coherent strategy to fight terrorism and political and military leaders have to work together; the 21st Constitutional Amendment is worrisome. It is not just a shortsighted kneejerk response or an extraordinary measure against terrorism as claimed by the Prime Minister of Pakistan.[27] Quite the contrary, it resembles a well planned, gradual strategy intended to build up a formal role of the military in the country's political landscape.[28] To some, the political leadership in Pakistan has abdicated its democratic responsibilities and the 21st amendment was a monument to the betrayal of the civilian, democratic cause.[29] It will have serious implications for the rule of law and the democratic structure of Pakistan.[30]

The Impact of Military on Judiciary

The Pakistan Army has ruled the country for nearly half of its total 70 years old history and has imposed Martial Law five times over the country. Every Martial Law regime has abrogated the Constitution and clipped the wings of the higher judiciary by curtailing its jurisdictions, assaulted the independence of the judiciary by arbitrary removal of the independent judges and degraded the dignity of the judiciary by making open interference in the proceedings of the court.[31] During the military regimes, the higher judiciary was allowed to function albeit deprived of the power to challenge the military regimes and their courts. No civil court could question the proclamation of Martial Law or extra constitutional emergency or any order made in pursuance of the proclamation made by the military dictators. In its journey from 1947 till date there have been many occasions in Pakistan when the military has intervened directly into the function of the higher judiciary or coerced the judges to give verdicts in favour of military regimes.

First Martial Law Regime

Within 18 months of democratic functioning, the President of Pakistan Iskandar Mirza issued a Proclamation on October 7, 1958 abrogating the Constitution. He dismissed the Federal and Provincial Governments, dissolved the Central and Provincial Legislatures, banned all political activities placed the whole country under Martial Law. General

Muhammad Ayub Khan was appointed as the Chief Martial Law Administrator. Laws (Continuance in Force) Order of 1958 restored the laws as they were applicable before the issue of the Proclamation. By this Order, the jurisdiction of all courts including the Supreme Court and the High Courts was restored and it was directed that the country would be governed as far as possible in accordance with the 1956 Constitution.[32] However, no court in Pakistan could call in question the Proclamation, any order made in pursuance of the Proclamation, any Martial Law Order or Regulations or any finding, judgment or order of a Military Court.[33]

Under the provisions of the Martial Law Regulation, military courts of criminal jurisdiction were established. These courts were empowered to try any persons for the violation of Martial Law Regulations and also for offences under ordinary law. The military courts were parallel to the existing civil courts in the country. The Martial Law Regulations also barred appeals and ousted the jurisdiction of all courts including the Supreme Court from calling in question the proceedings of the military courts.

A new Constitution was devised by the military government under the directions of the Chief Martial Law Administrator General Ayub Khan and promulgated on March 1, 1962. The Constitution came into force on June 8, 1962 after the Martial Law was lifted. However, the power of judicial review was denied to the judiciary under the Constitution. By a Constitutional Amendment in March 1963, the power of judicial review was restored and the Fundamental Rights were made justiciable. The Constitutional Courts were empowered to declare any law passed by Legislatures null and void on the ground that it was repugnant to any Fundamental Right. Thus the Supreme Court became the custodian of the Constitution and Fundamental Rights.

Second Martial Law Regime

After a nationwide protest, Ayub Khan stepped down as President on March 25, 1969 handing over reins of power to another Army Chief General Yahya Khan. Immediately after taking over Yahya Khan placed the country under Martial Law. The Proclamation of Martial Law abrogated the 1962 Constitution, dissolved the National

Assembly and the Provincial Assemblies, and dismissed the central and provincial governments. General Yahya took over as Chief Martial Law Administrator (CMLA) and the President of Pakistan. The Fundamental Rights were abrogated and the orders of Martial Law authorities or any proclamation could not be questioned in any court. In addition, a system of military courts parallel to the existing criminal courts was established. In 1971, after losing East Pakistan to Indian military, General Yahya stepped down and handed over power to Mr. Zulfikar Ali Bhutto as the leader of the majority party in the remaining Pakistan (West Pakistan).[34]

Prime Minister Bhutto introduced the new Constitution in 1973 having most of the provisions relating to the judiciary contained in the Constitutions of 1956 and 1962. The Constitution also provided that the superior courts shall not have any jurisdiction except as conferred on them by the Constitution. Another important provision was that the judiciary at lower level was to be separated progressively from the executive within three years.[35]

In the March 1977 election to the National Assembly, the sitting Prime Minister's party (Pakistan People's Party-PPP) won the election but the alliance of the opposition parties (Pakistan National Alliance-(PNA) charged that the election was rigged by the government of Zulfikar Ali Bhutto. PNA, boycotted the provincial assemblies' election, started countrywide strikes and agitations and demanded fresh election under the supervision of judiciary. Tension escalated and during the night between July 4 and 5, the armed forces led by the Army Chief General Zia-ul-Haq, took over the administration of the country.

Third Martial Law Regime

The third Martial Law was imposed by General Zia on July 5, 1977. Zia arrested Bhutto who was later hanged for conspiring to murder a political opponent.[36] An important step of General Zia, detrimental to the judicial independence, was the establishment of the Federal Shariat Court for the purpose of Islamisation of laws in Pakistan.[37] During General Zia's military regime, Tribunals were constituted consisting of a Judge of High Court and a Brigadier from the army to decide the allegations of misconduct against politicians and bureaucracy. General Zia enjoyed the blessings of the Chief Justice of Pakistan on almost all important legal issues. He secured the cooperation of the Judiciary by appointing the Chief Justices of the High Courts as acting Governors of their respective provinces. General Zia got the certificate of validity of his Martial Law from the judiciary.[38] The Balochistan High Court in *Suleman v. President Special Military Court* declared that the two Constitutional Amendments to Articles 212 and 199 (passed on October 16, 1979 and May 27, 1980 respectively) were illegal because these Amendments failed to pass the test of necessity laid down in the Supreme Court's judgment in the case of Begum Nusrat Bhutto.[39] General Zia effectively extinguished judicial powers by promulgating Provisional Constitution Order (PCO) 1981.[40] The PCO put a formal end to the necessity regime as sanctioned by the Supreme Court in Begum Nusrat Bhutto's case.

In March 1981, General Zia in the capacity of CMLA, issued the Provisional Constitution Order (PCO) which served the Constitution of Pakistan for years to come. The important features of the PCO were: (i) All Fundamental Rights under the 1973 Constitution and the provisions for their enforceability were taken out; (ii) The Supreme Court could transfer cases from one High Court to another High Court, (iii) Martial Law authorities and military courts and their acts and orders were placed beyond the limits of the writ jurisdiction of the High Courts; (iv) All Judges of the Higher Courts, including the Chief Justices, were required to take fresh oath under the PCO; those who did not take oath were to cease to hold office; and (v) the Judges, who took the oath under the PCO, were to be bound by the provisions of the PCO and could not call into question the validity of its provisions.[41] Martial Law and the prohibition of political parties remained in force until 1985. Soon after, President Bhutto's daughter, Benazir, returned from exile to lead the Pakistan People's Party. When General Zia died in 1988 she was elected Prime Minister. In 1990 she was dismissed on charges of incompetence and corruption.

During the period from 1989 to 1999, Benazir Bhutto and Nawaz Sharif occupied the chair of Prime Minister on different occasions. However, both were unable to govern without interference from the army and the military intelligence services, which under Zia had vastly expanded their domestic political role in Pakistan. During this period, the Eighth Amendment to the Constitution introduced in 1985 by Zia was repealed.[42]

Fourth Martial Law Regime

In October 1999, when Prime Minister Sharif ordered the dismissal of Chief of Army Staff General Pervez Musharraf, the latter executed a bloodless military coup and assumed executive powers. Musharraf claimed that coup was necessary to restore both the economy and the deteriorating political situation.[43] On October 14, 1999, Musharraf declared a state of emergency and issued the Provisional Constitutional Order which suspended the Federal and Provincial Parliaments, held the Constitution in abeyance, designated himself as Chief Executive and barred any court from making an order against him or any other person exercising powers under his authority.

A number of petitions were filed by Nawaz Sharif and other PML leaders in the Supreme Court under Article 184(3) of the Constitution challenging the military take over in October 1999 and seeking restoration of Assemblies. All these petitions were entertained and fixed for hearing on January 31, 2000. On May 12, 2000, the Supreme Court unanimously validated the October 1999 coup and granted General Musharraf executive and legislative authority for three years from the date of the coup. [44]. In June 2001 President Rafiq Tarar resigned and General Musharraf declared himself President.

In April 2002 Musharraf held a referendum to determine whether he would serve a term of five years as President, even though a referendum is not the mechanism stipulated in the Constitution for electing a President. The referendum result largely supported Musharraf, but it was widely acknowledged that it was a fraud on the Constitution of Pakistan.[45] In January 2004, Musharraf won a vote of confidence from the Electoral College, the body designated by the Constitution to elect the President, consisting of the members of both Houses of Parliament and the four Provincial Assemblies. Having previously announced in the Legal Framework Order of 2002 that he would relinquish his military role, Musharraf reneged on this promise in late 2004 when he announced that he would continue as President and Chief of Army Staff until 2007.[46]

Since the departure of Musharraf in 2008, the military has pledged its commitment to protecting democracy. Yet it has consistently undermined the civilian government to maintain military prerogatives and, if not establish direct control of the state. It has also attempted to secure a power-sharing arrangement guarantying military authority over key sectors such as Defence, Foreign Affairs, or Internal Security. As a result, most analysts regard the Pakistani army as the true center of power in those matters. Following the 2008 elections, the Pakistani military has successfully inserted itself into the political sphere during the post-Musharraf administrations.

During the period of last 60 years, the higher judiciary in Pakistan has succumbed to the pressure from the Generals and CMLA's and given verdicts favouring the military regimes. A brief account of some of the cases is as follows.

- In *Dosso case* (1958) the Pakistan Supreme Court used jurist Kelson's theory of revolutionary legality to validate illegal military coup and abrogation of the 1956 Constitution. By validating the Martial Law the court preserved its own limited powers but gave another setback to the judicial independence.[47]
- In *Asma Jillani case* (1972), while reviewing the Martial Law of 1969 and suspension of the 1962 Constitution, the Supreme Court not only reversed its previous verdict but also repudiated the doctrinal basis on which the Martial Law was legitimised. A detailed history of the Martial law in the British was mentioned and its comparison has been made with the past days. The judiciary utilised this opportunity, not only to rectify the wrongs of the Army Generals but also to determine its appropriate place in the democratic setup.[48]
- In *Nusrat Bhutto case* (1977), the Supreme Court once again used the doctrine of state necessity to legalise the suspension of the constitution and justify the military coup. The Supreme Court unanimously validated the imposition of martial law and proved an honorable protection for military adventure in civil government.[49]

- In *Federation of Pakistan v Saifullah Khan*, the Supreme Court held that the dismissal of Mohammad Khan Junejo's government by General Zia in May 1988 was unconstitutional but it refused to restore the National Assembly. The Chief Martial Law Administrator, General Ziaul Haq introduced several constitutional amendments that changed the basic structure of the Constitution and harmed the independence of the judiciary. The regime fell heavy on the judiciary. All these provisions and actions taken under them undermined the independence of the judges and damaged the image of judiciary in the country.[50]
- On August 6, 1990, President Ghulam Ishaq Khan, under Article 58(2)(b) of the Constitution, had dissolved the National Assembly and the government of Benazir Bhutto. The said dissolution order was challenged. The Supreme Court, in *Ahmed Tariq Rahim v. Federation of Pakistan* by majority, upheld the dissolution of the National Assembly.[51]
- In *Zafar Ali Shah* case, the Supreme Court validated the suspension the Assemblies in the interest of the state for the welfare of the people. By taking oath under Provisional Constitutional Order (PCO), the judiciary let its independence be subverted by the military regime. The Supreme Court suffered the most in terms of integrity and prestige. The Supreme Court held: ".....we are of the view that the machinery of the Government at the Centre and the Provinces had completely broken down and the Constitution had been rendered unworkable. A situation arose for which the Constitution provided no solution and the armed forces had to intervene to save the State from further chaos, for maintenance of peace and order, economic stability, justice and good governance and to safeguard integrity and sovereignty of the country dictated by highest considerations of State necessity and welfare of the people. The impugned action was spontaneously welcomed by all sections of the society."[52]

Pakistan military considers itself as the sole guardian of the country's national sovereignty and physical, political and moral integrity. However, to come to a conclusion that the Pakistan military would be able to curb the terrorism and religious extremism in the country in a period of two years by prosecuting and hanging few hundred individuals is a farfetched idea. The questions are being raised that if Pakistan army could not curb terrorism with a military dictator in power for a decade, what magic solution do military courts offer now?[53] The January 2016 terrorist attack at Bacha Khan University (Khyber Pakhtunkhwa) is a strong reminder that the latest Constitutional Amendment is not effective. No country in the world, with howsoever strong military it may have, has been able to curb terrorism by using violent means. Such as selective execution of individuals, with Pakistan army could not achieve its objective militarily, is now trying to achieve by 'unjust' legal means.

Taking the real composition of Pakistan's power structures into account, the 21st Amendment has paved the way for military dominance in judicial affairs and has also reduced the significance of all higher courts in Pakistan. It is similar to what Martial Law Administrator did in the past in Pakistan. The 21st Amendment is not only indicative for the willingness of the army's top brass to direct the political process openly but also to convey the truth that the country is once under the auspices of military rule.[54] The establishment of military courts for trial of civilians in Pakistan implies that (i) the civilian judicial system is untrustworthy; (ii) in the battle for supremacy, the military is the winner; (iii) the civilian leadership is incapable in providing security to a common man or addressing the core internal security interests; and (iv) the military courts could be used to suppress the voices of dissent in Sindh and Balochistan.[55] While one may argue that the 21st Amendment does not just violate the separation of powers under the scheme of the Constitution in Pakistan; but it strongly suggests that military courts in Pakistan are superior when compared to civilian systems of justice.[56]

The situation is advantageous to the Pakistan army. In case military courts get extension after January 2017, which is most probable, the military can claim credibility of their FGCM trial mechanism. If the military courts are not given extension after January 2017, the credibility of the political system would suffer as the army can always claim that after the special courts started functioning, there has not been ghastly incident similar to that of Peshawar killings. In both the situations, the judiciary would be the victim; for any future terrorist activity indirect blame could be apportioned to the judiciary. Experts feel that the Supreme Court's legitimising the 21st Amendment and trial of civilians by military courts has conveyed the message that the custodians of the country's civil legal system have admitted that they cannot dispense justice in cases related to Islamic terrorism. They have bowed to the pressure and handed over the 'reins of justice' to the army.[57]

Notes

1. In its seventy years of existence, Pakistan has had three Constitutions, adopted in 1952, 1962, and 1973. The 1956 Constitution replaced the Governor General with a President, but power in the hands of a Prime Minister elected by a National Parliament. It preserved most of the British Indian constitutional structure and declared Pakistan to be an Islamic Republic. The Constitution of 1962 created a stronger presidency and an elaborate system of local government. The Constitution of 1973 underwent a major amendment in 1985. As General Zia's Martial Law was being lifted, the powers of President were increased in comparison with those of the Prime Minister. Thus the Prime Minister could be removed by the President, and all the provincial Chief Ministers by the Governor. Prime Minister's authority was again revised in 1997 by Nawaz Sharif, only to be once again subordinated by that of the President in 2002 by General Musharraf's extra-constitutional Legal Framework Order (LFO). In 2004, as result of negotiations, much of the LFO was incorporated into the Constitution by majority vote of Pakistan's Electoral College.
2. The Eighteenth (2010) and Nineteenth (2011) Constitutional Amendments in Pakistan have brought fundamental changes in the process of appointment of the Judges in Superior Judiciary. The amendments created the Judicial Commission and the Parliamentary Committee to fill actual or potential vacancies in the Superior Courts of Pakistan. The Supreme Court examined the 18th Amendment (2010) and referred the matter to the Parliament with certain suggestions. The Parliament approved some of them by enacting Nineteenth Constitutional Amendment. However, the Parliament refused to surrender the parliamentary committee's power to reject a nomination.
3. Waseem Amir and Raja Asghar, With excuses, law makers vote for military courts, *Dawn*, January 7, 2015, available at http://www.dawn.com/news/1155432/with-excuses-lawmakers-vote-for-military-courts, accessed on January 12, 2015.
4. Article 10-A of the Constitution is largely inspired by Article 6 of the European Convention on Human Rights. In Pakistan the legislators have introduced two fundamental concepts i.e. of due process and fair trial. The scope of these two concepts has much wider meaning than fair trial. Shamshad Ahmad, The Tale of Democracy in Pakistan,6 September 16, 2013, available at: http://www.criterion-quarterly.com/the-tale-of-democracy-in-pakistan/, accessed on December 22, 2015.
5. According to Human Rights Watch millions of workers in Pakistan are held in contemporary forms of slavery. Although slavery is unconstitutional in Pakistan and violates various national and international laws, state practices support its existence. Throughout the country employers forcibly extract labour from adults and children,

restrict their freedom of movement, and deny them the right to negotiate the terms of their employment. Employers coerce such workers into servitude through physical abuse, forced confinement, and debt-bondage. The state offers these workers no effective protection from this exploitation. The state rarely prosecutes or punishes employers who hold workers in servitude. Moreover, workers who contest their exploitation are invariably confronted with police harassment, often leading to imprisonment under false charges. Contemporary Forms of Slavery in Pakistan, Human Rights Watch/Asia, July 1995, available at: https://www.hrw.org/reports/pdfs/c/crd/pakistan957.pdf, accessed July 22, 2015.

6. By incorporating the right to information, the framers of the 18th Amendment have opened up the business of the government to public scrutiny. However by making it subject to regulation and reasonable restrictions imposed by law, in theory, the framers have left open the door for a wide interpretation of the words "reasonable restriction". Security considerations and regulation in the name of national interest may defeat the purpose of this fundamental right.
7. The Constitution (Twenty First) Amendment Act, 2015 (Act 1 of 2015) added the following proviso to Article 175 of the Constitution: "Provided that the provisions of this Article shall have no application to the trial of the persons under any of the Acts mentioned at serial No. 6, 7, 8 and 9 of sub part III or Part I of the First Schedule, who claims, or is known, to belong to any terrorist group or organisation using the name of religion or a sect." Explanation: In this proviso, the expression 'sect' means a sect of religion and does not include any religious or political party regulated under the Political Parties order, 2002. By the same Act, First Schedule of the Constitution was amended to include in sub-part III of Part I after entry number 5, the following new entries namely: "6. The Pakistan Army Act 1952, 7. The Pakistan Air Force Act, 1953, 8. The Pakistan Navy Ordinance, 1961, and 9. The Protection of Pakistan Act, 2014".
8. Prior to the amendment to the Army Act, only persons of the armed forces and other persons on "active service"; or persons seducing and attempting to seduce persons in the Pakistani military from their allegiance to the Government of Pakistan could be tried by a Court Martial. The amendment to the Pakistan Army Act, 1952, adds to the list of persons who can be tried by Courts Martial those who commit offences related to terrorism who belong to "any terrorist group or organisation using the name of religion or a sect". For more details on the person subject to the Army Act, 1952, see chapter 2 of the book.
9. The Pakistan Army (Amendment) Act, 2015, November 2015, available at: http://www.na.gov.pk/uploads/documents/1449574923_658.pdf., accessed on December 01, 2015.
10. The 18th Amendment to the Constitution had introduced a number of far-reaching changes to the Constitutional scheme. Some of the important changes introduced were: increasing provincial autonomy through abolition of the Concurrent Legislative List (Fourth Schedule of the Constitution), reforming the appointments mechanism to superior courts (High Courts, Federal *Shariat* Court and Supreme Court, Article 175-A), changes to representation of religious minorities in the Parliament (Article 51(6)(e)), and powers of heads of political parties over legislators concerning voting on certain specified matters (Article 63-A).
11. Waqqas Mir, Saying not what the Constitution is … but what it should be: Comment on the Judgment on the 18th and 21st Amendments to the Constitution, *LUMS Law Journal*, Vol. 2, 2015, pp. 64-76.

12. Ashraf Sajjad, Pakistan Reinforces Resolve to Fight Terror, ISAS Insight, No. 288, August 28, 2015, National University of Singapore.
13. *Brig. (Retd) F B Ali v. The State*, PLD 1975 SC 506; *Sh. Liaquat Hussain v. Federation of Pakistan*, PLD 1996 SC 504.
14. *Federation of Pakistan v. Raja Muhammad Ishaque Qamar*, PLD 2007 SC 498.
15. Section 24A, the General Clauses Act, 1897: Exercise of power under enactments. (1) Whereby or under any enactment a power to make any order or give any direction is conferred on any authority, office or person such power shall be exercised reasonably, fairly, justly and for the advertisement of the purposes of the enactment. (2) The authority, office or person making any order or issuing any direction under the powers conferred by or under any enactment shall, so far as necessary or appropriate, give reasons for making the order or, as the case may be for issuing the direction and shall provide a copy of the order or as the case may be, the direction to the person affected prejudicially.
16. Copy of the judgment available at: http://www.supremecourt.gov.pk/web/user_files/File/Const.P.12of2010.pdf, accessed on December 20, 2015.
17. Petitions challenging the 21st Amendment were dismissed in a majority 11-6 vote of the 17-member Supreme Court. In a 14-3 majority vote, petitions challenging the 18th Amendment were also dismissed by the bench. Judges provided seven opinions and two additional notes on the ruling. 13 out of the 17 judges ruled that the Supreme Court can strike down a Constitutional Amendment if it repeals, alters or abrogates the 'salient features' of that document. Four judges ruled that the Court has no power to examine the validity of Constitutional Amendments and hence they dismissed the petitions. Eight other judges joined these four in dismissing petitions but these eight judges ruled that while the power to strike down Constitutional Amendments exists, it is not being exercised in the current cases. The remaining five judges ruled that not only does the Supreme Court have the power to examine the substance of Constitutional Amendments, but that various parts of the 18th and 21st Amendments ought to be struck down. Waqqas Mir, Saying not what the Constitution is ... but what it should be: Comment on the Judgment on the 18th and 21st Amendments to the Constitution, available at: http://lums.edu.pk/sahsol/lumslawjournal/page.php/saying-not-what-the-constitution-is-waqqas-mir, accessed on January 22, 2016.
18. Iqbal Nasir, Military courts get Supreme Court nod, *Dawn*, August 5, 2015, available at: http://www.dawn.com/news/1198533, accessed on November 22, 2015.
19. Sahgal Arun, Military Courts in Pakistan: A Soft Coup by the Pakistan Army? January 14, 2015, available at: http://www.idsa.in/idsacomments/MilitaryCourtsinPakistan_asahgal_140115, accessed on May 22, 2015.
20. Ashraf Sajjad, Pakistan Reinforces Resolve to Fight Terror, ISAS Insight, No. 288, August 28, 2015, National University of Singapore.
21. Pakistan: Supreme Court decision upholding 21st Amendment a blow to human rights and judicial independence, International Commission of Jurists, August 7, 2015, available at: http://www.icj.org/pakistan-supreme-court-decision-upholding-21st -amendment-is-a-blow-to-human-rights-and-judicial-independence/, accessed on November 22, 2015.
22. Wolf O., Siegfried, Formal Institutionalisation of Military Rule: The 21st Amendment in Pakistan, May 14, 2015, Pakistan Security Research Unit (PSRU), Briefing Paper 71, Durham University; Counter-terrorism Strategies in Pakistan: Opportunities and Pitfalls, Asia Report No. 271, July 22, 2015, International Crisis Group, Belgium.

23. A senior military officer, convening a military court has the absolute power to decide the charges against an accused, composition of military courts, and order for review of the finding and sentence of a Court Martial. The court members and Judge Advocate, if any, function under his direct command influence. Though empowered to award sentence of death to a civilian, there is no legal requirement that the court members be law qualified. The Appellate Military Courts also have similar shortcomings. The Constitutional Amendment has confirmed the dominance of military over the civilian judicial system.
24. Wolf Siegfried O., Pakistan: Between Coup and Constitutional Engineering, Sharnoff's Global Views, January 15, 2015.
25. Shah Aqil, Constraining consolidation: military politics and democracy (2007-2013), *Democratisation*, April 29, 2013, available at: http://dx.doi.org/10.1080/13510347.2013.781586, accessed on November 12, 2015.
26. A number of international counter-terrorists experts have strong opinion that Pakistan's security forces have nurtured many terrorist groups on the country's soil for a long time. It is well known that the Pakistan army has created *Mujahdeen* to fight both India and Russia (in Afghanistan) at the behest of USA, following the policy of strategic depth. It now coerced the Government to cope with unprecedented threat to the integrity of Pakistan by the raising of arms and insurgency in name of religion and sects, and foreign and locally funded anti-state elements including warriors in the name of the religion or sect. Accordingly, a clause was inserted in the 21st Amendment, that any person who is or claims or is known to belong to any terrorist group or organisation using the name of religion or a sect, commits an offence mentioned in Protection of Pakistan Act, 2014 can be tried under the Army Act, 1952. Chaudhry Sharafat A., The role of military agency in Pakistan's foreign policy: A case of post Musharraf Era, available at: http://www.hsadvocates.com/wp-content/uploads/2015/10/4-The-Role-of-Military-Agency-in-Pakistan-Foreign-Policy.pdf, accessed on January 12, 2016.
27. In Senate, Prime Minister Nawaz Sharif made a statement, "This bill is about military courts trying hardcore terrorists who kill Pakistanis....this is an important day for Pakistan when the nation decided that terrorists will be taken out from the roots. Further, "I want to thank all the party heads and their parliamentary representatives for attending committees and sharing their thoughts and advice on this highly important bill. This bill was created with the help of everyone's common agreement....Through this bill; we can overcome the last 60 years of unrest which should have ended years ago." Parliament passes 21st Constitutional Amendment, Army Act Amendment, *Dawn*, January 6, 2015, available at: http://www.dawn.com/news/1155271, accessed on March 22, 2015.
28. Wolf Siegfried O., Pakistan: Between Coup and Constitutional Engineering, Sharnoff's Global Views, January 15, 2015.
29. Editorial: A sad day, *Dawn*, January 3, 2015, available at: http://www.dawn.com/news/1154719, accessed on January 12, 2015.
30. Sahgal Arun, Military Courts in Pakistan: A Soft Coup by the Pakistan Army? January 14, 2015, available at: http://www.idsa.in/idsacomments/MilitaryCourtsinPakistan_asahgal_140115, accessed on May 22, 2015.
31. Besides curtailing the jurisdiction of the courts, arbitrary removal of the judges, blatant interference in the proceedings of the courts damaging the credibility of the court, the military dictators in Pakistan have also introduced detrimental changes in the constitutional structure of the judiciary. Shah Amanullah, Critical

Study of the Factors Undermining Independence of the Superior Judiciary in Pakistan, Unpublished Thesis, Gomal(?) University, Pakistan, July 2011, pp.226-227.

32. The Laws (Continuance in Force) Order 1958 which was the principal constitutional document for the period of Martial Law provided that subject to the Martial Law Regulations and Orders, all courts would continue in being and would exercise the same powers and jurisdictions as before but they could not challenge the martial law authorities.
33. The Laws (Continuance in Force) Order 1958 Para 3.
34 Shah Amanullah, *Critical Study of the Factors Undermining Independence of the Superior Judiciary in Pakistan*, unpublished thesis, July 2008, p. 37.
35. The judiciary at higher level was already separated from the Executive but it was not separated at magisterial level. Administration of justice particularly criminal justice at the lower level was being carried out by Executive Magistrate under the control and supervision of the home department of the Provincial government. In spite of expiry of the period fixed in the Constitution, no step was taken by the government for separation of the judiciary from the executive. Shah Amanullah, *Critical Study of the Factors Undermining Independence of the Superior Judiciary in Pakistan*, unpublished thesis, July 2008, p. 37.
36. General Zia used judiciary to eliminate his arch rival, Zulfikar Ali Bhutto. Zia was aware that Justice Mushtaq was aggrieved and held a grudge against Bhutto. He favoured Justice Mushtaq and appointed him the Chief Election Commissioner and later acting Chief Justice of Lahore High Court. Bhutto was tried before a full bench of five judges headed by acting Chief Justice Mushtaq. Mushtaq had carefully selected the bench which convicted Bhutto and sentenced him to death. The Supreme Court under another annoyed Chief Justice Anwer-ul-Haq rejected Bhutto's appeal and endorsed the decision of Lahore High Court. Shah Amanullah, *Critical Study of the Factors Undermining Independence of the Superior Judiciary in Pakistan*, unpublished thesis, July 2008, pp. 233-234.
37. A Constitutional Amendment was made on February 7, 1979, through a President's Order confirming jurisdiction on the High Courts to examine any law or provision of law whether the same was repugnant to the injunctions of Islam as laid down in the Holy Quran and the Sunnah. Shah Amanullah, *Critical Study of the Factors Undermining Independence of the Superior Judiciary in Pakistan*, unpublished thesis, July 2008, pp. 46-47.
38. Shah Amanullah, *Critical Study of the Factors Undermining Independence of the Superior Judiciary in Pakistan*, unpublished thesis, July 2008, p. 231.
39. *Suleman v. President Special Military Court* 1980 N. LR. Civ. Quetta 873.
40. CMLA's Order No: 1 of 1981 promulgated on March 24, 1981.
41. Former Chief Justice AR Cornelius, commenting on the unfortunate episode called it "the rape of the judiciary", quoted by Hamid Khan, (*Constitutional and Political History of Pakistan*, Karachi: OUP, 2001), p. 651.
42. The Eighth Constitutional Amendment had allowed the President to dissolve the National Assembly and thereby remove the Prime Minister and Cabinet.
43. Differences between Prime Minister Nawaz Sharif and General Musharraf were raised over Kargal war with India. On October 12, 1999, the Prime Minister Nawaz Sharif removed General Musharraf when he was on a foreign visit to Sri Lanka and appointed a new COAS, but the army did not accept this change and very swiftly took over the control of the country. Nawaz Sharif and some his Cabinet

Members were arrested. Cohen, Stephen P, The Future of Pakistan, The Brookings Institution, January 2011, Washington, p. 9.

44. In response to petitions filed in the Supreme Court to challenge these actions, Musharraf issued an order requiring superior court Judges to swear an oath to uphold the Provisional Constitutional Order. On January 26, 2000, 13 Judges including five Members of the Supreme Court, were dismissed for not taking the oath. The newly constituted Supreme Court deemed Musharraf's coup to be legal, and, following the doctrine of necessity the Supreme Court sanctioned both the Proclamation of Emergency and the Provisional Constitutional Order. The Supreme Court held that the 1973 Constitution remained the supreme law but that it was in abeyance and that Musharraf had the authority to amend it. On October 10, 2000 Nawaz Sharif was convicted of the crimes of hijacking and terrorism and sent into exile in Saudi Arabia.
45. Nine months after joining the Western coalition against terrorism, General Musharraf, is isolated in his own land, increasingly a figure of ridicule and the focus of a growing anti-Western fury that is shared by Islamic militants and the middle class alike. General Musharraf's dutiful carrying out of Washington's demands is galvanising a widespread feeling here that he has largely traded away Pakistan's sovereignty to the US and that Pakistan's new policy toward Kashmir is the latest in a series of humiliations he has endured at America's hand. A nationwide referendum on his rule two months ago was regarded so widely as fraudulent that the general was forced to acknowledge the nation's anger publicly. Dexter Filkins, As Pakistani's Popularity Slides, 'Busharraf' is a Figure of Ridicule, *The New York Times*, July 5, 2002.
46. On July 20, 2007, the Chief Justice of Pakistan was removed by General Musharraf. He was restored to his office at a time when the military was still ruling the country (*Chief Justice of Pakistan Iftikhar Muhammad Chaudhry v President of Pakistan through Secretary* 2010). General Musharraf claimed to have accepted the verdict, but on November 3, 2007, he declared Extra-Constitutional Emergency and promulgated Provisional Constitution Order (PCO) 2007. Constitution was suspended, judges of High Courts and Supreme Court were asked, on the basis of choose and pick, to take new oath under PCO 2007. On November 23, 2007, the reconstituted Supreme Court validated the imposition of emergency and the promulgation of the Provisional Constitution Order issued by the Chief of the Army Staff General Pervez Musharraf, and justified all the steps taken after the emergency on November 3, 2007. In *Sindh High Court Bar Association Case* (2009) the Supreme Court declared all the actions "taken by General Pervez Musharraf including the appointment of PCO judges to be unconstitutional" and held that "the doctrine of necessity inapplicable to an illegal assumption of power (*Sindh High Court Bar Association v Federation of Pakistan* PLD 2009 SC 879, p.1200;1080).
47. *State v. Dosso* PLD 1958 SC 533.
48. *Miss Asma Jillani v. The Government of the Punjab* PLD 1972 SC 139.
49. *Begum Nusrat Bhutto v. Chief of Army Staff and Federation of Pakistan* PLD 1977 SC 657.
50. *Federation of Pakistan v Saifullah Khan* PLD 1989 SC 166.
51. *Ahmed Tariq Rahim v. Federation of Pakistan* PLD 1992 SC 646.
52. *Syed Zafar Ali Shah v. General Pervez Musharraf, Chief Executive of Pakistan*, PLD 2000 SC 869.
53. Pakistan's military courts a solution or a problem? *Dawn*, available at: http://www.dw.com/en/pakistans-military-courts-a-solution-or-a-problem/a-18633959, accessed on January 10, 2016.

54. Wolf, Siegfried O., Formal Institutionalisation of Military Rule: The 21st Amendment in Pakistan, Pakistan Security Research Unit, Durham University, Briefing Paper 71, May 14, 2015, pp. 6-7.
55. Sahgal Arun, Military Courts in Pakistan: A Soft Coup by the Pakistan Army? January 14, 2015, available at: http://www.idsa.in/idsacomments/MilitaryCourtsinPakistan_asahgal_140115, accessed on May 22, 2015.
56. Kaiser Fawad, Military jurisdiction over non-military persons, *Daily Times*, February 16, 2016, available at:http://www.dailytimes.com.pk/opinion/16-Feb-2015/military-jurisdiction-over-non-military-persons, accessed on February 23, 2016.
57. Empowering military courts to try terrorism cases does not acknowledge, let alone resolve, any of the problems [Pakistan is facing]. Instead, it is yet another example of the state's resort to 'exceptionalism' to justify a knee-jerk response to terrorism that Pakistan has been guilty of many times before. Omer Reema, Rethinking Justice, *Dawn*, February 01, 2016, available at: http://www.dawn.com/news/1236633/rethinking-justice, accessed March 10, 2016. Also see: Pakistan's military courts -a solution or a problem? *Dawn*, available at: http://www.dw.com/en/pakistans-military-courts-a-solution-or-a-problem/a-18633959, accessed on January 10, 2016.

6

Enforced Disappearance

Introduction

Enforced disappearances has been defined as the arrest, detention or abduction of an individual by state authorities or their agents followed by a refusal to acknowledge the deprivation of liberty or by concealing the fate or whereabouts of the person, which places the person outside the protection of the law. Enforced disappearances are not the violation of merely one right, but constitute a multiple human rights violation. Among the rights an enforced disappearance violates are the right to liberty and security of the person, the protection from torture and other ill-treatment; the right to recognition as a person before the law; and the right to a prompt, fair, and public trial. Enforced disappearances also often constitute a grave threat to the right to life. These rights are protected by the international treaties such as ICCPR and the UN Convention Against Torture (CAT), which have been ratified by Pakistan in 2010. In addition, the International Convention for the Protection of All Persons from Enforced Disappearance (CPED), 2010, which has not yet been ratified by Pakistan, exclusively deals with the protection from enforced disappearance.[1]

Enforced Disappearances in Pakistan

There have been a number of reports about the prevalence of enforced disappearances in Pakistan. The Asian Human Rights Commission (ACHR) has reported that more than 8,000 persons from political and nationalist parties, students, lawyers, doctors, journalists and human rights defenders are reported missing after their arrest by the military, the Frontier Corps or by other law enforcement agencies. Pakistan military's premier intelligence agency, the Inter-Services Intelligence (ISI), has been blamed for disappearances and extra judicially killings.

More than 100 nationalists from the Sindh province have been reported missing after their arrest by the intelligence agencies and dozens of those disappeared persons have been killed extra judicially. Religious groups claim that more than 2,000 activists have been made to disappear by the military and government intelligence agencies. In Balochistan Province, [2] between July 2010 and January 2014, more than 700 extra-judicial killings and abductions by paramilitary forces or following enforced disappearances by Pakistan's law enforcement and security agencies have been recorded. Journalists, teachers, political activists, students and human rights defenders have been targeted in particular. The trend in the increase of enforced disappearances has been a direct cause for the proportional increase in instances of custodial torture and extra judicial killings. [3]

The United States Country Reports on Human Rights Practices described the situation of lawlessness in Pakistan[4]: "There were many reports that authorities committed arbitrary or unlawful killings. Security forces reportedly committed extrajudicial killings in connection with conflicts in Balochistan, Federally Administered Tribal Region (FATA), and Khyber Pakhtunkhwa (KP). The most serious human rights problems were extrajudicial and targeted killings, disappearances, torture, lack of rule of law (including lack of due process, poor implementation and enforcement of laws, and frequent mob violence and vigilante justice), and sectarian violence. Societal discrimination against national, ethnic, and racial minorities persisted, as did discrimination based on caste, sexual orientation, gender identity, and HIV status. Respect for worker's rights was minimal." The report continues, "Alleged politically motivated killings of Baluch nationalists continued in Balochistan and Karachi. For example, the Voice of Baluch Missing Persons (VBMP) in September compiled a list of 3,556 Baluch activists it claimed were abducted or killed since 2005. The VBMP claimed the army or security agencies killed 471 of these persons while holding them in custody. The South Asia Terrorism Portal (SATP) reported that journalists, teachers, students, and human rights defenders also were targeted in Balochistan."

The report further states, "There were reported kidnappings and forced disappearances of persons from various backgrounds in nearly all areas of the country. Some police and security forces reportedly held prisoners incommunicado and refused to disclose their location. In KP's Peshawar High Court, more than 400 *habeas corpus* petitions from the families of missing persons remained pending, and the court regularly conducted hearings on these cases. Government and NGO statistics on the number of persons who disappeared in Balochistan continued to diverge. NGOs compiled a list of 3,356 Baluch whom security agents allegedly abducted or killed while in custody. The VBMP claimed the total number of persons who have disappeared could be above 19,000."

According to Human Rights Watch,[5] Pakistan had a tumultuous year in 2014 as sectarian attacks continued with impunity and military operations in North Waziristan displaced more than one million people. Ongoing rights concerns in Balochistan province related to enforced disappearances, extrajudicial killings, and torture remained unaddressed. Lack of government response to enforced disappearances by the security forces fostered a long-standing culture of impunity.[6] Despite rulings from the Pakistan Supreme Court in 2013 demanding justice for victims of enforced disappearances, Pakistan's government has failed to meet its constitutional and international law obligations. In an earlier report, the Human Rights watch has explicitly dealt about the problem of disappearances in Pakistan and has concluded that it is widespread and is not limited to Balochistan province. A Pakistan official's statement to Bashir Azeem, the 76-year-old Secretary General of the Baluch Republican Party, during his unacknowledged detention in April 2010 brings out the ground reality: "Even if the President or Chief Justice tells us to release you, we won't. We can torture you, or kill you, or keep you for years at our will. It is only the Army Chief and the Intelligence Chief that we obey."[7]

The Amnesty International in its latest report[8] has brought out that despite clear rulings by the Supreme Court to the government in 2013 demanding the recovery of victims of enforced disappearances, the authorities did not take any action to prevent these violations. The state security forces exploited the provisions of Protection of Pakistan Act, resulting in men and boys being subjected to enforced disappearance across Pakistan and particularly in the provinces of Balochistan, Khyber

Pakhtunkhwa and Sindh.[9] Several victims were later found dead, bearing bullet wounds and torture marks. The government did not implement Supreme Court orders and failed to take action against the members of security forces responsible for enforced disappearances.[10]

The Amnesty International in its earlier report had stated that since Pakistan became a key ally in the US-led "war on terror" in late 2001, hundreds of people accused of links to terrorist activity have been arbitrarily detained and held in secret facilities.[11] They are possibly held in secret detention in Pakistan or other countries, and their whereabouts remain unknown. The Baluch community has been especially targeted for abductions, enforced disappearances and extrajudicial executions. Non-Baluch communities in Balochistan have also faced the same human rights violations, although in smaller numbers. Baluch political and human rights activists, lawyers, journalists and student leaders are among those who have been targeted for enforced disappearance, abduction, arbitrary arrest, and torture and other ill-treatment. The violence takes place in a context of increasing political unrest and Pakistani military operations in Balochistan. The families of those missing continue to fear for the lives of their loved ones, aware that torture and other ill-treatment is routine in Pakistani prisons and jails. They are victims of enforced disappearance: denied all access to the outside world, including lawyers, families and courts, and held outside the protection of the law.

The Human Rights Commission of Pakistan[12] has also reported deteriorating human rights situation in Balochistan province of Pakistan. According to report, Frontier Corps and intelligence agencies were generally believed to be involved in enforced disappearances of people as the dumping of bodies continued with impunity in the region. Kidnapping for ransom was a profitable enterprise and the law enforcement and security agencies completely failed to deal with the situation.[13]

Visit by the UN Working Group

At the invitation of the Pakistan government, the UN Working Group on Enforced or Involuntary Disappearances visited Pakistan in 2012.[14] During its 10-day visit, the Working Group visited Islamabad, Lahore, Karachi, Quetta and Peshawar and had meetings with government officials, civil society groups and families of victims of enforced disappearance.[15] A few highlights of the report are as follows:

- The cases of enforced disappearance filed with the Working Group allegedly occurred since mid-1980s in the north-western region, in relation to the conflicts in Afghanistan; and in relation to the military operations carried out in Karachi and their aftermath (Sindh Province).
- In Balochistan, some sources alleged that more than 14,000 people are still missing, while the provincial Government did not agree with the figure. Most of the cases concerned the alleged disappearance of members of the political party Muhajir Qaomi Movement (MQM), who were allegedly arrested by the police or by other security forces.
- A number of families were promised that, if they did not file a case, their loved ones would be released, which did not happen. While others were threatened that, if they did file a case, their loved ones would be harmed, or another member of their family would also be abducted. Witnesses who were called to testify in court were threatened and, in some cases, victimised. In a few cases, the lawyers defending the families were reportedly themselves victims of enforced disappearance.
- The abduction, often taking place in front of witnesses, is reported to have been perpetrated by law enforcement agencies, such as the police, the Frontier Corps (FC) or the Rangers, jointly with members of intelligence agencies in civilian clothing. Most of the time, intelligence agencies, such as Inter-Services Intelligence (ISI) or Military Intelligence (MI) are alleged to be directing the operations.
- It was claimed by the federal and provincial authorities that most of the "missing persons" were in fact not victims of enforced disappearance; some of those persons had been under criminal charges and had chosen to go into hiding, a few had fled to another country to join illegal armed groups, and others had been the victims of abduction by non-state actors for various reasons. As reported by the government agencies, cases of enforced disappearances by the state actors were very few and were the result of misconduct and *ultra vires* behaviour of some agents of the state.

- Under Article 3 of the Declaration on the Protection of All Persons from Enforced Disappearance, the State must take effective measures to prevent and terminate acts of enforced disappearance in any territory under its jurisdiction. However, no specific measures were taken by the federal and provincial authorities in Pakistan to address the issue of reparation of victims of enforced disappearances.
- The Working Group was concerned that some of the persons with whom the delegation had met were later threatened or intimidated.
- A mother of a disappeared person asked the Working Group to convey a message to all persons in charge of Public Affairs in Pakistan. She asked, "If your child disappeared, what would you do?" This question summarised the ordeal that families endure. According to the Working Group, the relatives of the disappeared persons have the right to the truth, the right to justice and the right to reparation, and it is the duty of the State of Pakistan to take all necessary measures to make those rights effective.

Involvement of Security Forces

Almost every human rights report has alleged the involvement of Pakistan military, paramilitary, police forces, and intelligence services in enforced disappearances and extrajudicial killings in various part of Pakistan. During the regime of General Pervez Musharraf, there were hundreds of such disappearances that still remain unaccounted for.[16] According to Amnesty International, in 2010, the Ministry for the Interior admitted to 965 disappearance cases for which there were some records, although there are differing claims on figures made by families, human rights groups and the state, ranging up to 7,000.[17] Although the military and intelligence agencies refute every accusation, the Pakistani press has reported the use of death squads, composed of Baluch guns-for-hire, resembling the Al Shams and Al Badr militias that the Pakistani military employed during the Bangladesh war. The Pakistan intelligence agencies have allegedly created the death squads operating in Balochistan to counter the Marris, Mengals, and Bugtis.[18] Despite the restoration of democracy after the departure of Musharraf, the Pakistan military remains the dominant political authority and pays no heed to the commands of the civilian government. The military's harsh response to the Baluch insurgency has led to violence, widespread human rights abuses, mass internal displacement and the deaths of hundreds of civilians and armed personnel. According to the US intelligence estimates, around 25,000 army and paramilitary forces are involved in counterinsurgency operations in Balochistan, which has amplified the problem of enforced disappearances, that too with impunity.[19] Other provinces in Pakistan have also witnessed the involvement of security personnel in enforced disappearances and extrajudicial killings.

On November 10, 2007, General Pervez Musharraf promulgated an ordinance making Amendments to the Army Act giving wide powers to security forces and military courts. Outdated draconian laws of Gen. Ziaul Haq's era were activated, given new life and made punishable by the military courts. The Army Act, 1952, already had a provision to hold Court Martial of civilians but only when at least one of the accused belonged to the armed forces. The amendments enhanced the already excessive powers of the Army for arrests and detention and trying of civilians by military courts on charges of terrorism, anti-national activities, sedition, attacks on military personnel. The ordinance was in fact passed to settle scores with lawyers, human rights activists and journalists and was made effective from January 2003. The powers given to military and security forces were abused and served as a powerful tool to strangle the dissented voices. Media offices were attacked and put under surveillance; while media personnel were regularly subjected to torture, kidnapping, illegal detention, beatings, and death threat from the security forces, insurgents and violent political stakeholders.

Witnesses to enforced disappearances have described the perpetrators as armed men in civilian clothes, usually arriving in one or more four-door pickup trucks. In a number of cases the abductions were carried out by, in the presence of, or with the assistance of uniformed personnel of the frontier corps, a paramilitary force. It has also been reported that police assisted by being present at the scene or securing an area while plainclothes intelligence officers abducted individuals who later "disappeared." According to representatives of the intelligence agencies, including the ISI, military intelligence, and the intelligence bureau were involved in kidnapping and enforced disappearances.

Even after return of democracy in 2008, the Pakistani military has successfully inserted itself into the political sphere. The use of political violence by the Pakistani intelligence agencies, through their support to terrorist groups has been extensively acknowledged. Citizens have been abducted, tortured, and ultimately killed, with their bodies often abandoned miles away from the place where they were abducted. Insurgents are not the only victims; sympathisers of militant groups, suspected nationalists, students, teachers, lawyers, journalists, and, more generally, all educated citizens are systematically targeted in what increasingly resembles a genocide aimed at eradicating ethnic identities and preventing any possible resurgence of Baluch nationalism. Military operations have been stopped, but "kill-and-dump" operations remain in use across the state. Pakistan's military and intelligence agencies constantly demonstrate complete contempt for the state institutions, including the Supreme Court.[20]

In 2011, Pakistan enacted the Action in Aid of Civil Power Regulations, which retrospectively provides legal cover to detentions by the military since 2008. It is applicable in FATA region and authorises the armed forces to handle detainees under civilian supervision when called upon by the government. The regulation deprives citizens the right to a fair trial by an impartial tribunal, legalises detention without trial by intelligence agencies and is violative of international human rights law. The regulation also violates the Pakistan's Constitution because under its broad provisions the military authority can circumvent legal due process.[21]

Human Rights Obligations

Human Rights are derived from the inherent dignity and humanity of a person and their protection is imperative for the proper functioning of the state. At a basic level, human rights enshrine people with equality irrespective of their gender, race, religion, political thinking, etc. As formulated in constitutions; human rights are those fundamental rights that are afforded to the people in order to enable them to live their lives in peace and harmony, without prejudice or persecution. The Constitution of Pakistan imposes an obligation on the state to protect the rights of its people, including women, children and minorities, in reality such protection have not been fully translated. This has resulted in a criticism of the standard of human rights in Pakistan by the international organisations.

On June 23, 2010, Pakistan signed and ratified the International Covenant on Civil and Political Rights (ICCPR) and the Convention Against Torture (CAT),[22] however, made sweeping reservations to several provisions of both of these core International Human Rights Treaties. The Pakistan government entered reservations to eight of the ICCPR's 27 substantive Articles, and to seven of the CAT's 16 substantive Articles.[23] The reservation made by Pakistan to ICCPR relate to, amongst others, equality between men and women, the right to life, including restrictions on the imposition of the death penalty, the prohibition of torture, freedom of thought, conscience and religion, freedom of expression, the right to liberty of movement and freedom in the choice of residence, restrictions on the expulsion of aliens lawfully in the territory of a State Party, the right to take part in public affairs, the right to vote and to be elected and the right to have access to public service on terms of equality subject to the *Sharia* laws and/or the constitutional and/or national laws in force in Pakistan. Many of these reservations are incompatible with the object and purpose of the ICCPR. Moreover, through a reservation to Article 40 of the ICCPR,[24] Pakistan seeks to avoid reporting under the Covenant and to disregard the fundamental role of the UN Human Rights Committee in evaluating the state's observance of its ICCPR obligations. Such a reservation is unprecedented and similarly incompatible with the object and purpose of the Covenant.

As regard, reservation to Articles 3, 4, 6, 12, 13 and 16 of the CAT, the Government of Pakistan has made the application of essential obligations under the Convention subject to the Sharia laws and/or the constitutional and national laws in force in Pakistan. This makes it unclear to what extent Pakistan considers itself bound by the obligations of the treaty and raises concerns as to the commitment of Pakistan to the object and purpose of the Convention.

On September 20, 2011, in a communication to the UN Secretary-General, the Pakistan government notified that it had decided to partially withdraw the reservations, made upon ratification, to Articles 3 and 25 of the ICCPR.[25] Subsequently, the Government of Pakistan notified the Secretary-General that it had decided to partially withdraw the reservations, made upon ratification, to Articles 6, 7, 12, 13, 18, 19 and 40 of the Covenant.[26] As regards reservation to the CAT, the Government of Pakistan notified the Secretary-General on September 20, 2011 that it has decided to withdraw the reservations to Articles 3, 4, 6, 12, 13 and 16 of the CAT.[27]

As to the reservations[28] entered in relation to Articles 3 (equal right of men and women), Pakistan has declared that the provisions of Articles 3 shall be so applied to the extent that they are not repugnant to the Provisions of the Constitution of Pakistan and the *Shariah* laws. This reservation to Article 3 made by Pakistan is unspecific and deceptive. The reservation refers to a domestic legal document which is not easily understood by other state parties and which is subject to changes and interpretation. By mentioning that Article 3 of the ICCPR only apply as far as it is in line with Pakistan's Constitution, the reservation introduces a de facto hierarchy of norms by which national law supersedes international obligations. Pakistan's reservations may be regarded as unlawful and inapplicable. Pakistan's reservations to the ICCPR are, therefore, incompatible with international human rights law and the government should withdraw it.[29] Pakistan is also bound by the obligations under the Convention on the Rights of the Child, the Convention on the Elimination of All Forms of Discrimination against Women, and the International Convention on the Elimination of All Forms of Racial Discrimination. These international treaties oblige Pakistan to ensure the protection of a host of important human rights to its citizens without any discrimination on the basis of religion. Upholding the integrity of the treaties and the functioning of the UN treaty system is in the interests of all states parties.

Derogations from human rights in accordance with the ICCPR may only occur in "time of public emergency which threatens the life of the nation and the existence of which is officially proclaimed." Any derogation must be only "to the extent strictly required by the exigencies of the situation, provided that such measures are not inconsistent with their other obligations under international law and do not involve discrimination solely on the ground of race, colour, sex, language, religion or social origin."[30]

Blasphemy Laws

The religious identity was the basis of an independent state for Muslims of British India. The founding fathers of Pakistan had a vision to create a secular state where Muslims could live freely without any domination. Jinnah reiterated this vision in his presidential address to the first Constituent Assembly on August 11, 1947: "You are free; you are free to go to your temples, you are free to go to your mosques or to any other place of worship in this state of Pakistan. You may belong to any religion or caste or creed that has nothing to do with the business of the State."[31] The successive governments after independence have promoted the use of Islam for political purposes resulting in a culture of intolerance and discrimination. During General Zia's dictatorship, the campaign of islamisation resulted in discrimination against religious minorities. Zia also introduced changes into the legal system, such as, the creation of the Federal *Shariat* Court, a separate electorate system, *hudood* laws and anti–blasphemy laws. Changes introduced Sections 295, 295a, 295b, 295C, 298a, 298b and 298C incorporated under offences relating to religion of the Pakistan Penal Code 1860, are popularly termed as anti-blasphemy laws.[32] The anti–blasphemy laws seek to punish the offence of insulting the prophet Mohammad and impose severe punishment including the death.

Pakistan's blasphemy laws have been criticised for being discriminatory against religious minorities. Minorities, Muslims, children, and persons with mental disabilities have all been charged under the law. Blasphemy law has been frequently abused to imprison people on grounds of religious enmity but also has proved an easy tool to have people imprisoned when the real motives are business rivalry or property disputes. There have been instances when the death sentence under Section 295C has been given to a juvenile, violating Article 6(5) of the ICCPR. In the case of *Salamat Masih v State* (1995), a 13-year old Christian boy and his co-accused were given death sentences after conviction under Section 295C by a sessions court. There have been protests by religious minorities to amend these laws. In 2011, the debate to amend the blasphemy laws resulted in the killings of Punjab Governor Salman Taseer and the Federal Minister for Minorities Shahbaz Bhatti.[33] Since 1990, at least 60 people have been murdered after being accused of blasphemy. These incidents have caused a major blow to the protection of human rights of religious minorities in Pakistan. At present, 17 people convicted of blasphemy are on death row; 19 others are serving life sentences.[34] The Constitution of Pakistan's guarantees the Fundamental Rights to life, liberty and equality before the law, as well as equal protection of the law. According to Hayee, blasphemy laws are inconsistent with international soft law on religious freedom; violate a number of legally binding human rights obligations of Pakistan; and also contravene the rights guaranteed in Article 20 of the Constitution of Pakistan.[35]

Respect for International Humanitarian Law

International Humanitarian Law (IHL)[36] protects those who are not, or who are no longer, taking part in the fighting; and puts restrictions on the means and the methods of warfare. The Geneva Conventions of 1949 remain applicable in international armed conflicts, and deal with the treatment of the wounded and sick in armed forces in the field (Convention I), the wounded, sick and shipwrecked members of the armed forces at sea (Convention II), prisoners of war (Convention III) and civilians, including those in occupied territories Convention IV). Similarly, the rules applicable in non-international armed conflicts are Article 3 common to the Geneva Conventions and Additional Protocol II of 1977 concern the treatment of persons not or no longer taking direct part in hostilities. In an internal conflict IHL binds the government, as well as the groups fighting against it. IHL lays down rules that are applicable to both State and non-State actors. It also provides that persons may be held individually criminally responsible for grave breaches of the Geneva Conventions and of Additional Protocol I, and for other serious violations of IHL, both in international and non-international armed conflicts. The Government of Pakistan has signed and ratified the four Geneva Conventions of 1949. Pakistan is not a party to the 1977 Additional Protocol II, which also deals with non-international armed conflicts, and therefore it is not applicable.

There is no denying the fact that the Pakistan's armed forces are involved in internal armed conflict in the provinces of Balochistan; between the military and Islamic militants along the Afghan border; and between the military and suspected *Taliban* militants in the SWAT valley region. They have been continuously deployed in crushing militants and terrorists as well as quelling protests in various parts of the country. Militants and terrorist groups have targeted armed forces, civilians, journalists, community leaders, law enforcement agents, and schools, killing hundreds and injuring thousands with bombs, suicide attacks, and other forms of violence.[37]

In 2014, the military launched Operation *Zarb-e-Azb,* a comprehensive operation in North Waziristan (FATA), to stem *Tehrik-i-Taliban* Pakistan (*TTP*) militancy. Militant and terrorist bombings in all four provinces and in FATA also resulted in hundreds of deaths and thousands of injuries. Political, sectarian, criminal, and ethnic violence in Karachi took lives of more than 2,034 persons in 2014. On December 16, 2014, militants attacked an Army-run Public School in Peshawar, killing at least 142 and injuring at least 250, most of them students. The *TTP* claimed responsibility for the attack and stated it was in retaliation for the military operation *Zarb-e-Azb*. Non-state militant groups have kidnapped boys and girls and used fraudulent promises to coerce parents into giving away children as young as age 12 to spy, fight, or die as suicide bombers. The militants sometimes offered parents money, often sexually and physically abused the children, and used psychological coercion to convince the children that the acts they committed were justified. There were reports of civilian casualties and extrajudicial killings committed by government security forces during operations against militant groups.[38]

Core obligations of Pakistan security forces as well as non-state actors during these conflicts are as follows:

- Persons taking no active part in the hostilities, including members of armed forces who have laid down their arms and those who are *hors de combat* for any other reason will in all circumstances be treated humanely without any adverse distinction based on race, colour, religion or faith, sex, or birth. The wounded and sick must be provided medical treatment.

- The following acts are prohibited in respect of above named individuals: (a) violence to life and person, in particular murder of all kinds, mutilation, cruel treatment and torture; (b) taking of hostages; (c) outrages upon personal dignity, in particular, humiliating and degrading treatment; and (d) the passing of sentences and the carrying out of executions without previous judgment pronounced by a regularly constituted court affording all the judicial guarantees which are recognised as indispensable by civilised peoples.

The Geneva Convention applicable in non-international armed conflict prohibit murder, torture, rape, bodily injury, or other cruel, humiliating or degrading treatment, enforced disappearances, taking of hostages, and the arbitrary deprivation of liberty. In addition no one may be convicted or sentenced, except pursuant to a fair trial affording all essential judicial guarantees. This includes a defendant's right to know the charges against him/her; to understand the court proceedings; to have the opportunity to conduct a genuine defence; and to be able to appeal against both conviction and sentence. Everyone charged with a criminal offence shall be presumed innocent until proved guilty according to law.

It has been alleged that the Government of Pakistan has provided absolute impunity to the army and security forces for the abuses including murder, extrajudicial killings, illegal detentions, torture and enforced disappearances during their deployment in non-international armed conflict. It is apparent that one of the most important provisions of the Geneva Conventions, dealing with grave breaches has not yet been incorporated by the Pakistan Government. There is a direct obligation under paragraph 1 of Article 49 (the First Geneva Convention), which provides: "The High Contracting Parties undertake to enact any legislation necessary to provide effective penal sanctions for persons committing, or ordering to be committed, any of the grave breaches of the present Convention." The grave breaches are listed in Article 50 of the Conventions and are as follows: willful killing, torture or inhuman treatment, including biological experiments, willfully causing great suffering or serious injury to body or health, and extensive destruction and appropriation of property, not justified by military necessity and carried out unlawfully and wantonly. Incidentally, during a non-international armed conflict the provisions of both international human rights law and IHL remain applicable.[39]

Enforced disappearance is also a crime under International Humanitarian Law, and is explicitly defined in the Rome Statute as follows: "Enforced disappearance of persons" means the arrest, detention or abduction of persons by, or with the authorisation, support or acquiescence of, a State or a political organisation, followed by a refusal to acknowledge that deprivation of freedom or to give information on the fate or whereabouts of those persons, with the intention of removing them from the protection of the law for a prolonged period of time. [40]The crime consists of two major alternative types of conduct—deprivation of liberty and withholding information. The perpetrator of the deprivation of liberty need not be the one who withholds information and vice versa, but all of them have to know the context of the act. There might be a number of persons responsible for the crime.[41] Though Pakistan has not signed the Rome Statute, but is bound to rules against enforced disappearance under national law as its components namely kidnapping, abductions, unlawful detention and wrongful restraint and confinement are made illegal under the Pakistan Penal Code, 1860.[42]

Informal justice systems lacking institutionalised legal protections continue to exist in Pakistan, especially in rural areas, and often resulted in human rights abuses. Women are often sentenced to violent punishment or death for honour-related crimes. In March 2013, a Pakistani soldier was publicly stoned to death on the order of a tribal court[43] in the country's northwestern Kurram region (FATA) for having an affair with a local girl.[44]

National Commission for Human Rights

With the adoption of the National Commission for Human Rights Act, 2012, and the recent appointment of members to the National Commission for Human Rights (NCHR), the government of Pakistan has created a Human Rights Institution with the power to promote and protect the Fundamental Rights of its citizens. The NCHR has quasi-judicial competence and the ability to investigate allegations of human rights abuse and state negligence. This includes the power to summon and examine witnesses; visit jails and places of detention; procure public records and court proceedings; forward cases to a magistrate for criminal proceedings; order reports from the Federal and Provincial Governments; and advise the federal government on the appointment of special prosecutors in human rights courts. It is hoped, that the NCHR will not only promote and protect human rights enshrined in Pakistan's Constitution, but also those included in the international instruments to which Pakistan is a state party.

Common Article 1 to the four Geneva Conventions of 1949 lays down an obligation to respect and ensure respect for the Convention in all circumstances. The non-international armed conflicts in Pakistan have resulted in enormous sufferings by killing of thousands of innocent civilians including women and children. The obligation to respect the Geneva Convention, to which Pakistan is a state party, means that it must do everything it can to guarantee that its own organs abide by the rules of IHL. The non-state actors in Pakistan are also bound by this obligation. However, common Article 1 goes one step further by introducing a commitment to ensure respect in all circumstances. This has two components: first, the parties to conflict must ensure that the provisions of Convention are respected at all times not only by its armed forces but also by military authorities and civilians. The second component postulates that third states have a duty to take action in order to ensure compliance with the provisions of Geneva Conventions.[45] In the case of armed conflict in Pakistan, the second component relates to the US military which is an ally to Pakistan in its fight against terrorism.[46] The US has an international obligation not only to avoid encouraging IHL violations committed by the armed forces of Pakistan but also to take measures to put an end to on-going violations and to prevent their occurrences.[47]

Notes

1. The international community has taken steps to combat enforced disappearance, both at the regional and international level, with the Declaration on the Protection of all Persons from Enforced Disappearance, 1992, the Inter-American Convention on Forced Disappearance of Persons, 1994, and the Rome Statute of the International Criminal Court, 1998, and the International Convention for the Protection of All Persons from Enforced Disappearance (CPED), 2010. The CPED defines the term enforced disappearance as the "arrest, detention, abduction or any other form of deprivation of liberty by agents of the State or by persons or groups of persons acting with the authorisation, support or acquiescence of the State, followed by a refusal to acknowledge the deprivation of liberty or by concealment of the fate or whereabouts of the disappeared person, which place such a person outside the protection of the law.
2. Balochistan has witnessed five successive insurgencies and unrests since 1947. Unfortunately due to narrow vision of national security since independence, Balochistan is gradually sinking into a quagmire with serious and long lasting implications for Pakistan. Mirza Lt. Gen. Zahid Latif, Balochistan—Past, Present and Future, *NDU Journal*, Pakistan, 2013, pp. 21-34.
3. Statement to mark the International Day of the Victims of Enforced Disappearances, Asian Human Rights Commission, August 23, 2014, available at: http://reliefweb.int/report/pakistan/statement-mark-international-day-victims-enforced-disappearances, accessed on June 30, 2015.
4. Country Reports on Human Rights Practices for 2014, United States Department of State, Bureau of Democracy, Human Rights and Labour, pp. 1-4.
5. Human Rights Watch, World Report 2015, pp. 418-424.
6. For instance, on March 18, 2014, plainclothes gunmen later identified as belonging to Pakistan's paramilitary Frontier Corps allegedly abducted Zahid Baloch, chairperson of the Baloch Student Organisation-Azad in the provincial capital, Quetta. His whereabouts and safety are unknown. Human Rights Watch, World Report 2015, p. 422.
7. In the report Human Rights Watch interviewed over 100 individuals in Pakistan, including family members of disappeared individuals, persons who had been held in unacknowledged detention and then released, local human rights activists, lawyers, and witnesses. *We Can Torture, Kill, or Keep You for Years: Enforced Disappearances by Pakistan Security Forces in Balochistan*, Human Rights Watch, July 2011, p. 1.
8. Amnesty International Report 2014/15.
9. On December 10, 2013, the Supreme Court bench headed by the Chief Justice ordered the federal government to produce all the thirty five 'missing persons' before it in seven days. The court held that such practices of enforced disappearances were a serious crime against humanity. Objecting to the verdict of the Court, the Ministry of Defence filed a review petition and pleaded that holding the Pakistan Army responsible for enforced disappearances by the Supreme Court would demoralise the troops engaged in combating terrorists in SWAT and Malakand. The review petition highlighted that the Supreme Court had failed to take into consideration that the armed forces were called in SWAT and Malakand under Article 245 of the Constitution to act in aid of the civil powers and to fight the worst form of terrorism in the area. Further, when the army is called to assist the civil authorities to carry out a constitutional duty, the jurisdiction of the High Court as well as the Fundamental

Rights guaranteed in the Constitution are suspended. In the review petition, the Ministry requested the Apex Court to revisit its verdict by accepting the contentions in the interest of Pakistan and the state and expunge all the findings, remarks and observations recorded against the army and its intelligence agencies. The Defence Ministry urged that the deletion of the observations and remarks should be done in such a manner as if these had never been incorporated in the judgment. Iqbal Nasir, Army seeks review of SC verdict in missing persons' case, *Dawn*, January 19, 2014, available at: http://www.dawn.com/news/1081304, accessed on January 12, 2016.

10. Amnesty International Report 2014/15, pp. 282-283.
11. Pakistani security forces have detained hundreds of residents of the Federally Administered Tribal Areas (FATA) on suspicion of co-operating with the Pakistani Taliban. There is no public information on the number of persons detained, or their current whereabouts, but credible media reports suggest that some 2,500 people were in detention in the first half of 2010. Amnesty International and other human rights groups believe that the numbers subjected to enforced disappearances could be much higher. These detainees are not held under any clear legal framework under Pakistan's law, given FATA's exceptional legal status and the inapplicability of many laws to the region. Given the well-documented record of abuse by Pakistan's security agencies, there are ample grounds to fear that these detainees could have been subjected to torture or other ill-treatment. The Bitterest of Agonies: End enforced disappearances in Pakistan, Amnesty International, Index ASA 33/010/2011, September 2011.
12. The Human Right Commission of Pakistan (HRCP) was established as an NGO in 1987. Since then it has developed to become an influential country wide human rights body. The HRCP has established a leading role in providing a highly informed and objective voice on a national level in the struggle for the provision of human rights for all and democratic development in Pakistan. HRCP's role in highlighting human rights abuses has been recognised not only on a national level but also internationally.
13. Hopes, Fear and Alienation in Balochistan, Report of an HRCP fact-finding mission, 2012, Human Rights Commission, Pakistan, p. 44.
14. The Working Groups was represented by Chairperson-Rapporteur Olivier Frouville and Osman El-Hajje and visited Pakistan from September 10-20, 2012. UN General Assembly, Human Rights Council, Report of the Working Group on Enforced or Involuntary Disappearances on its mission to Pakistan, UN Doc. A/HRC/22/45/Add.2 dated February 26, 2013.
15. The Working Group met a number of high-ranking government and security officials including the Chief Justice of Pakistan, Chief Justices of four High Courts, the Director General of Inter-services Intelligence and the Inspector General of Frontier Corps in Balochistan and Khyber-Pakhtunkhwa.
16. The military coup in 1999 that brought Pervez Musharraf to power increased general alienation among the Baluchs. This is because Baluchs see the army as lacking Baluch representation due to its domination by the interests of the Punjabi—the main ethnic group in Pakistan that accounts for approximately 45 percent of the country's population. A primary Baluch grievance is the construction of the megaport of Gwadar, which began in 2002 and is ongoing. In 2004, a renewed ethnic insurgency broke out, and violence has escalated since the killing of the Baluch leader Nawab Akbar Bugti by the army in 2006 and the unlawful detention and disappearance

of many additional Baluch leaders by the Pakistani government. Kupecz Mickey, Pakistan's Baluch Insurgency: History, Conflict Drivers, and Regional Implications, *International Affairs Review*, Vol. 20, No. 3, Spring 2012, pp. 95-110.

17. The Bitterest of Agonies: End enforced disappearances in Pakistan, Amnesty International, Index ASA 33/010/2011, September 2011, p. 2.
18. Bhattacharjee D., Pakistan's India Fixation on the Issue of Balochistan, Indian Council of World Affairs, Issue brief, 3 June 2015, p. 3.
19. Jetly Rajsree, "Resurgence of the Baluch Movement in Pakistan: Emerging Perspectives and Challenges," in Jetly Rajshree (ed.). 2009. *Pakistan in Regional and Global Politics*, New York: Routledge, p. 215.
20. Grare Frederic, The Challenges of Civilian Control over Intelligence Agencies in Pakistan, December 18, 2015, Bangladesh Institute of Law and International Affairs, book chapter available at: http://carnegieendowment.org/2015/12/18/challenges-of-civilian-control-over-intelligence-agencies-in-pakistan/inad, accessed on January 10, 2016.
21. Under section 4 of the Actions in Aid of Civil Power Regulation, 2011, the Armed Forces may undertake the following preventive measures during the action in aid of civil power: (i) warn the civilians to vacate the area; (ii) give warning to the residents to withdraw support for the miscreants; (iii) residents may be directed to point out the miscreants in hiding to the Armed Forces personnel; (iv) take special measures in respect of the life and safety of children, women and elderly persons; and (v) take feasible precautions in the choice of means and methods of attack with a view to avoiding and minimising collateral loss of civilian life and object. The armed forces are authorised to use necessary force, arms and ammunitions, weapons and air power etc., to achieve the objective during any armed action. Under Section 5 of the Regulations, if any abuse or misuse of the use of force during action in aid of civil power is alleged or attributed to any member of the Armed Forces, the same shall be investigated within the hierarchy of the Armed Forces.
22. The UN Covenant on Civil and Political Rights, 1966, and the Convention against Torture and other Cruel, Inhuman or Degrading Treatment or Punishment 1984; in addition, the Pakistan Government has also signed and ratified Convention on the Rights of the Child (on November 12, 1990) and Convention on the Elimination of All Forms of Discriminations Against Women (March 12, 1996). Pakistan also ratified the International Covenant on Economic, Social and Cultural Right (ICESCR) in 2008. However, till date no reports have been submitted from Pakistan. There are some core instruments that Pakistan has not signed; these are the International Convention on the Protection of the Rights of All Migrant Workers and Members of their Families, 1990, and the International Convention for the Protection of All Persons from Enforced Disappearance, 2006.
23. Pakistan entered reservations to eight of the 27 substantive Articles of the ICCPR (Articles 3, 6, 7, 12, 13, 18, 19, 25, as well as to Article 40) and to seven of the 16 substantive Articles of the CAT (Articles 3, 4, 6, 8, 12, 13, and 16, as well as to Article 28).
24. The Human Rights Committee, which oversees implementation of the ICCPR, in a statement issued on April 1, 2011 stated that Article 40 gives the Human Rights Committee the competence to consider and study reports submitted by the States Parties. This competence is of critical importance for the performance of the Committee's monitoring functions and essential to the *raison detre* of the Covenant. In its earlier General Comment 24 of 1994, the Committee stated that a

reservation that rejects the Committee's competence to interpret the requirements of any provisions of the Covenant would also be contrary to the object and purpose of the treaty.

25. These reservations read as follows: Article 3: The Government of the Islamic Republic of Pakistan declares that the provisions of Article 3 of the International Covenant on Civil and Political Rights shall be so applied as to be in conformity with Personal Law of the citizens and *Qanoon-e-Shahadat*. Article 25: The Government of the Islamic Republic of Pakistan states that the application of Article 25 of the International Covenant on Civil and Political Rights shall be subject to the principle laid down in Article 41 (2) and Article 91 (3) of the Constitution of Pakistan.
26. These reservations read as follows: Article 3, 6, 7, 18 and 19: The Islamic Republic of Pakistan declares that the provisions of Articles 3, 6, 7, 18 and 19 shall be so applied to the extent that they are not repugnant to the Constitution of Pakistan and the *Sharia* laws. Article 12: The Islamic Republic of Pakistan declares that the provisions of Articles 12 shall be so applied as to be in conformity with the Provisions of the Constitution of Pakistan. Article 13: With respect to Article 13, the Government of the Islamic Republic of Pakistan reserves its right to apply its law relating to foreigners. Article 40: The Government of the Islamic Republic of Pakistan hereby declares that it does not recognise the competence of the Committee provided for in Article 40 of the Covenant.
27. These reservations read as follows: Article 3: The Government of the Islamic Republic of Pakistan declares the provisions of Article 3 shall be so applied as to be in conformity with the provisions of its laws relating to extradition and foreigners. Articles 4, 6, 12, 13 and 16: The Government of the Islamic Republic of Pakistan declares that the provisions of these Articles shall be so applied to the extent that they are not repugnant to the Provisions of the Constitution of Pakistan and the *Sharia* laws.
28. A reservation is a unilateral statement purporting to exclude or modify the legal effect of certain provisions of an international treaty, including as it applies at the domestic level. Under the Vienna Convention on the Law of Treaties, such modifications are only allowed if entered at the time of ratification, and if they are in accordance with the object and purpose of the treaty. Neither the ICCPR nor the CAT expressly prohibits reservations. However, under Article 19 of the Vienna Convention on the Law of Treaties, a state may enter a reservation only if it is compatible with the object and purpose of the treaty. The Human Rights Committee in General Comment 24 (paragraph 18) has stated that because of the special character of human rights treaties, the normal consequence of an unacceptable reservation is not that the ICCPR will not be in effect at all for a reserving party. Rather, such a reservation will generally be severable, in the sense that the Covenant will be operative for the reserving party without benefit of the reservation.
29. Akstiniene Aiste, Reservations to Human Rights Treaties: Problematic Aspects Related to Gender Issues, *Jurisprudence*, Vol. 20, No. 2, 2013, pp. 451–468.
30. See: Article 4, the International Covenant on Civil and Political Rights. However, no derogations from Article 6, 7, 8 (paragraph 1 and 2), 11, 15, 16 and 18 may be made under this provision.
31. For more details see: Hamid Khan,*Constitutional and Political History of Pakistan*(Karachi: Oxford University Press, 2009).
32. Hayee Bilal, Blasphemy Laws and Pakistan's Human Rights Obligations, *UNDALR*, Vol. 14, 2012, pp. 25-54.

33. Salman Tasir, Governor of Punjab Province was brutally assassinated for seeking reforms to the country's controversial blasphemy law. He was shot 28 times in broad light in Islamabad. On February 29, 2016, the accused, a former Police Commando Mumtaz Qadri was hanged to death. Qadri had admitted killing and said he objected to the Governor's calls to reform the blasphemy laws. Anti-terrorism Court had convicted and condemned Qadri to death in 2011, a ruling upheld by the Islamabad High Court and the Supreme Court. Execution of Salman Taseer's assassin leads to protests, *The Hindu*, March 1, 2016.
34. In March 2014, a Lahore court sentenced Sawan Masih to death for blasphemy after he was accused of making derogatory statements regarding the Prophet Muhammad. In April 2014, these allegations prompted a mob of 3,000 persons to attack a Christian residential community in Lahore and torch hundreds of houses. On May 7, 2014, unidentified gunmen killed Rashid Rehman, a renowned human rights lawyer, in retaliation for representing people accused of blasphemy. In April 2014, a court in Toba Tek Singh sentenced to death a Christian couple, for allegedly sending "blasphemous" text messages. In November 2014, a mob beat to death a Christian couple after they allegedly committed blasphemy by burning pages of a Quran. Their bodies were later burned in the kiln of the factory in which they worked. In July 2014, a mob in Gujranwala burned down houses of the Ahmadi community killing three people and injuring eight others over alleged blasphemy. The provisions of Pakistan's Penal Code, which perpetuate discrimination against the Ahmadis, remain unchanged: the code explicitly prohibits Ahmadis from "indirectly or directly posing as a Muslim"; declaring or propagating their faith publicly; building mosques or referring to them as such; or making public calls to prayer. Human Rights Watch, World Report 2015, pp. 418-424.
35. Hayee Bilal, Blasphemy Laws and Pakistan's Human Rights Obligations, *UNDALR*, Vol. 14, 2012, p. 51.
36. International Humanitarian Law (IHL) is a set of rules which seeks, for humanitarian reasons, to limit the effects of armed conflict. It protects persons who are not or are no longer participating in the hostilities and restricts the means and methods of warfare. IHL is also known as the law of war or the law of armed conflict.
37. See: http://www.geneva-academy.ch/RULAC/applicable_international_law.php?id_state=166, accessed on March 22, 2016.
38. Pakistan: Country Reports on Human Rights Practices for 2014, United States Department of State, Bureau of Democracy, Human Rights and Labour, pp. 18-22.
39. Common Article 3 of the 1949 Geneva Conventions specifically applies in the case of conflicts "not of an international character." This means armed conflicts between governments and organised armed groups. Common Article 3 does not define "armed conflict." However, several criteria have been developed through practice, such as the following: (i) The parties to the armed conflict have to be identifiable, i.e. they must have a minimum of organisation and structure, and a chain of command. (ii) The armed conflict must have a minimum level of intensity. The parties would usually have recourse to their armed forces or to military means. The duration of the violence is another element that has to be taken into consideration. Common Article 3 stipulates the minimum protection that must be afforded to all those who are not, or who are no longer, taking an active part in hostilities (e.g. civilians, members of armed forces of the parties to the conflict who have been captured, are wounded, or have surrendered). It provides for humane and non-discriminatory treatment for all such persons, in particular by prohibiting acts of violence to life

and person (specifically murder, mutilation, cruel treatment and torture), the taking of hostages, and outrages upon personal dignity, in particular humiliating and degrading treatment. It prohibits also the passing of sentences and the carrying out of executions without judgment being pronounced by a regularly constituted court providing all judicial guarantees recognised as indispensable. Finally, it imposes an obligation on the parties to collect the wounded and sick and to care for them.

40. The Rome Statute of the International Criminal Court, 1998, Article 7.1(i).
41. Vitkauskaite-Meurice Dalia and Zilinskas Justinas, The Concept of Enforced Disappearances in International Law, *Jurisprudence*, Vol. 2, pp.197–214.
42. The Pakistan Penal Code, 1860 does not contain the crime of enforced disappearance. Section 359 and those thereafter relate to the crimes of kidnapping and abduction. The crime of kidnapping is of two kinds: kidnapping from Pakistan and kidnapping from lawful guardianship (Sections 359-361). Abduction, regulated by Section 362, is defined as "whoever by force compels, or by any deceitful means induces, any person to go from any place." Section 364 also punishes "kidnapping or abducting in order to murder." Section 365 targets "whoever kidnaps or abducts any person with intent to cause that person to be secretly and wrongfully confined", while Section 369 also punishes "whoever knowing that any person has been kidnapped or has been abducted wrongfully conceals or confines such person."
43. A traditional jigra (tribal council) deals with various issues affecting those in tribal areas including land and property disputes, inheritance, alleged violations of honour, and intra-tribal or inter-tribal killings. Jigra is a traditional or tribal justice system, being practiced by the Pakhtun ethnic group that lives in Pakistan and Afghanistan with 'Jigra' being the most preferred form of informal or parallel justice/dispute resolution mechanism in many Pakhtun dominated areas of Pakistan.
44. In 2012, Anwar Din, a 27-year-old-soldier was posted at Parachinar area of Kurram (FATA) and met Intizar Bibi, 19, a local tribal girl. In 2013, while on leave, Anwar came to meet Intizar Bibi and was confronted by the villagers. The local jigra, or tribal court, sentenced Anwar to death. He was taken to local graveyard where he was stoned to death and buried. The jigra had ruled that the woman must also be shot to death. The jigra had also requested that another Pakistani soldier, Saif Ullah, be handed over for helping the couple meet and coordinate the planned elopement. Pakistan soldier stoned to death over affair, March 13, 2013, available at: http://www.independent.co.uk/news/world/asia/pakistan-soldier-stoned-to-death-over-affair-8533184.html, accessed on January 10, 2015.
45. For more details see: Dorman Knut and Jose Serralvo, Common Article 1 to the Geneva Conventions and the Obligations to prevent IHL Violations, *International Review of the Red Cross*, Vol. 96, No. 895/896, pp. 707-736.
46. Pakistan Government under General Pervez Musharraf had permitted the US military to use drones against its citizens in the Federally Administered Tribal Areas (FATA). The US has publically announced using drones in Pakistan for both surveillance and attacks against terrorist groups and has carried out more than 400 drone strikes inside Pakistan. As claimed, these drone strikes have killed a number of militants in Pakistani, but also scores of innocent civilians, in part because of so-called "signature" strikes that target groups of men based on behaviour patterns associated with terrorist activity rather than known identities. Pakistan's attitude towards drones borders on the schizophrenic. The Pakistan military leadership, in particular its military, seeks greater control over target selection. This is often to punish enemies, but sometimes, allegedly, to protect militants who enjoy good

relations with, or support from the military. Apparently the Pakistan military has made peace deals with such militant groups. Although the use of drones for military activity could be effective, it has resulted in large numbers of deaths and casualties of innocent civilians in Pakistan. For more details see: Patrick B. Johnston and Anoop K. Sarbahi, The Impact of US Drone Strikes on Terrorism in Pakistan, 2015, available at: https://esoc.princeton.edu/files/impact-us-drone-strikes-terrorism-pakistan-and-afghanistan, accessed January 10, 2016; Drones: Myths and Reality in Pakistan, Asia Report No. 247, dated May 21, 2013.

47. The US government has preserved its relationship with the Pakistan military, even when it committed genocide in East Pakistan (now Bangladesh); committed grave breaches of the Geneva Conventions of 1949 during the Kargil War; and was responsible for enforced disappearances/ extrajudicial killings in internal armed conflict in various parts of Pakistan. The US has remained an accomplish of the Pakistan military in its wrongdoings, thus shirking the responsibility contained in the first Article of the Geneva Conventions of 1949, which states: "The High Contracting Parties undertake to respect and to ensure respect for the present Convention in all circumstances."

7

International Humanitarian Law

Introduction

Pakistan has 644,000-strong armed forces and nearly 500,000 reservists. In the 70 years of its existence, Pakistan has fought and lost four major wars. Its territory in the east was lost to a secessionist movement (now Bangladesh). Pakistan military is actively engaged in armed conflict fighting terrorist and militants in various parts of the country and outside. The USA has a few military bases on Pakistan's soil and is also fighting militants in the northwest region of Pakistan associated with the *Taliban* and *Al Qaeda*. As the USA is funding, equipping and training Pakistani military forces, the US military is also involved in these conflicts. Pakistan military and its intelligence establishments have created and supported various terrorists groups which carried out deadly attacks on Indian soil—including suicide attacks against the Indian Parliament in 2001, against civilian establishments in Mumbai in 2008, and at Air Force Station in Pathankot in 2016.[1]

International Humanitarian Law (IHL), also known as the "law of war" or "law of armed conflict", is a body of law which regulates the conduct of combatants during an armed conflict. It protects those who do not or are no longer taking part in hostilities and limits the means and methods of warfare in order to alleviate human suffering during armed conflict.[2] Pakistan government has signed and ratified a number of international treaties relating to IHL. These are: the four Geneva Conventions of 1949;[3] the Hague Convention for the Protection of Cultural Property, 1954 and its Protocol of 1954; the Biological Weapons Convention, 1972; the Chemical Weapons Convention, 1993; the Convention Prohibiting Certain Conventional Weapons (CCW), 1980 and its Protocols I to V; and the Convention Prohibiting Environmental Modification Techniques, 1976. It has signed the Optional Protocol on the Involvement of Children in Armed Conflict, 2000, on September 26, 2001, but failed to ratify the same.

IHL binds all parties engaged in an armed conflict. In international conflicts IHL must be observed by the states involved, whereas in an internal conflict IHL binds the government, as well as the groups fighting against it or among themselves.[4] Thus, IHL lays down rules that are applicable to both state and non-state actors. It also provides that persons may be held individually criminally responsible for grave breaches of the Geneva Conventions and of Additional Protocol I, and for other serious violations of IHL, both in international and internal armed conflicts.

Violations of IHL During International Armed Conflict

During the secessionist movement in East Pakistan in 1970-71, Pakistan military was accused of genocide and the worst kinds of violations ever witnessed by the humanity. In the ensuing War-of-Independence, over 300,000 civilians were butchered in the East Pakistan, millions rendered homeless, and nearly 10 million went as refugee to India. According to a Pakistan army officer who served in East-Pakistan with 3 Commando Battalion, the directions to him were, "kill as many bastards as you can and make sure there was no Hindu left alive." When he replied that he would not kill unarmed civilians, he was told, "Kill the Hindus. It is an order for everyone and do not show your commando finesse..."[5] General Tikka of Pakistan army was branded as "Butcher of Bengal". On the night between March 25/26, 1971, General Tikka struck in East Pakistan. He let loose everything at his disposal. The military action was a display of brutality, stark cruelty, more merciless than the massacre by anyone in the history. He adopted a scorched earth policy. His orders to troops were specific in that he wanted the land and not the people. Soldiers were encouraged to rape as many as possible.[6]

Sexual Assaults

In Bangladesh, various women from different socio-economic backgrounds have narrated their violent experiences of rape by the Pakistani army and local collaborators during 1970-71. Various researchers who reported on the number of rapes committed by Pakistani military, states them to be between as low as 200,000 to as high as 400,000. Adam Jones, a scholar states that girls of eight and grandmothers of seventy-five had been sexually assaulted: “Pakistani soldiers had not only violated Bengali women on the spot; they abducted tens of hundreds and held them by force in their military barracks for use during night... Some women may have been raped as many as eighty times in a night.” In seven days after liberation, about 300 girls were recovered from different places around Dacca where they had been taken away and kept confined by the Pakistani army personnel. On December 26, 1971, the Red Cross recovered 55 emaciated and half-dead girls on the verge of mental derangement from various hideouts of the Pakistani army in Dacca Cantonment. At a government shelter many of the rape victims had babies (often referred to as war babies) and many had to be aborted.

The Government in Pakistan never prosecuted any military personnel for unspeakable atrocities committed on civilians in East Pakistan, which became an independent country in 1971. In order to investigate abrupt surrender of Pakistan army in East Pakistan, the Prime Minister Bhutto constituted Hamud-ur-Rahman commission to expose the surrender of the armed forces and their role in killing and humiliation of Bengalis. The final report of the commission was submitted in November 1974, which recommended public trial of nine military Generals and Court Martial of six Generals and other officers. [7] The refusal of Pakistan army to deal with its 1971 atrocities may be partly due to its desire to save nearly 200 military personnel identified for war crimes. Pakistan's reaction to recent trial of war criminals of 1971 in Bangladesh who played a key role in genocide, rape and arson has been negative since the beginning.

Kargil War

In mid-November 1998, Lt. Gen. Mahmud, then commanding 10 Corps of Pakistan was allowed by the Chief of Army Staff (COAS), Gen. Pervez Musharraf, to execute a plan to occupy terrain in the Dras-Kargil sector in Jammu and Kashmir, vacated every winter by the Indian military. The rationale was that it would provide a fillip to the Kashmiri freedom movement. The plan was approved in principle, with instructions to commence preparations. The knowledge of this plan was initially confined to the four senior officers of the Pakistan Army.[8] The rest of the army, the Chief of Air Staff (CAS), and the Chief of Naval Staff (CNS) were unaware of plans for the operation. The preparations for infiltration proceeded in secret.

The Pakistan army occupied 132 posts in an area of about 130 square kilometers over a front of over 100 kilometers, and a depth ranging between seven to fifteen kilometers in Dras-Kargil sector. The total number of troops occupying these posts was nearly 1000, four times this number provided the logistical backup to undertake the operation. The occupants were soldiers of the Northern Light Infantry (NLI) and special services group, while there were some local *Mujahideen* assisting as labour to carry logistical requirements.[9] In April 1999, the first formal briefing of the entire operation was made to the Prime Minister, in the presence of the other services. A decision was taken in Pakistan to deny that the intrusion had been perpetrated by military troops, and instead put the blame on the *Mujahideen*.[10]

In early May 1999, the Indian army learnt that intruders had occupied the heights close to the Dras region. A patrol of seven soldiers under the command of Capt. Kalia with three local porters sent to investigate the intrusion was wiped out. In the ensuing battle, the Indian army occupied all the posts and forced the Pakistan military to make a hasty retreat from the Dras-Kargil sector. On July 26, 1999, the last of the Pakistani intruders was evicted. Pakistan army was accused of committing the gross violations of Geneva Conventions during the Kargil War.

Captain Saurabh Kalia[11] and other members of patrol were captured by Pakistani troops during a reconnaissance in May 1999. Instead of treating them as prisoner of war, the Pakistani Army subjected Captain Kalia and his soldiers to horrendous torture during which the ear drums were pierced with hot iron rods, eyes punctured and genitals cut off. The autopsy of the bodies also revealed that before brutal killing, they were burned with cigarettes butts. Their limbs were also chopped off, teeth broken and skull fractured during the torture. Even their nose and lips were cut off. Their mutilated bodies were handed over to the Indian Army on June 9, 1999.[12] During the ensuing battle the Pakistan army personnel committed perfidy by wearing civilian clothes. In addition, the dead bodies of few Indian soldiers were booby-trapped with explosives.[13]

Pakistan military, for some inexplicable reasons, tried to disclaim responsibility for the incursion and gross violations of Geneva Conventions. Not only did this caused considerable politico-diplomatic embarrassment to Pakistan, it also made other truthful assertions suspect. According to Pakistan Prime Minister Nawaz Sharif, after the Kargil War, Pakistan lost the international community's sympathy....Pakistan army was described as rough army in the international media.[14] According to an estimate, Pakistan army's northern light infantry was perished in this misadventure, altogether 2,000 soldiers were killed and hundreds wounded. However, Musharraf for a longtime maintained that Pakistan army was not involved in Kargil.[15]

The retreating NLI troops had left behind the bodies of their comrades at the high-altitude mountain ridgelines that they had surreptitiously occupied. Some of these were half buried in shallow pits. Some others had simply been covered by rocks and some were left out in the open. Since Pakistan had taken a position that there was no involvement of Pakistani armed forces in the operation, and those who participated in it were Kashmiri *Mujahedeen* and Pakistani volunteers, there was no procedure under the laws of war whereby India could handover the bodies of the disowned soldiers who died fighting, for Pakistan. These bodied were buried according to Islamic rites.[16] The illegal occupation of Kargil heights by the Pakistan army (in the guise of civilian) under the command of General Musharraf and their subsequent conduct during the ensuing battle with India amounted to gross violations of Geneva Conventions and a 'war crimes' under the International Humanitarian Law.[17]

The UN Peacekeeping Missions

Pakistan is one of the top contributors of forces for the UN Peacekeeping missions. The peacekeeping, however, has a dark side: a large number of sexual exploitation and abuse against civilians by UN personnel has been reported in the last two decades. A UN Office of International Oversight Services Reports from May 2015 recorded 480 allegations of abuse between 2008 and 2013. The Pakistan's military and security forces forming the part of UN contingents have also been accused of these violations. While the UN has paid lip service to stopping such sexual violence, the action taken by the troop contributing countries has generally not been made public.

Few Pakistani military personnel from the UN Mission in the Democratic Republic of the Congo were accused of major human rights violations. The crimes involved rape and forced prostitution of women and young girls across the country, including inside a refugee camp in the town of Bunia in northeastern Congo. The victims were defenceless refugees, many of them children, who had already been brutalised and terrorised by years of war and who looked to the UN for safety and protection. It was reported that Pakistani peacekeepers paid the bribe to witnesses to change their testimony.[18]

On March 13, 2012, three police personnel of Pakistan serving with the UN peacekeeping mission in Haiti—MINUSTAH, were sentenced to one year's imprisonment for raping of a 14-year-old Haitian boy. According to the media, the Haitian government had requested the lifting of immunity for the Pakistani officers and the Senate had passed a resolution requesting that they be tried in Haitian courts. The trial was eventually held in Haiti, following the military justice procedure of Pakistan. However, as reported by Reuters, "Haitian government authorities were given no advance notice of the military trial" and there were allegations that had the Pakistani police officers been tried in a Haitian court they would likely have faced much harsher penalties. Once again, this example shows how important it is, for the good image of peacekeeping troops and their deputing State to ensure that the judicial proceedings are fair and transparent.[19] The UN was informed that three accused will be imprisoned and given a dishonorable discharge on their return to Pakistan.[20]

The peacekeepers are deployed in the areas which suffer a breakdown of law and order, poverty, and population displacement. The individuals living in such areas face various forms of conflict-related human suffering and trauma. They heavily rely upon peacekeepers for subsistence. This dependency makes members of the local population extremely vulnerable to exploitation and abuse by peacekeepers. Investigations of sexual exploitation and abuse by peacekeeping personnel revealed that allegations of sexual exploitation and abuse do not come alone. They are always linked to other forms of misconduct or abuse of power. This necessitates that the police and military hierarchies must address sexual exploitation and abuse not only as violations of human rights, but also as a problem of internal discipline and management of the forces by their Commander. Since the UN does not have the capacity to give such training to all peacekeeping personnel, countries contributing armed and security forces to peacekeeping missions are responsible for training their contingents prior to deployment.

Internal Armed Conflict

During the decade prior to the withdrawal of Soviet troops from Afghanistan in 1989, Pakistan military was deeply involved in supporting the *mujahedeen* to resist Soviet aggression. The military ruler of Pakistan, General Zia-ul Haq, inflicted serious harm to the social structure of Pakistan by pursuing policies that not only served the *mujahedeen* in Afghanistan but also promoted the intense radicalisation of his own country. Zia aligned Pakistan with the US in the Afghani *jihad* without considering its adverse effect on the Pakistan's policy.[21] The monster created and nurtured by the military has anchored its tentacles all over. The *Tehrik-e Taliban* Pakistan (*TTP*), a network of militant groups mostly from to the tribal belts of Pakistan has been involved in a large number of terrorist attacks throughout Pakistan. A few Punjab and Kashmiri-based militant organisations also have developed a nexus with the *TTP* and the remnants of *Al-Qaeda*. They are engaged in major acts of violence.[22]

The menaces of Islamic militancy have now spread across the Pakistan and are not confined to Jammu and Kashmir and Afghanistan. They are determined to pursue their global *jehadi* agenda.[23] The killing of 72 and injuries to over 300 persons in a suicide blast that took place in Lahore's crowded Gulshan-i-Iqbal park on Easter Sunday (March 27, 2016) evening is a reminder of the spread of militancy in Pakistan.[24] In a knee-jerk decision taken after the blast, it was reported that Pakistan army and rangers will conduct a widespread operation across Punjab to target militants, their facilitators and their hideouts. Pakistan army and security forces have been involved in internal (non-international) armed conflict[25] across Pakistan since the last two decades.[26]

The extent and nature of the hostilities between the *TTP* and Pakistan's security forces demonstrate that there is currently an internal armed conflict in Pakistan, between the government and the *TTP* as well as other armed groups. The common Article 3 to the Geneva Conventions of 1949 and the principles of IHL recognised as customary law applicable in internal armed conflicts therefore govern the conduct of Pakistan, the *TTP*, and other armed groups. As the *TTP* continues to attack US targets and US drone strikes on *TTP* targets continue, the hostilities between the US and the *TTP* have reached to higher level of intensity over the past few years. The hostilities between the US and the *TTP* can be characterised as an intervention into the ongoing internal armed conflict between Pakistan and the *TTP*. The conflict remains an internal armed conflict because the US is intervening on the side of the state actor.[27] It can also be termed as internalised non-international armed conflict. There are ample evidence to show that the Pakistan military and security forces as well as non-state armed groups have committed war crimes, other violations of IHL and gross human rights abuses with impunity in the internal armed conflict. Some of these allegations are as follows.

Religious Minorities

In Pakistan, religious minorities, both Muslim and non-Muslim are facing the laws and practices that has resulted in discrimination and persecution.[28] In February 2015, *TTP* claimed responsibility for an attack on a Shiite mosque in Peshawar that killed at least 20 worshippers and injured 60. In March 2015, a suicide attack on two churches in Lahore claimed by *Jamaat ul Ahrar*, a splinter group of the *TTP*, killed at least 22 people. Following the attack, a group of Christians in the same neighbourhood killed two Muslim men. On May 13, 2015, nearly 50 Ismailis while travelling on a bus in Karachi were killed; and various groups, including *TTP*, Jundullah and the armed group Islamic State (IS), claimed responsibility.[29] Blasphemy laws have been applied to people of all religions but were disproportionately used against religious minorities. The members of Ahmadiyya faith face criminal prosecution if they propagate, profess or practice their religion openly. There have been serious allegations of forced conversions and marriages of Hindu girls to Muslim men, particularly in Sindh.

Violence Against Women

In Pakistan, women and girls are facing violence and threats. During the period January to June 2015, at least 4,308 cases of violence against women and girls were reported in various parts of Pakistan. This includes 709 cases of murder; 596 of rape and gang rape; 36 of sexual assault; 186 of honour crimes; 1,020 of kidnapping and at least 40 cases of acid attacks. Despite efforts in recent years to enact legislation protecting women from violence, laws remained in force under which female rape victims can be convicted for adultery. The criminal justice system denies equality and protection to women.

Killings and Displacements of Civilians

Since 2001, the conflict in northwest Pakistan has killed and injured thousands of civilians, displaced millions, and destroyed countless homes and livelihoods. The warring parties include Pakistan's army and security forces, the US military, and the militant organisations. In 2009 alone, an estimated 2,100 civilians were killed in terror attacks and many more injured.[30] Unfortunately, the civilian casualties receive too little attention from the Pakistan government, the US, the United Nations, and other international organisations. Civilian losses in Pakistan are often long-lasting and complex. The loss of a husband can deprive the family of its only source of income. An injury can require expensive medical treatment, care by other family members, and prevent survivors from working in the household or finding a job. A house destroyed can mean homelessness, but also the loss of a family's most important financial asset, forcing them into cycles of debt and dependency. As a result of the current and past armed conflict, more than one million people remained displaced in Pakistan.

As on July 2015, there were more than 1.8 million people displaced by insurgency, counter-insurgency and other related violence in Pakistan.

These internally displaced persons (IDPs) are mainly concentrated in the country's north-western Khyber Pakhtunkhwa (KP) province and Federally Administered Tribal Areas (FATA) (up to 1.5 million), but also live in Balochistan province and other parts of the country (up to 275,000). These figures exclude unregistered IDPs living in KP and FATA and IDPs living in other parts of Pakistan, including in urban centres such as Karachi.[31] Keeping in view the ongoing conflict in other parts of the country the actual figure may be as high as 2.5 million. For IDPs, there are few employment opportunities. Access to assistance is hampered by cumbersome registration and lack or loss of identification documents. It has affected children's education. The operating environment for humanitarian actors in Pakistan remains volatile, with fragile security, as well as access, social and economic challenges likely to affect humanitarian operations.[32]

In Pakistan, all three warring parties, its military and security forces, the US military and militants are responsible for loss of civilian lives and their displacements.[33] Militants have shown little regard for civilian life, deliberately attacking them, using terrorism tactics in populated areas, engaging Pakistani forces from civilian property, preventing civilians from leaving conflict areas, and using them as human shields. The members of Pakistan army and security forces have deployed heavy weaponry including the air power against militants without regard for discrimination or proportionality, leading to significant civilian losses. As reported, during 2008 to 2011, the Pakistan Air Force has flown nearly 5,500 bomb strikes in FATA.[34] All warring parties have engaged in extrajudicial killings in FATA, often resulting in civilian casualties.[35]

Missing Persons

After the attack on Afghanistan on October 7, 2001, the Bush administration offered head money for key *Al Qaeda* and *Taliban* suspects. The Pakistan military, as an ally to the US, arrested a large number of suspected militants and cashed in thousands of dollars. According to Musharraf, Pakistan military captured 672 individuals and handed over 369 to the US and earned millions of dollars.[36] This is a conservative figure. Under the domestic laws of Pakistan, the security forces are allowed to detain suspects, but need to maintain record of those arrested and let their relatives know the whereabouts of the detainees. The details of persons arrested by the military are not available in any government record.

Enforced Disappearances and Extra Judicial Killings

Pakistan military; its premier intelligence agency, the Inter-Services Intelligence (ISI); police as well as various non-state actors have been accused for disappearances and extra judicially killings. Enforced disappearance is often categorised as multiple human rights violations which simultaneously covers the violation of several human rights such as: the right to security and personal dignity; the right not to be subjected to torture or other cruel, inhuman or degrading treatment or punishment; the right to humane conditions of detention; the right to legal representation; the right to a fair trial; the right to a family life; and even the right to life, when the abducted person is killed.[37] Chapter V of the book covers the issue in greater details.

Use of Drones

The United States has used armed drones to attack in the border area between Afghanistan and Pakistan. These attacks have resulted in the deaths of hundreds of unintended victims, including children. The US has defended its actions asserting that drone attacks are precise and cause only limited collateral damage. However, this is far from truth. It has been estimated that during the initial period of drone engagement, the US was killing 50 unintended targets for each intended target.[38] The Stanford Report on the US drone attacks in Pakistan argues that drone strikes are damaging and counterproductive.[39] In fact the border area between Afghanistan and Pakistan became a drone-testing ground for the US and its allied forces.[40] For the US, drones were a cheap form of aerial reconnaissance and attack which avoided endangering pilots' lives.[41]

There has been serious international criticism of the use of armed drones in Pakistan. Pakistan's military leadership has apparently supported the use of drones in its territory behind the scenes, however, in the recent past they have publicly criticised it. Musharraf also lied to the world and blamed that the US military was never authorised by him to use drones in Pakistan's territory. He later retracted, stating he had allowed only a couple of drones' attacks.[42] The Pakistani military and the civilian government have insisted in public that they do not support the US drones that attack militants in the tribal areas, even though they have acquiesced to the strikes in private. As reported, General Kayani, who succeeded Pervez Musharraf had also asked for American surveillance drones to fly over South Waziristan, where the army was fighting the *Taliban*. The army public information unit later clarified that General Kayani had not asked for the support of 'armed' drones for military operations.

The Pakistan army launched its first drone strike in September 2015, claiming it killed three leaders of armed groups in North Waziristan.[43] Earlier, a US drone strike of May 16, 2015 which resulted in a number of casualties in the Mana area of North Waziristan Agency, was condemned by the Pakistan Government stating it was a clear violation of its sovereignty and territorial integrity.[44] Brushing aside the protest from Pakistan that its sovereignty has been violated, a US drone strike on May 21, 2016 in Balochistan--an area that was normally off limits of the US drones--killed Taliban chief Akhtar Mohammad Mansour.[45] Civilian casualties caused by US drone strikes are particularly difficult to verify.[46] For people on the ground, these attacks have been counterproductive, alienating the local population and encouraging recruitment into the ranks of the militants, and therefore, destabilising Pakistan.[47] Drone strikes often drive survivors and families of victims to seek revenge.

Responsibilities Toward Victims of Drone Strikes

The US drone strikes in Pakistan have killed nearly 4,000 individuals, including an unknown number of civilians. The Pakistan has also recently used its indigenous drones against suspected militants operating from tribal areas. The US and Pakistan government have failed to account for and provide redress and compensation for civilian harm from these strikes. Whatever tactical gains may be achieved by drone strikes, there are serious doubts whether they would address the threats of terrorism or bring security and peace to the people of tribal region in Pakistan. There is a large variation in the number of drone casualties, both of civilians and alleged terrorists, reported by various NGOs, the US and the Pakistan government. The recording of casualties is the obligation of the Pakistan government as well as the US military under IHL, [48] and this is supported by existing customary law,[49] as well as the rights of the victims under the IHRL framework.[50] There is a binding legal obligation upon the parties to an armed conflict to record every casualty, whether civilian or combatant, and whether it is an international or non-international armed conflict. The obligations are: (i) search for all civilians missing as a result of the hostilities; (ii) collect the casualties of armed conflict from the area of hostilities as soon as circumstances permit; (iii) if possible, return the remains of those killed to their relatives; (iv) the remains of the dead are not to be despoiled; (v) property found on the bodies of the dead is to be returned to their relatives; (vi) the dead are to be buried individually, with dignity and in accordance with their religious or cultural beliefs; and (vii) the graves are to be maintained and protected.[51]

The soldiers serving in the military face other serious dilemma. In addition to their physical wounds, they have to deal with a society that doesn't appreciate their service. The conflict with the *Taliban* pits soldiers against fellow Muslims and fellow Pakistanis, and against the local population that views the armed conflict in the tribal areas as imposed by the US and against Islamic values. There is a strong feeling in the Pakistan's tribal belt that the conflict in FATA is a dirty war against the region's tribal peoples and financed by the US.[52] Pakistan must avoid the temptation of using armed drones against its own citizens. There is no supportive evidence that drone strikes cause a decrease in violence.

In this war of terrorism, since 2004, more than 4,000 military and security personnel have been killed and nearly 13,000 wounded. The Pakistan military is responsible for disappearances, unlawful detention, extrajudicial killing, bombardment of villages, and mass displacement of tribal peoples in Pakistan. The *TTP* has targeted and killed thousands of civilians since 2002; in some cases these killings have been deliberate while in others civilians were killed and their property destroyed as a result of indiscriminate firing and suicide bombing.[53] The Pakistan's military and security forces as well the *TTP* and its affiliated armed groups have been responsible for gross violations of common Article 3 to the Geneva Conventions. Attacking civilians and civilian objects is prohibited under the Geneva Conventions and customary IHL.

Law to Prosecute Military Offenders

In Pakistan, individual military members may be held criminally responsible not only for committing war crimes, but also for attempting, assisting in, facilitating or aiding and abetting the commission of war crimes. They may also be held responsible for planning and instigating the commission of war crimes. Commanders and other superiors may be held criminally responsible for war crimes committed pursuant to their orders. The military commander has a duty to take all necessary and reasonable measures within his power to repress the crimes. In the event the commander holds disciplinary power, he is required to exercise it, within the limits of his competence.

The armed and security forces of Pakistan are extensively involved in internal conflicts. Pakistan is also one of the largest contributors to UN peacekeeping forces. It has not signed the 1998 Rome Statute of International Criminal Court; however, it has ratified a few international instruments relating to IHL and the protection and preservation of human rights.[54] There are no explicit provisions in the Constitutions of Pakistan regulating the incorporation of international law in their military legal systems. A military violator cannot be prosecuted effectively as the military justice systems of Pakistan does not contains serious crimes of international concern like 'war crimes', 'torture', 'enforced disappearances', etc. The concept of superior responsibility has not been incorporated in the military or criminal law of Pakistan. Some of offences which could be considered as breaches of IHL and listed in the military law of Pakistan are as follows.

Breach of IHL	**Offence under the Pakistan Army Act, 1952**	**Punishment under the Army Act, 1952**
Offences against property or person	Section 27: Destroying property or harming inhabitant of a country where serving	14 years of rigorous imprisonment (RI)
Offences against property	Section 29: Breaking into house in search of plunder	14 years of rigorous imprisonment (RI)
Disobedience	Section 33: Disobedience of lawful command	14 years of RI
Any act of fraud or theft in relation to property	Section 40: Fraudulent offences in respect of property	5 years of RI
Inhuman treatment, wilfully causing great suffering	Section 41: Disgraceful conduct of a cruel, indecent or unnatural kind	10 years of RI
Irregular confinement	Section 51: Detaining a person in arrest or confinement	2 years of RI
Torture, inhuman treatment.	Section 55: Violation of good order and discipline	5 years of RI
Making perfidious use of protective emblem	Section 52: Unbecoming behaviour	Dismissal
Murder, rape, or other civil offences on active service	Section 59: Civil offences	Death

The principle of 'complementarity' built into the Rome Statute ensures that the ICC does not displace the responsibility of the states to prosecute the most serious crimes of international concern.[55] However, to reserve the right to do so, a State must conform to the international standard. Seen in this context, it would be advisable for Pakistan to amend its military Acts to create a basis of culpability for commanders equal to the international standard. It would be beneficial from a policy standpoint for the Pakistan military to try those who violate the IHL as criminals under domestic law rather than as war criminals. Moreover, asserting that domestic jurisdiction exists to cover alleged violations of IHL may prevent jurisdiction from being asserted by another country or an International Tribunal. It is essential that concepts such as 'command responsibility', the 'war crimes' listed in Article 8 of the Rome Statute are incorporated in the military legal systems of Pakistan. The Government of Pakistan must also develop a 'manual on the laws of war' consistent with the military doctrine to ensure that the military personnel as well as civilians are familiar with the laws of war, and structure and administration is in place to ensure compliance with the law.

Notes

1. Pakistan's Southern Punjab was once known for a tolerant society, but over the past few decades, state support for jihadist proxies, financial support from foreign, particularly Saudi and other Gulf countries, combined with an explosive mix of political, socioeconomic, and geostrategic factors, has enabled jihadist expansion there. Bordering on insurgency-hit and lawless regions of the country and also sharing a border with India, it has long provided a convenient base where these outfits can recruit, train and plan and conduct terror attacks. The region hosts two of Pakistan's most radical Deobandi groups, Jaish-e-Mohammed, held responsible by India for the January 02, 2016 attack on its Pathankot airbase. *Pakistan's Jihadist Heartland: Southern Punjab*, Asia Report No. 279, May 30, 2016, International Crisis Group, Brussels, Belgium, pp. 1-2.
2. IHL does not address whether a nation is justified in using military force but instead assumes the presence of armed conflict and is therefore only concerned with humanising conflict, balancing military necessities with the preservation of human dignity.
3. The Geneva Conventions, which today serve as the foundation for modern IHL, are the only international treaties that have been adopted by every nation in the world. Their universal acceptance illustrates the importance of this body of law as a cornerstone of international relations. Based on four central tenants: (i) military necessity (only targets offering a definitive military advantage can be attacked); (ii) distinction (fighters must at all times distinguish between military targets and civilian persons and buildings); (iii) proportionality (attacks cannot cause collateral damage which is excessive to the military advantage gained from the attack); (iv) the prevention of unnecessary suffering (belligerents must not use means and methods of warfare which cause superfluous injury or unnecessary suffering), IHL is a critical ceiling on the use of force during armed conflict. Gary Solis,. *The Law of Armed Conflict: International Humanitarian Law in War* (New York: Cambridge University Press, 2010) pp. 250-286.
4. The Latin phrase *jus in bello* describe the law governing the conduct of hostilities. The rules of *jus in bello* are: (i) weapons prohibited by international law must not be used; (ii) distinction between combatants and non-combatants must be followed and only combatants may be targeted; (iii) the armed forces must use proportional force, i.e. proportional to achieving the end; (iv) prisoners of war must not be harmed and must be treated humanely; (v) no unlawful methods of war are permitted; and (vi)

the armed forces are not justified in breaking these rules in response to the enemy breaking them.

5. Ahmed Ishtiaq., *The Pakistan Military in Politics: Origins, Evolution, Consequence* (New Delhi: Amaryllis, 2013).
6. General Niazi openly encouraged soldiers of Pakistan army in their unsoldierly, inhuman and carnal indulgences. 'What is your score, Shera (tiger)?' He would ask the soldier with a satanic glint in his eyes. The score referred to the number of women the soldiers might have molested. Niazi argued brazenly in support of rape cases, 'You cannot expect a man to live, fight and die in East Pakistan and go to West Pakistan for sex?' The soldiers were under orders not to show any mercy to subversive, anti-state element, Bengalis or non-Bengalis. Ahmed Ishtiaq, *The Pakistan Military in Politics: Origins, Evolution, Consequence* (New Delhi: Amaryllis, 2013), pp. 184-185.
7. Jalalzai Musa Khan, *The Prospects of Nuclear Jihad in Pakistan* (New York: Algora Publishing,2015), pp. 134-135.
8. General Pervez Musharraf, the Chief of Army Staff (COAS); Lt. Gen. Mahmud, then commanding 10 Corps; Lt. Gen. Aziz, the Chief of General Staff (CGS); and Major General Javed Hassan, General Officer Commanding (GOC), Frontier Constabulary of the Northern Areas (FCNA). While preparations for executing the plan began in November/December 1999, the subject was casually broached with Prime Minister Sharif at some point in December. He was presented with the same argument that the freedom struggle in Kashmir needed a fillip, which could be provided by an incursion into these (temporarily unoccupied) territories. Sharif, being the type of person he is, accepted the statement at face value. The military leadership had not presented a complete analysis of the scale of the operation or its possible outcome, nor had they set out its political aim and how it would be achieved. Qadir Shaukat, An Analysis of the Kargil Conflict 1999, *RUSI Journal*, April 2002, pp. 24-135.
9. The documents captured by the Indian army revealed that main invading force has come from four Northern Light Infantry (NLI) battalions and two companies of the Special Services Group under the Force Commander Northern Area (FNCA). The regular army battalions were 4 NLI based in Gilgit, 6 NLI located at Skardu, 5 NLI based in Minimarg and the 3 NLI based at Dansam. It was supplemented by *Mujahideen*. Additional brigade has been moved into the FNCA as reserve. Baweja Harinder, *A Soldier's Diary: Kargil, The Inside Story*, (New Delhi: The India Today Group, 2000) p. 140.
10. Qadir Shaukat, An Analysis of the Kargil Conflict 1999, *RUSI Journal*, April 2002, p. 26.
11. Captain Saurabh Kalia, Sepoys Arjunram Baswana, Mula Ram Bidiasar, Naresh Singh Sinsinwar, Bhanwar Lal Bagaria and Bhika Ram Mudh of 4 Jat Regiment were among the first casualties during the Kargil war. The ill-fated patrol had moved down the Kaksar Langpa area in Kargil on May 14, 1999 and declared missing a day later. They were in captivity of Pakistan army for almost 22 days till June 7, 1999. The Pakistani government, however, maintained that Captain Kalia and his soldiers died due to extreme weather and their bodies were found in a pit.
12. Pakistan Army punctured eyes, cut off genitals of Captain Saurabh Kalia and his soldiers but Centre refuses to act, available at: http://www.ibnlive.com/news/india/pakistani-army-punctured-eyes-cut-off-genital-and-limbs-of-captain-saurabh-kalia-and-his-soldiers-after-capturing-them-999802.html. The Government of India had requested

the International Committee of the Red Cross to conduct the post mortem of the dead bodies, but the request was denied on the grounds that it was an impartial and independent organisation and would not like to get involved in bilateral issues.

13. These are based on personal knowledge of the author about the war. Perfidy is prohibited in armed conflict. The term perfidy refers to acts misleading the adverse party into belief that there are situations affording protection under the IHL. Moral and legal duty requires the combatants to protect the innocent civilians. See: Article 37, the 1977 Additional Protocol I to the Geneva Conventions of 1949. It is prohibited in all circumstances to use booby-traps which are in any way attached to or associated with sick, wounded or dead persons. Fleck Dieter (ed.). *The Handbook of International Humanitarian Law* (Oxford: Oxford University Press, 2008), p. 150.
14. Ahmed Ishtiaq, *The Pakistan Military in Politics: Origins, Evolution, Consequence* (New Delhi: Amaryllis, 2013) pp. 293-294.
15. American intelligence had already confirmed a military presence there. Tapes obtained in Pakistan of a conversation between the COAS and the CGS during a trip to China added further confirmation. To top it off, Pakistan gave gallantry awards (including the highest military award in Pakistan) to soldiers who had died in the Kargil. Pervez Musharraf in his autobiography has admitted the use of NLI in Kargil. Musharraf Pervez. *In the Line of Fire: A Memoire* (New York: Free Press, 2006), pp. 87-98.
16. It has been reported by a former Indian military officer that casualties belonging to Pakistan army were honoured with the Pakistani flag and given a decent burial by the Indian troops. Kanwal Gurmeet, Pakistan's Strategic Blunder at Kargil, *CLAWS Journal*, Summer 2009, pp. 53-72.
17. Under Article 130 of the third Geneva Convention of 1949, willful killing, torture or inhuman treatment, willfully causing great suffering or serious injuries to body or health of a prisoner of war amounts to grave breaches of the Convention. In addition Article 10 (Protection and care of wounded); Article 37.1 (c) (Feigning of civilian, non-combatant status); Article 44 (protection of prisoner of war); Article 51 (Protection of civilian population from the dangers of attack and violence); Article 75 (prohibition of murder and torture) of 1977 Additional Protocol I to the Geneva Conventions were violated by the Pakistan army under the command of General Musharraf. These violation amount to grave breaches of Geneva Conventions of 1949 and the 1977 Additional Protocol I, and are 'war crimes' under Article 8 of the Rome Statute of the International Criminal Court.
18. The exploitation of some of the most vulnerable people in the world-refugees in a war-ravaged country-is a shameful episode and a betrayal of trust that will haunt the United Nations for years to come. Gardiner Nile, The UN Peacekeeping Scandal in the Congo: How Congress Should Respond, Report of March 1, 2005, available at: http://www.heritage.org/research/lecture/the-un-peacekeeping-scandal-in-the-congo-how-congress-should-respond., accessed on June 10, 2015.
19. Bergsmo Morten and Tianying Song (ed.)., Military Self-Interest in Accountability for Core International Crimes, Brussels: Torkel Opsahl Academic E-Publisher, 2015), pp. 351-352.
20. Pakistan UN peacekeeping role at risk after 3 punished in Haiti sexual abuse case, The Express Tribune, March 14, 2012, available at: http://tribune.com.pk/story/349652/pakistan-risks-un-peacekeeping-role-after-3-found-guilty-of-sexual-abuse-in-haiti/. Also see: Burke Roisin, The Impunity Dilemma: Sexual Offences by UN Peacekeepers, available at: http://asiapacific.anu.edu.au/regarding-

rights/2015/06/05/the-impunity-dilemma-sexual-offences-by-un-peacekeepers/., accessed on June 10, 2015.

21. Masood Talat, Pakistan's Fight Against Terrorism, *Defence Against Terrorism Review*, Vol. 4, No. 1 Spring and Fall 2012, pp. 13-30.
22. Pakistan has failed to identify the perpetrators of the attacks on the Army Public School in Peshawar and Bacha Khan University, allowing its media to indulge in rampant speculation that placed blame for attack outside Pakistan. It has been now revealed that Tariq Gidar Group (TGG), a Pakistan Taliban linked group based in Darra Adam Khel is responsible for these two massacres. The US state department has placed the TGG as well as Jama'at ul Dawa al-Quran (JDQ) on a Specially Designated Global Terrorist (SDGTs) list amid continuing criticism that Pakistan is not doing enough to end the scourge of terrorism. US designates two more Pakistani outfits as terror groups, *Pakistan Telegraph*, 27 May 2016, available at: www.pakistantelegraph.com/index.php/sid/244396313, accessed 27 May 2016.
23. Mir Amir, *Talibanisation of Pakistan: From 9/11 to 26/11* (New Delhi: Pentagon Security International, 2009).
24. At least 72 people were killed in a suicide blast that took place in Lahore's crowded Gulshan-i-Iqbal park on Sunday (March 27, 2016) evening, police confirmed on Monday. At least 300 others were injured. In the wake of the attack, the Punjab government declared an emergency in Lahore and announced three days of mourning. Schools and markets were closed in the provincial capital on Monday. A First-Information Report was lodged by the Counter-Terrorism Department Lahore against four suspects under Section 7 of the Anti-Terrorism Act and various sections of the Pakistan Penal Code. Attack was claimed by the *Tehreek-i-Taliban* Pakistan Jamaatul Ahrar, who also claimed last year's twin suicide bombings at churches in Lahore's Youhanabad area, which killed at least 15 people and sparked violent protests across the city. At least 72 killed in suicide blast as terror revisits Lahore, *Dawn*, available at: http://www.dawn.com/news/1248259, accessed on March 28, 2016.
25. Common Article 3 to the Geneva Conventions of 1949 does not define non-international (or internal) armed conflict. The most common and contemporary definition of armed conflict is from the Appeals Chamber of the International Criminal Tribunal for the former Yugoslavia in *Tadic* case, where the tribunal held that an internal armed conflict exists whenever "there is protracted armed violence between governmental authorities and organised armed groups or between such groups within a State." *Prosecutor v. Tadic*, case No. IT-94-1, Decision on Defence Motion for Interlocutory Appeal on Jurisdiction, ICTY, dated October 2, 1995, accessed on December 12, 2016.
26. In order to establish the existence of an armed conflict in Pakistan, factual conditions need to be examined. First, there is protracted violence in Pakistan since 2002. The TTP and its affiliated armed groups are inflicting heavy losses on the Pakistan's army and security forces. The Pakistani security forces are using tanks, jets, and gunship helicopters to suppress the TTP's fighters in SWAT, Buner, Dir, Kurram Agency, and North and South Waziristan. Thousands of people have left their homes and taken refuge in the neighbouring areas of Afghanistan and some settled in districts of the NWFP. The International Committee of the Red Cross (ICRC) has declared Dir as a war zone and consistently refers to the situation as an armed conflict. Second, the armed conflict is between the TTP and the security forces of Pakistan. Third, the conflict is taking place within the territory of Pakistan. The conflict in Pakistan

possesses the three basic elements of an internal armed conflict. The conflict even meets the more stringent requirements of an internal conflict contained in Article 1 of the Additional Protocol II as the TTP controls different regions and carry out concerted attacks on the Pakistani forces and other targets. Shah, Niaz A., *War Crimes in the Armed Conflict in Pakistan, Studies in Conflict & Terrorism, Vol. 33, No. 4, 2010,* pp. 288-289.

27. Blank Laurie R. and Benjamin R. Farley, Characterising US Operations in Pakistan: Is the United States Engaged in An Armed Conflict? *Fordham International Law Journal*, Vol. 34, No. 2, 2011, pp. 151-189.
28. Amnesty International Report 2015-2016, available at: http://amnesty.org/en/countries/asia-and-the-pacific/pakistan/report-pakistan/, accessed on March 30, 2016.
29. At least 43 people were killed and 13 others wounded on May 13 1975? when armed men opened fire inside a bus carrying members of the Ismaili community near Safoora Chowk in Karachi. Sindh Police Inspector General Ghulam Haider Jamali said that 60 people were on board the bus when six gunmen entered and executed 43 passengers. The armed men used 9 mm pistols in the massacre and managed to flee after the attack. Ali, Imtiaz, 42 Killed in attack on bus carrying Ismailis in Karachi, *Dawn*, 14 May 2015, available at: http://www.dawn.com/news/1181698, accessed on May 22, 2015.
30. According to Pakistan Institute of Peace Studies, 2,123 civilians were killed and 5,551 injured in terrorist attacks in Pakistan in 2009. Out of this 1,403 civilians killed and 3,351 injured in terrorist attacks in NWFP/KPK and FATA in 2009. Total of persons killed in terrorist attacks in Pakistan in 2009 were 3,021.
31. Conflict-related displacement since 2004 has been caused by fighting between the Pakistani military and non-state armed groups (NSAGs), clashes between NSAGs, sectarian violence between Sunni and Shia Muslims, tribal and local clashes over resources, and human rights abuses committed by both the military and NSAGs. Information on numbers of IDPs in FATA and KP is regularly updated, while numbers on Balochistan are scarcer. Internal Displacement Monitoring Centre, available at: http://www.internal-displacement.org/south-and-south-east-asia/pakistan/figures-analysis, accessed on April 2, 2016.
32. UNHCR: 2015 UNHCR country operations profile – Pakistan, available at: http://www.unhcr.org/pages/49e487016.html, accessed on April 2, 2016.
33. Artillery shelling and mortar fire were the most common causes of harm suffered by civilians during military operations. Pakistani military jets and helicopters have been accused of bombing or opening fire in civilian areas and not properly distinguishing between civilians and combatants. Civilians have also been targeted in airstrikes based on faulty intelligence. For instance, on April 10, 2010, Pakistani jet fighters bombed targets in Sra Vela, a village in Khyber Agency, believing they were hitting a meeting attended by a high-level militant Commander. Instead, they hit the home of a pro-government family with three brothers serving with government forces. A second bomb hit crowds of neighbours as they tried to help those injured in the first strike. At least 60 civilians were killed and 30 injured in the airstrikes. Civilian have also been caught in crossfire during the fighting between militants and the Pakistani military in populated areas. Rogers Christopher, *Civilians in Armed Conflict: Civilian Harm and Conflict in Northwest Pakistan,* (Washington: Campaign for Innocent Victims in Conflict (CIVIC), 2010), pp. 18-19.

34. The Chief of the Pakistan Air Force Air Chief Marshal Suleiman informed that PAF has flown more than 500 F-16 sorties with the DB-110 pod, and 650 with the Star Safire EO/IR sensor on the C-130. The Air Force has dropped more than 10,600 bombs, and 4,600 targets have been destroyed. PAF conduct 5,500 bombing runs in FATA since 2008, *The Tribune*, November 14, 2011, available at: http://tribune.com.pk/story/291762/paf-conducted-5500-bombing-runs-in-fata-since-2008/, accessed on June 10, 2015.
35. Rogers Christopher, *Civilians in Armed Conflict: Civilian Harm and Conflict in Northwest Pakistan,* (Washington: Campaign for Innocent Victims in Conflict (CIVIC), 2010), p. 15.
36. Musharraf, Pervez, *In the line of fire: A memoir*(New York: Free Press, 2006).
37. Boot M. and Hall C. K., "Crimes against Humanity", in Triffterer O. (ed.). 2008. *Commentary on the Rome Statute of the International Criminal Court: Observer's Notes, Article by Article*, p. 221.
38. Between 2006 and early 2009, 700 persons died in attacks killing 14 intended targets. David Kilcullen and Andrew McDonald Exum, Death From Above, Outrage Down Below, *New York Times*, March 17, 2009.
39. Some myths regarding drone strikes in Pakistan are as follows: Myth 1: Drones kill terrorists with minimum civilian deaths. From the date compiled by the credible sources, it is clear that the ratio of innocent Pakistani citizens killed in the US drones is staggering and alarming. Myth 2: Drone is an effective counterterrorism measure. The former CIA Director Michael Hayden has stated that that drone strikes have made Pakistan's FATA 'neither safe nor a haven' for Al-Qaeda and its affiliated networks. However, the reality is that with the increase of drone strikes, the corresponding number of casualties of government forces (including NATO) also increased in Afghanistan and Pakistan. Myth 3: US Drone strikes are legitimate in FATA. As regard the legitimacy of drone strikes in the FATA, none of the independent agencies has declared these as legitimate under any law. The legal experts also question drone strikes against mosques, schools, funerals and large community gatherings to target a suspected terrorist or "double tap" targeting. According to Christopher Heyns, the UN special representative on extrajudicial, summary or arbitrary executions, "if civilian 'rescuers' are indeed being intentionally targeted, there is no doubt about the law: those strikes are a war crime." Myth 4: US has conducted unilateral drone strikes in FATA. General Musharraf has admitted that on occasions his government colluded with the US over drone strikes. Anne Patterson, ex US ambassador to Pakistan, in a cable sent to Washington had disclosed that in her meeting with Prime Minister Yousaf Raza Gillani on drones; Gillani remarked: "I don't care if they do it as long as they get the right people. We'll protest in the National Assembly and then ignore it." In fact the use of indigenous lethal drones by Pakistan in FATA in September 2015 had been most unfortunate use of air power against own citizens. Consistent drone strikes are a blot on credibility of Pakistan's military. In May 2013 the Pakistani Peshawar High Court declared that the drone strikes perpetrated by CIA are considered illegal. Maan Zahid Nawaz, Pakistan's Drone Dilemma, *NDU Journal*, Pakistan, 2014, pp. 77-96.
40. On November 3, 2002, the US used a drone outside a combat area to fire laser-guided Hellfire missiles at a passenger vehicle traveling in a thinly populated region of Yemen. The drone was operated by CIA agents based in Djibouti. The US Air Force, at that time, operated the US's drones, but the Air Force was concerned about legal issues raised by the Yemen operation, so the CIA carried out the strike.

All six passengers in the vehicle were killed. The US officials claimed that one of six men was a suspected Lieutenant in *Al-Qaida*; another was an American citizen in his early twenties. In January 2003, the United Nations Commission on Human Rights received a report on the Yemen strike from its Special Rapporteur on extrajudicial, summary, or arbitrary killing. The rapporteur concluded that the strike constituted a clear case of extra judicial killing. UN Doc. E/CN.4/003/3, paras. 37 - 39.

41. Drones have a number of advantages for any military force. They spare pilots' lives. Pilots operate the drones with a joystick at a comfortable place far from the war zone. Thus, even if a drone is shot down, there is no loss of human life. They are also relatively cheap and easy to manufacture. Drones cost less than manned military aircraft. Cost of a US Predator in 2009 was about $4.5 million, 30 times less than a fighter jet. Further, drones can be used for any battlefield operation: surveillance, reconnaissance, precision attacks, targeted killings, etc. A drone can be used to carry out dull, dirty or dangerous battlefield operations, referred to as the Three Ds. For more details see: O'Connell Mary Ellen, *Unlawful Killing with Combat Drones: A Case Study of Pakistan, 2004-2009*, Notre Dame Law School Legal Studies Research Paper No. 09-43, 2010.
42. Though the present government in Pakistan had never consented to the use of Drones by the US military, it has been reported that an "un-reconciled consent" was accorded during Pervez Musharraf's regime. This was clarified, as Musharraf admitted to having given the CIA permission to launch drone attacks inside his country, directly contradicting repeated claims by the Pakistani government that it has never authorised drone strikes. He stated that Pakistan gave permission "only on a few occasions, when a target was absolutely isolated and [there was] no chance of collateral damage ... maybe two or three times only." In March 2013, following a visit to Islamabad Ben Emmerson QC, the UN's special rapporteur on counterterrorism and human rights, said he had been given assurances that there was no "tacit consent by Pakistan to the use of drones on its territory." On its part, the US administration has defended the legality of its drone activities and said that strikes are conducted only with the consent of the states involved. Jon Boone and Peter Beaumont, "Pervez Musharraf admits permitting 'a few' US drone strikes in Pakistan," *The Guardian*, April 12, 2013, available at: http://www.guardian.co.uk/world/2013/apr/12/musharraf-admits-permitting-drone-strikes.
43. At least three suspected militants were killed while a militant hideout was destroyed in Shawal valley of North Waziristan in the first ever air strike by a Pakistan made drone "Burraq". The armed drone was used for the first time since its development in November 2013. Pakistan had long aspired to have the US armed drones for bolstering its counter-terrorism capacity, but was only offered surveillance drones. Haider Mateen, Three killed in military's first drone strike in North Waziristan, *Dawn*, September 7, 2015, available at: http://www.dawn.com/news/1205455, accessed on September 15, 2015.
44. Pakistan Condemns US Drone Strike in North Waziristan, May 18, 2015, notification issued by the Ministry of Foreign Affairs, Government of Pakistan, Islamabad, available at: http://www.mofa.gov.pk/pr-details.php?mm=Mjc5NA, accessed on March 12, 2016.
45. Adam Entous, How the US Tracked and Killed the Leader of the Taliban, *The Wall Street Journal*, May 25, 2016.
46. The majority of drone strikes occur in North and South Waziristan, areas inaccessible to foreigners as well as most Pakistanis. The casualty estimates are based on media

reports, which in turn rely on a range of sources from government and army officials to militant commanders and local stringers. With no significant on-the-ground presence, the US relies on electronic and aerial surveillance, informants, and Pakistani intelligence agencies for information on civilian casualties resulting from its drone operations. There is a significant difference among the counts of the total number of civilians killed in the drone attacks, as opposed to militants killed. The Long War Journal counts civilians as about 7 percent of the total victims of drone attacks, while Pakistan Body Count finds that more than 80 percent of the victims are civilians.

47. Abbas Hassan, *Pakistan 2020: A Vision For Building a Better Future*, Asia Society, Pakistan 2020 Study Group, May 2011, p. 52.
48. Under IHL, there are extensive obligations to account for military casualties in armed conflict. The Geneva Conventions of 1949 are now universally ratified and their provisions with respect to the dead are binding on states as well as non-state actors. These provisions include the obligation to search for and collect the wounded and dead, to record their details and transfer information to the other party when appropriate. The 1977 AP I contains detailed rules concerning provisions for missing persons, which involve the recording of information. One of the rights under the 1977 AP I, Article 32 is the 'right of families to know the fate of their relatives'. AP I encourages the parties to try to make joint arrangements for joint to search for, identify and recover the dead from battlefield areas. Such teams are to be respected and protected while carrying out their duties (Article 33 (4), 1977 AP I).
49. The customary humanitarian law makes it obligatory for the parties to armed conflict to search for and collect the dead, prevent them from being despoiled and facilitate of return of their remains to their next of kin. The dead must be disposed of in a respectful manner and their graves respected and properly maintained. With a view to the identification of the dead, each party to the conflict must record all available information prior to disposal and mark the location of the graves (Rules 112-116). Jean-Marie Henckaerts and Louise Doswald-Beck, *Customary International Humanitarian Law, Volume I: Rules* (Cambridge: Cambridge University Press, 2005), pp. 406-420.
50. The Universal Declaration of Human Rights (UDHR), 1948, is the basis on which all other treaties are formed and its core ensures the protection of these essential human rights. The International Covenant on Civil and Political Rights 1966 (ICCPR), the International Covenant on Economic, Social and Cultural Rights 1966 (ICESCR) and the UN Convention Against Torture and Other Cruel, Inhuman or Degrading Treatment or Punishment 1984 are the mechanisms of enforceability within the system and give traction to the principles enshrined in the UDHR. All these treaties recognise the sanctity of human life and the significance of the family unit as the cornerstone of society.
51. The mortal remains must be respected. It is an obligation to protect the dignity of persons. Any outrages against personal dignity can constitute an offence under the Rome Statute Article 8 (2) (b) (xxi) and 8 (2) (c) (ii). For more details see: Anna Petrig, 'The war dead and their gravesites', *International Review of the Red Cross*, Volume 91, No. 874, June 2009, pp. 341-370.
52. *Pierson Charles, Pakistan Army, available at:* http://www.counterpunch.org/2014/03/31/wall-street-journal-%E2%99%A5-pakistani-army/, accessed on March 10, 2016.

53. Hostage taking and kidnapping by the *TTP* and its allies has been a common practice. *TTP* has kidnapped members of the security forces, government officials and those who have pro-government opinion. In addition they have killed around 400 people on the ground of suspected spying for the US. The *TTP* has committed serious war crimes and has also violated the laws of Pakistan and the law it regards as its own, i.e., the Islamic law of *qital*. Shah Niaz A., *Islamic Law and the Law of Armed Conflict: The Armed Conflict in Pakistan* (London: Routledge, 2011) pp. 122-124.
54. The modern law of international human rights is based on the UN Charter, supplemented by the 1948 Universal Declaration of Human Rights (UDHR); the 1948 Convention on the Prevention and Punishment of the crime of Genocide; the 1966 International Covenant on Civil and Political Rights (ICCPR), and the International Covenant on Economic, Social and Cultural Rights (ICESCR); the 1989 Convention on the Rights of the Child (CRC); the 1984 Convention against Torture and Other Cruel, Inhuman or Degrading Treatment (CAT); and the 2010 UN Convention for the Protection of All Persons from Enforced Disappearance. Human rights law is also complemented during times of armed conflict by International Humanitarian Law.
55. The very impetus for a permanent International Criminal Court (ICC) arose from the numerous instances in which powerful perpetrators ignored established international norms with impunity. To attain the goal of international justice, Article 1 of the Rome Statute states that the court will "be a permanent institution and shall have the power to exercise its jurisdiction over persons for the most serious crimes of international concern .... and shall be complementary to national criminal jurisdictions. The term 'complementarity', has not been defined in the Rome State; however Article 1 implies that the ICC is intended to supplement the domestic punishment of international violations, rather than supplant domestic enforcement of international norms. Newton, Michael A., Comparative Complimentarity: Domestic Jurisdiction Consistent with the Rome Statute of the International Criminal Court, *Military Law Review*, Vol. 167, March 2001, pp. 20-73.

8

The Future

The State of Pakistan, intended to transform the lives of British Indian Muslims by providing them a homeland sheltered from Hindu oppression was borne on August 14, 1947. After gaining independence, Pakistan adopted the Government of India Act, 1935 as its Provisional Constitution. The Indian Independence Act, 1947 had provided that all laws enforceable in the pre-partition India would continue as valid laws for the new dominion. At independence, the top posts of Pakistan were occupied by Jinnah as Governor-General and his close associate Liaquat Ali Khan as Prime Minister. However, both suffered untimely deaths. Pakistan could frame its Constitution in 1956, which came into force on March 23, 1956. It renamed the state as the Islamic Republic of Pakistan. Under the new constitution, Iskander Mirza, a former soldier became the President. He abrogated the Constitution within 30 months of his rule. He was displaced in a coup by General Ayub Khan in 1958. Since then the Pakistan's journey of 70 years is riddled with many successful as well as unsuccessful military coups.[1] Every military coup was justified on the grounds of national security, corrupt and incompetent political leadership, and military being the only establishment which could protect the interest of the country.[2] The Pakistani army forms the bulk of Pakistan's armed forces, and is the key player in country's internal affairs as well as its offensive and defensive capabilities.

Pakistani military and political leaders have portrayed India as the nation's most significant military threat. The Indian threat has led Pakistani leaders to seek the US military assistance. The US and Pakistan relationship has witnessed many ups and downs. During the 1990s, Pakistan military intelligence establishment, the ISI supported numerous Kashmir-oriented militant groups as well as the *Taliban* in Afghanistan. In 1999, an unsuccessful attempt was made by the Pakistan army to occupy strategic heights in Kargil (Jammu and Kashmir), which were left unoccupied by the Indian army during peak winter season. This resulted in a blame game between the Prime Minister Nawaz Sharif and General Musharrf. In a bloodless coup Musharraf assumed control of the country. After the September 11, 2001 attacks, Musharraf consented to US demands to renounce formal Pakistani support of the *Taliban* and agreed to be a full partner in the global war on terror. In exchange, the US resumed aid to the Pakistani military.[3] A former Pakistan army officer writes:

> To countervail India's growing economic and military power, Islamabad has used militant proxies to lock up Indian forces. However, some of the asymmetric that were meant to advance Islamabad's strategic interest have grown fairly strong and autonomous so that they are even challenging the authority of the state. They have now turned inwards and are responsible for many acts of violence within Pakistan and abroad. Thus the narrow security orientation pursued during military rule in Pakistan has now become a major security challenge. The weak civilian government and the law enforcement agencies are not capable of countering this menace of militancy. More recently, as violence has become a fundamental threat to the safety of everyone, there is a growing realisation that domestic extremism represents an even greater threat to the country than India does.[4]

According to Pervez Musharraf, "America wanted Pakistan to produce Islamic warriors that could be deployed in the Afghanistan jihad. We obliged without thinking out the consequences such brainwashing would carry for our own society. We trained them to become jihadists. We trained them to kill. We sent them into Afghanistan and in the India-administered Kashmir. Now, they have unleashed their terror on our own people. They are killing our soldiers and will stop at nothing to impose their brutal ideology on us."[5]

Since 2004, the Pakistani military under the pressure from the US has been engaged in antiterrorism operations in North and South Waziristan, FATA and the Khyber Pakhtunkhwa (KP)[6]. In addition, the military is also engaged in handling notorious gangs of criminal and insurgents in other parts of the country.[7] These operations have resulted in heavy military as well as civilian casualties and the creation of monster, the *TTP* or Pakistani *Taliban*.[8] In June 2014, the Pakistan military launched Operation *Zarb-e-Azb* against the *TTP*.

The Pakistan military has made certain claims of success in the areas of armed conflict. The Director General Inter Services Public Relations (ISPR) has stated that after start of Operation *Zarb-e-Azb*, phenomenal successes have been achieved. In a period of last 18 months, 3400 terrorists have been killed and 837 hideouts of terrorists have been destroyed. However, this success came at a heavy price, 488 officers and men of Pakistan military and security forces have lost their lives, besides 1914 have been injured. In addition, over 13,200 Intelligence Based Operations (IBOs) have been carried out across the country in which 183 hardcore terrorists were killed and 21,193 were arrested.[9] The Pakistan military has used aircraft as well as heavy artillery in the conflict zone but has never declared any collateral damage. The fatalities in terrorist violence in Pakistan from 2003-2015 have been enumerated in the following table.[10]

Fatalities in Terrorist Violence in Pakistan 2003-2015

Year	Civilians	Security Force Personnel	Terrorists/ Insurgents	Total
2003	140	24	25	189
2004	435	184	244	863
2005	430	81	137	648
2006	608	325	538	1417
2007	1522	597	1479	3598
2008	2155	654	3906	6715
2009	2324	991	8389	11704
2010	1796	469	5170	7435
2011	2738	765	2800	6303
2012	3007	732	2427	6211
2013	3001	676	1702	5379
2014	1781	533	3182	5496
2015	940	339	2403	3682

The restrictions on journalist and other independent observers, however, make it nearly impossible to verify the military's claims. If military claims that it has killed 10 high profile terrorists in an air attack, there is no one to verify the claim. The rise of terrorism has made Pakistan one of the most dangerous countries on the planet to not just practice journalism but also to exercise the Constitutionally guaranteed Fundamental Rights to freedom of expression and access to information. Pakistan's three most powerful intelligence outfits–the Inter Services Intelligence (ISI), the Military Intelligence (MI), and the Intelligence Bureau (IB)—are known to recruit informants among journalists. The link between journalists and the intelligence agencies is a complex one; journalists need information, and therefore have an interest in maintaining a good relationship with intelligence agencies. In return, journalists are asked to provide information themselves to intelligence agencies. This relationship becomes more complicated when journalists refuse to toe the line or probe areas considered sensitive by the intelligence agencies. Journalists have been arrested, brutalised, and, in some cases, have even died under mysterious circumstances over the years.[11]

The terrorist attacks on security personnel, minorities, and educational institutions continue in Pakistan. The recent spate of terrorist attacks clearly indicated that terrorists may have regrouped once again for striking in sensitive areas. In early January 2016 a suicide bomber riding a motorcycle struck a crowded police checkpoint on the outskirts of Peshawar, killed 11 people. Another 21 people were wounded in the blast, which took place on a road leading to Afghanistan. On January 20, 2016, few terrorists stormed Bacha Khan University in Charsadda, 20 miles from Peshawar, gunning down 22 people, most of them students and teachers. On Easter Sunday, March 27, 2016, a suicide bomber blew himself in a park in Lahore killing 72 innocent civilians and injuring 340 others. No one doubts that more atrocities will follow this year and next.[12]

The Army Corps Commanders' Conference held in Pakistan on November 19, 2015 underlined the need for matching/ complimentary governance initiatives for long term gains of military operation and enduring peace across the country. The areas of concern were delays in finalisation of FATA reforms and prioritising ongoing joint investigations.[13] FATA's political empowerment and reforming the Pakistan's criminal justice system remains the most crucial steps to improve the situation in the country.

FATA has also been ravaged by the American drones strikes killing and maiming thousands. Now the indigenous drones are killing Pakistan's citizens. By an estimate nearly 4,000 individuals have been killed; and 1,800 have been injured in drone attacks, only a few of them being hardcore terrorists. There has been no transparency and accountability in these strikes and no compensation has been paid.[14] The courts in Pakistan have also failed to redress the grievances of families whose members have been killed or injured. The US must ensure that armed drone operations in Pakistan comply with International Law. It must disclose key targeted killing standards and ensure effective investigations in every case where an innocent civilian is killed or injured. The Pakistan government needs to create a mechanism to compensate the families of those who have become victims of the drone strikes.

The military is actively engaged in non-international (internal) armed conflict in Pakistan. With the involvement of American forces in anti-terrorists operations in Pakistan, the conflicts could be categorised as internationalised non-international armed conflict. For the duration of armed conflict, the International Committee of the Red Cross (ICRC) must be provided access to detainees. The ICRC should also be given opportunity to collect evidences relating to war crimes, if any.[15] The Army Act, 1952, describes acceptable conduct of the military personnel, but does not include the offences listed as war crimes under the Rome Statute of the International Criminal Court. The military legal system therefore must be updated.[16] The Government of Pakistan must issue a 'Manual' on the laws of war to clarify the understanding of International Treaty and Customary Law applicable to military operations. [17] Military Manuals are designed to describe legal and policy rules applicable in armed conflicts; both international and internal as well as the UN peace operations. It would benefit both the armed forces and the members of the civil society and contribute to the progressive development of law of war.

Pakistan's human rights record continues to be subject to strong criticism by human rights organisations. While Islamic extremists are responsible for a number of atrocities, the state has allegedly been involved in many violations.[18] Critics claim that the crack-down on Islamist terrorism during 2014-2015 has been accompanied by a rise in extra-judicial executions, disappearances, torture and other human rights abuses.[19] Involvement of security forces in enforced disappearance has been on record.[20] Under the "kill-and-dump" operations undertaken at the behest of intelligence agencies, citizens are captured, tortured, and ultimately killed, with their bodies often abandoned many miles away from the place where they were. As reported, most of the disappearances have been perpetrated by Pakistan's main intelligence agencies and the Frontier Corps, which often act in conjunction with the local law enforcement agencies.[21] In fact, the insistence of the higher judiciary to investigate such disappearances and prosecute the perpetrators was strongly opposed by the military regime and led to serious threats to the human rights defenders.

According to Pakistan Institute for Peace Research, which has analysed the 20-point National Action Plan (NAP), there is no direct relation between the decline in terror attacks and resumption of death penalty in Pakistan.[22] Though the military and political leadership in Pakistan has been vowing to take action against every non-state armed group, including those attacking across the border, the government's subsequent action and statements suggests lack of clarity on dealing with certain groups. The strengthening and activation of the National Counter Terrorism Authority (NACTA) was one of the main concerns of the NAP; however, there is a serious confusion in the functioning of the NACTA. It is not clear whether it falls under the Prime Minister or Interior Minister and has no office or funds.[23]

The Pakistan's armed forces, besides fighting wars and militancy, are also involved in multiple business activities within the borders of the country. The military's business empire has a decentralisd structure operating at three levels and in three segments of the economy: agriculture, manufacturing and the service sector. The Pakistani military's private business empire, as estimated in 2007, was worth as much as US $20 billion.[24] The Ministry of Defence is at the apex of the economic activities and most of the establishments are being run by the retired senior military officers. The military officers who have spent their life in dealing with weapons, tactics and administration cannot be expert in managing finances, organising production and dealing with the civilian market.[25]

The retired or serving military officers governing the business organisations are an obstacle to the growth of modern corporate sector in Pakistan. It is said that the Pakistan military personnel lives a dual identity: one, as a military man; two, as a business man. While army officers continue to insist in public that their priority is the former; facts on the ground suggest the priority is the latter.[26] The military uses the same rationale to justify its economic role that it has used for its political intervention; that the politicians are corrupt while the military is not.[27]

The military controls one-third of heavy manufacturing industries and owns more than 12 million acres of public land.[28] The perks and privileges, land grants, and post-retirement employment opportunities in business ventures conferred on to senior military officers has progressively resulted in increased corruption in the armed forces. There is hardly any genuine audit of military's financial gains. The possibility that the ISI, Pakistan's spy agency, using this money to sponsor terrorist attacks in the neighbouring countries cannot be ruled out altogether.[29] The judiciary has also succumbed to corrupt practices. The members of the judiciary have been encouraged to acquire residential plots in the housing colonies established by the military. In a few instances the higher judicial officers have been offered land as reward.[30]

The Pakistan Army has recently sentenced two Lieutenant Generals allegedly involved in corrupt practices. These officers were employed in the National Logistics Cell (NLC) and were accused of illegally investing Rs 4.3 billion in the stock market and causing a loss of Rs 1.8 billion.[31] In another case, the Chief of the Army Staff has ordered action against retired military officers and civilians involved in the Rs 62 billion defence housing scam.[32] In April 2016, the Army Chief has administratively removed 6 officers of the army, including a Lieutenant General, a Major General and three Brigadiers, allegedly involved in corrupt practices.[33] An anonymous person appropriately describes the military corrupt practices in Pakistan: *bhookay reh gayay main tay tu, lutt kay lay gaya G.H.Q!*[34]

After the 21st Constitutional Amendment the military has established 11 courts for the trial of suspected terrorists and nearly 150 cases have been referred to these courts. The procedure followed in Field General Court Martial has been equated with a trial held at International Criminal Court for war crimes committed under the Rome Statute.[35] The procedures laid down in the Pakistan Army Act, 1952 and the Pakistan Army Rules, 1954, are summary in nature, denying the right to a fair trial available to an accused under the Rome Statute. Also the officers constituting summary courts and the Appellate Courts are not trained in law. There are no independent Civilian Appellate Forum and the military commander exercises undue command influence over the officers constituting military court. The summary military courts represent the failure of the elected government to fulfill its democratic responsibility and ceding its mandate to the military.

The Security Council resolution 1373 of 2001 requires States to ensure that any person who participates in the financing, planning, preparation or perpetration of terrorist acts or in supporting terrorist acts is brought to justice. The States adopt various mechanisms to counter terrorist activities and use criminal and non-criminal proceedings, or measures in respect of which access to judicial procedures are applicable. The UN guide on the "Right to a Fair Trial and Due Process in the Context of Countering Terrorism,"[36] has identified following guidelines concerning the right to a fair trial and due process in the context of countering terrorism.

- Regardless of nationality all individuals must have effective access to justice.
- Criminal charges must be determined by a competent, independent and impartial tribunal established by law. Trial by military or special tribunals must comply with human rights standards in all respects, including legal guarantees for the independent and impartial functioning of such tribunals.
- The right to a fair trial involves the right to a public hearing. Any restrictions on the public nature of a trial, including for the protection

of national security, must be both necessary and proportionate, and assessed on a case-by-case basis. Such restrictions should be accompanied by adequate mechanisms for observation or review to guarantee the fairness of the hearing.

- Every person charged with a criminal offence has the right to be presumed innocent until proved guilty according to the law.
- Anyone charged with a criminal offence cannot to be compelled to testify against himself, or to confess guilt.
- The right to a fair hearing, in both criminal and non-criminal proceedings, involves the right to a trial 'without delay' or 'within a reasonable time'. The right to a timely hearing includes the right to a timely judgment.
- Everyone charged with a criminal or a terrorist offence, has the right to be tried in his or her presence. Trials *in absentia* should occur only in exceptional circumstances and only if all due steps have been taken to inform the accused of the proceedings sufficiently in advance.
- All persons have the right to representation by competent and independent legal counsel of their choosing, or to self-representation. The right to representation by legal counsel applies to all stages of a criminal process, including the pre-trial phase. Any restrictions on the right to communicate privately and confidentially with legal counsel must be for legitimate purposes, must be proportional and should not undermine the overall right to a fair hearing.
- In criminal proceedings initiated by the State, every person shall have the right to adequate time and facilities to prepare his or her case. In criminal proceedings the prosecution must disclose any relevant material in its possession, or to which it may gain access, including exculpatory material. Restrictions on the disclosure of information may be justified in certain cases and subject to conditions that sufficiently guarantee the right of the person to respond to the case.
- Every person shall have the right to call and examine witnesses, including expert witnesses. The use of anonymous witnesses must be restricted to cases where this is necessary to prevent intimidation of witnesses or to protect their privacy or security and must in all cases be accompanied by sufficient safeguards to ensure a fair trial.

- Any person convicted of a terrorist offence shall have the right to a genuine review of the conviction and/or sentence by a higher tribunal established by law.
- Violation of fair trial rights must result in the provision of effective remedies to the person whose rights have been violated. Compensation must be provided where a conviction has resulted from a miscarriage of justice.

The right to a fair trial is one of the fundamental guarantees of human rights and the rule of law, aimed at ensuring the proper administration of justice. Justice must be administered in a way that achieves fairness for all, regardless of the identity of the parties to the proceedings. Under IHL, common Article 3(1)(d) of the Geneva Conventions governing internal armed conflicts prohibits the passing of sentences and the carrying out of executions without previous judgment pronounced by a regularly constituted court, affording all the judicial guarantees which are recognised as indispensable by civilised peoples. This provision is considered to reflect customary international law. Pakistan and the US have signed and ratified the four Geneva Conventions of 1949. Article 1 common to four Geneva Conventions states that the High Contracting Parties undertake to respect and to ensure respect for the present Convention in all circumstances. The phrase 'to respect and to ensure respect' applies first to the High Contracting Parties themselves, their armed forces, other persons and groups acting on their behalf, and their populations as a whole. Fair trial guarantees contained in Article 14 of the ICCPR continue to apply during armed conflict.[37] Terrorism-related conventions also require compliance with the right to a fair trial and the rule of law. Denial of the right to a fair trial can constitute a war crime in certain circumstances.[38] The Rome Statute of the ICC also includes the basic requirements for a fair trial in the context of international criminal law.[39]

The Constitutional Amendment provides that the Army Act, 1952, under which summary military courts operate, is exempt from the application of Article 8 of the Constitution, which states that laws that violate fundamental rights shall be void. It also provides that constitutional provisions relating to the independence of the judiciary will not be applicable in terrorism-related cases that are tried by military courts. The Army Act also bars civilian courts from hearing appeals against the decisions of military courts, and Article 199 of the Constitution states that High Courts may not intervene in cases where an application is made by or in relation to a person who is for the time being subject to any law relating to the armed forces.

The Constitutional Amendment establishing the military courts was challenged before the Supreme Court for violating the basic structure of the Constitution by unduly restricting individual Fundamental Rights. Many analysts in Pakistan believe that the Supreme Court let down the cause of human rights and the rule of law when it upheld the legality of the trial of civilians before military courts.[40] The summary military courts were set up under the dictates of the military leadership. Unfortunately, the higher judiciary in Pakistan except for a brief period has remained under the shadows of military dictators.

According to International Commission of Jurists, in the 18 months since FGCM were empowered to try terrorism-related offences, they have convicted at least 81 people, possibly including children, in secret trials.[41] In most cases, the Field General Court Martial has awarded the sentence of death. While a few executions were temporarily stayed by the High Court,[42] and the Supreme Court,[43] majority of the condemned individuals have been hanged. The proceedings of summary military courts have been treated as confidential and their copies have not been provided to the accused or their counsel.[44] The Amnesty International has reported that Pakistan has executed one individual every day after the moratorium on the death penalty was lifted by the government.[45]

According to the International Commission of Jurists the proceedings before Pakistani Field General Court Martial fall short of national and international standards requiring fair trials before independent and impartial courts on the following grounds: (i) Judges are part of the executive branch of the State and continue to be subjected to military command; (ii) The right to appeal to civilian courts is not available; (iii) The right to a public hearing is not guaranteed; (iv) A duly reasoned, written judgment, including the essential findings, evidence and legal reasoning, is denied; (v) The procedures of military courts, the selection of cases to be referred to them, the location and timing of trial, and details about the alleged offences are kept secret; and (vi) The death penalty is implemented after unfair trials.[46]

PILDAT, a Pakistan based think-tank, is of the opinion that extraordinary situations call for extraordinary measures; however, the establishment of special military courts, in principle, is indeed a negative development for Pakistan's democracy that blurs the lines between the judiciary and the executive under the separation of powers enshrined in the Constitution. Trial by a military court cannot achieve the objectives until the investigation, prosecution and the operation branches are not reformed and protected from terrorist's threats. Establishment of military courts for two years as a parallel justice system negates the credibility and effectiveness of the existing civilian judicial system.[47]

The United Nations Human Rights Bodies have expressed their grave concern over the special laws and establishment of military courts for the trial of civilians in the country.[48] The Protection of Pakistan Act (PoPA) empowers security forces, including the army, police and Rangers, involved in the fight against terrorism, with the authority to arrest without warrant, to order preventive detention without adequate safeguards, and in some cases, to even detain individuals secretly, and to retroactively apply the law to legitimise illegal detentions. In view of the human rights bodies, the absence of judicial oversight may open the door to discretionary and arbitrary interpretation or application of the law. The PoPA also grants immunity to the law-enforcement officers who might be responsible for serious human rights violations such as arbitrary detention and enforced disappearance. These provisions are incompatible with a number of international human rights norms and standards, including the ICCPR, which Pakistan ratified on June 23, 2010 and the UN declaration on the protection of all persons from enforced disappearance. The UN bodies have also objected to section 6 of the PoPA which empowers the government of Pakistan and law-enforcing agencies to preventively detain individuals suspected of being involved in "scheduled offences" for 90 days.

The Institute for Peace Research has expressed concerns over the secret proceedings of Court Martial as they mark a dark spot on the country's nascent democracy. The country's existing criminal legal system is sufficient for taking action against those involved in 'hate speech', however, the law-enforcement agencies are untrained and lack gadgets to collect evidence. As regard terror financing, there has not been any convictions in the last few years in Pakistan. The issue remains untouched because the government has not been able to interfere in the economic web of terrorists organisations. Easy access to heavy weapons in Pakistan is a major challenge for the security forces' counter-terrorism drive. According to one estimate, 20 million illegal weapons are in circulation in Pakistan.[49] Sectarian terrorist groups and insurgents have recently adopted the tactics of suicide bombing and targeted killings as the foremost instrument of terrorism. Although the military has made claims of having restored security in parts of FATA, no action has been taken for administrative reforms in these areas.[50]

The counter-terrorism operations will have to be followed up by building effective local governance and economic development in the tribal regions. The civilian government has not given sufficient attention to this aspect and seems to be relying on the army to undertake the task. Pakistan military may be able to contain the insurgency by use of force but should be ready to face significant and complex security threats in coming years.[51] Enacting draconian counter-terrorism legislation, trying and sentencing civilians in military courts and hanging them without transparency will never end terrorism in the country. A militarised approach to bring FATA peace is beyond the bounds of possibilities. Without structural and governance reform,[52] the root causes of terrorism and extremism will remain unaddressed and *jihadis* will exploit the absence of rule of law. According to Hoodbhoy, F-16s or drones cannot dent the enemy's real armour, his ideology. Military force, though sometimes indispensable, cannot eliminate those who live only to die. Direct military action or use of hard power has its place in the battlefield; however, while fighting an insurgency or irregular warfare, the employment of unconventional method like negotiations would be the most appropriate. There are ample examples in the history to demonstrate that military action has remained ineffective in defeating insurgency.[53] To destroy terrorism will require a massive change of public attitudes and a complete repudiation of Pakistan's current policy.[54]

The perceived threat from India has historically justified the military's dominance in Pakistan, and it will continue to be so in the near future. The power sharing deal between civilian and military leaders will keep the potential for a future military coup low.[55] The civilian government will always function under the fear of possibility of a military coup. In January 2017, the Constitutional and military law amendments for the trial of civilians would most likely be extended for a period of one year.

Successive military and civilian governments in Pakistan have used the resources towards selfish interests. They have done little for the well-being of the common people. Pakistan military continues to play an influential role in the country's internal security at the same time retaining its vast business interests in the country. There is no possibility of transformation of Pakistan at the hands of Generals. The civilian political system is not powerful enough to bring about any transformation in the civil-military relationship, in which military serves to democratically elected political leaders. The Pakistan Planning Commission's visionary statement that "all segments of society: politicians, bureaucrats, military, judiciary, media, private sector, professionals and civil society to align and synergise their energies and resources towards a shared destination",[56] may not come true for another two decades. The present stalemate is most likely to continue in Pakistan.

According to Mushtikhan Amhar, "Sages have said there are three main problems of Pakistan- Allah, America and Army-in alphabetical order. The military court is the common thread in all three. So in the setting up of the military courts Allah has played a role as it came in the wake of the horrific Peshawar killings in December 2014, the army has played a role-perhaps bigger than Allah and America-as it created the Taliban to control Afghanistan-and of course, nothing moves in Pakistan without the tacit blessings of wise guys in America."[57] The Army lacks the capability to fix Pakistan's problems. However, it is unwilling to give other state institutions and the political system the opportunity to learn and grow. Military's own performance, when in power, has been lugubrious. As a result of which Pakistan has been labeled as one of the failing States.[58] To sum up, Pakistan is a victim of ... "an Army conquering its own country".[59] In national interest, Pakistan Army must obey the civilian power.

Notes

1. The successful coups were by General Ayub Khan (1958), Yahya Khan (1969), Zia ul-Haq (1977) and Pervez Musharraf (1999). The unsuccessful coup were by low ranking officers: Rawalpindi conspiracy (1951), Islamic-minded General and junior officers (1995) and by a group of middle level and junior officers (2004). Cohen Stephen Philip, *The Idea of Pakistan* (Washington DC: Brooking Institution Press, 2004), p. 7.
2. Most military officers view politicians as fools. They are skeptical of the parliamentary democracy in a society where politicians can dupe, bribe or coerce the common illiterate Pakistani to vote for them. Shah Aqil, The Army and Democracy: Military Politics in Pakistan (Place: Harvard University Press, 2014), pp. 22-24.
3. The US's alliance with Pakistan military has three significant consequences for Pakistan: (i) Because the US military sees Pakistan in the context of its Middle East strategy, Pakistan has become more oriented toward the Middle East even though it is geographically and historically a part of South Asia. (ii) The intermittent flow of US military and economic assistance has encouraged Pakistan's military leaders to overestimate their power potential. This has contributed to their reluctance to accept normal relations with India even after learning through repeated misadventures that Pakistan can, at best, hold India to a draw in military conflict and cannot defeat it. (iii) The ability to secure military and economic aid by fitting into the current paradigm of American policy has made Pakistan a rentier state, albeit one that lives off rents for its strategic location. Husain Haqqani, *Pakistan: Between Mosque and Military*(Washington DC: The Brookings Institution Press, 2005), p. 203.
4. Masood Maj. Gen. Talat [Pakistan Army], Pakistan's Fight Against Terrorism, *Defence Against Terrorism Review*, Vol. 4, No. 1, Spring & Fall 2012, p. 14.
5. As quoted in Ahmed Ishtiaq, *The Pakistan Military in Politics: Origins, Evolution, Consequence*, (New Delhi: Amaryllis, 2013), pp. 351-352.
6. North West Frontier Province (NWFP) is now called Khyber Pakhtunkhwa (KP).
7. In April 2016, Pakistan army took over an operation to dislodge a criminal gang headed by Chotoo, holding 24 policemen as hostages on an island hideout in the centre of the Indus River in the Province of Punjab. The security operations involved more than 1,600 security forces personnel as well as the use of air power. The small gangs, after kidnapping businessmen and professionals from areas as far as Karachi, Balochistan and Rahimyar Khan, used to sell them to Chotoo for Rs 400,000 to Rs 500,000. Gabol Imran, The Rise of Chotoo and his gang, *Dawn*, April 16, 2016, available at: http://www.dawn.com/news/1252447/the-rise-of-chotoo-and-his-gang, accessed on April 18, 2016.
8. In June 2012, *TTP* militants released a video showing severed heads of 17 Pakistani soldiers who they claimed to have killed in a cross-border attack on a check post in Pakistan. The video prepared by the *Taliban's* media wing showed 17 severed heads of soldiers placed on a white sheet while masked men stand behind clutching assault rifles captured from the soldiers. The beheading, claimed by the *TTP* took place when *Taliban* militants from Afghanistan infiltrated into the northwestern district

of Upper Dir. *Taliban* releases video of beheaded Pakistani soldiers, *Dawn*, June 27, 2012, http://www.dawn.com/news/729939/taliban-release-video-of-beheaded-pakistani-soldiers, accessed on March 1, 2015.

9. Director General ISPR Press Release No PR380/2015-ISPR dated December 12, 2015, available at: https://www.ispr.gov.pk/front/main.asp?o=t-press_release&id=3127#pr_link3127, accessed on April 10, 2016.
10. Available at: www.satp.org/satporgtp/countries/pakistan/database/casualties.htm, accessed on May 2, 2016.
11. Grare Frederic, *The Challenges of Civilian Control Over Intelligence Agencies in Pakistan*, December18, 2015, Bangladesh Institute of Law and International Affairs, book chapter available at: http://carnegieendowment.org/2015/12/18/challenges-of-civilian-control-over-intelligence-agencies-in-pakistan/inad, accessed on January 10, 2016. Over 100 journalists and media workers have been killed in the line of duty in Pakistan since 2000 and over 2,000 injured, kidnapped, arrested or harassed and intimidated in the same period. The non-state actors as well as the military intelligence services have been blamed for this. On April 19, 2014, Hamid Mir, a senior anchorperson for Geo News TV channel was attacked minutes after landing in Karachi from Islamabad. He was shot at and received six bullets in his body. The journalist's family charged intelligence agency ISI chief Lt. Gen. Zaheerul Islam of masterminding the attack. In retaliation, the military got the channel banned for one month and fined Rs 10 million for treason. On August 28, 2014, Irshad Mastoi, bureau chief of online news agency was shot dead in his office in Quetta along with one reporter by unidentified gunmen. Express News TV channel has been targeted repeatedly in recent time. Its Peshawar Bureau Chief Jamshed Bhagwan was thrice attacked when bombs were planted outside his residence. Three of the channel's staffers were gunned down in Karachi and *TTP* claimed responsibility for the attacks. Dera Bugti-based Baluch journalist Manzoor Bugti, working for Pakistan Television, remained unaccounted for since he disappeared in Quetta on November 7, 2014. State of Media in Pakistan, Key Trends of 2014 and Main Challenges in 2015, available at: http://www.fnpk.org/state-of-media-in-pakistan-key-trends-of-2014-and-main-challenges-in-2015/, accessed on April 15, 2016.
12. Hoodbhoy Pervez, Can Pakistan's F-16s fight terror? *Dawn*, April 16, 2016, available at: http://www.dawn.com/news/1252330/can-pakistans-f-16s-fight-terror, accessed on April 19, 2016.
13. Delhi Policy Group, Update, Pakistan Update, February 2016.
14. The principles of Islamic *Sharia* could be regarded as a valid source of jurisprudence of the law of armed conflict. Islamic *Sharia* recognises the concept of reparation and compensation for victims of crimes. It provides detailed rules for compensation in lieu of any harm inflicted against the physical (and also moral) integrity of persons. In this respect, the Islamic criminal justice system is based on the principle that "no blood goes in vain in Islam". Victims of violent crimes or families of deceased victims are entitled to *diyya*, that is, compensation either from the perpetrator himself or from his family or tribe.
15. Soofi Ahmer Bilal, 'Legal Challenges to Military Operations in Pakistan: The Case of the Federally and Provincially Administered Tribal Areas', in Yusuf Moeed (ed.).,*Pakistan's Counterterrorism Challenge* (Washington DC: Foundation Books, 2014), p. 131.
16. Pakistan's current body of legal system is cumbersome and confusing. The British colonial era criminal and civil procedural laws are the main source of law in

Pakistan's courts today. The three laws governing the Army, the Air Force and the Navy also belong to the British era, which were legislated for the mercenary forces. These laws, other than *Islamisation*, have remained static. The procedural aspects of these laws are not in public domain.

17. The necessity of a Manual is envisaged in Article 1 of the 1899 Hague Convention II, with respect to the laws and customs of war on land makes it obligatory on a State Party to issue "instructions ... which shall be in conformity with the "regulations ... attached to the present Convention". Use of the term "instructions" manifested a direct commitment by the State Parties to issue instructions consistent with treaty obligations providing elaboration and explanation. The provision does not obligate the Governments merely to reprint the texts of treaties it has ratified. The 1949 Geneva Conventions, to which Pakistan is State Party, also necessitates preparation of a law of war manual.

18. Violence, abuse, and social and religious intolerance by militant organisations and other nongovernmental actors has contributed to a culture of lawlessness in many parts of the country, particularly in the provinces of Balochistan, Sindh, Khyber Pakhtunkhwa the FATA. Militants and terrorist groups killed hundreds and injured thousands with bombs, suicide attacks, and other violence. There have been many reports that security forces committed abductions, torture, enforced disappearances and arbitrary or unlawful killings. Other human rights problems included poor prison conditions, arbitrary detention, lengthy pretrial detention, a weak criminal justice system, lack of judicial independence in the lower courts, and infringement on citizens' privacy rights. Pakistan: Country Reports on Human Rights Practices for 2014, The US Department of State, Bureau of Democracy, Human Rights and Labour,pp. 1-4.

19. ICG, Revisiting counter terrorism strategies in Pakistan: opportunities and pitfalls, Asia Report No. 271, July 22, 2015.

20. Forced disappearances, an extremely sensitive issue in Pakistan, had been a daily practice of government services under the military regime, especially of General Pervez Musharraf. It became routine in Pakistan since September 11; accused of anti-terrorist activities, the persons were abducted, detained and tortured in illegal places of detention or were handed over to US authorities. The abduction by Pakistani secret services and the disappearance of anonymous citizens, political opponents and human rights defenders affects large parts of civil society and leaves many families in mourning. It is very difficult to quantify these disappearances because of the pressure exercised against those who dare to expose them, the difficulty to provide evidence and information on those responsible and places of detention used, and lastly because the disappearances are more prevalent in areas prohibited to access by human rights defenders. According to *Asian Human Rights Commission* (AHRC), estimated the total number of persons disappeared since 2001 could be several thousands. Bouvier Delou and Cosadia Fatma-Boggio, Pakistan: A Long March for Democracy and Rule of Law 2007-2008, International Federation for Human Rights (FIDH), January 2009, p. 19.

21. *We can Torture, Kill, or Keep You for Years: Enforced Disappearances by Pakistan Security Forces in Baluchistan*, Human Rights Watch (HRW), July 2011, p. 26.

22. Executive Summary of comprehensive package of NAP, Pakistan Institute for Peace Studies, December 14, 2015, available at: http://pakpips.com/art.php?art=166, accessed on January 12, 2016; The database of the Human Rights Commission of Pakistan also reveal that out of the 195 people executed from December 19, year? to July 31, 2015, only 22 were terrorists; the remaining 173 were common criminals. Militants in minority in Pakistan execution drive, deterrent effect debated, *Reuters*, 26 July 2015; also see: hrcp-web.org/hrcpweb/who-has-been-executed. Accessed on month date,year.

23. The reactivation of the National Counter Terrorism Authority (NACTA) is part of the Pakistan government's 20-point National Action Plan (NAP) on counterterrorism that was announced after attack on Army Public School in December 2014. The NACTA was established under the NACTA Act of 2013 with the view to curb the menace of terrorism from the country. It is a Federal organ and its main is to coordinate and prepare comprehensive national counterterrorism and counter-extremism strategies. NACTA is headed by a national coordinator. Security analysts believe that NACTA is still a dormant body. Ministry of Interior in the past had been asking the Finance Ministry to release funds for reactivation of the authority. The NACTA has no office building and was housed in the premises of the National Police Bureau because a single police officer was heading both institutions. For more details see: http://nacta.gov.pk/updates.htm, accessed on April 10, 2016.
24. For more detailed analysis, see: Siddiqa Ayesha, *Military Inc: Inside Pakistan's Military Economy*, (London: Pluto Press, 2007).
25. Pakistan's President Musharraf, at the inauguration of a desalination plant for the Defence Housing Authority (DHA) at Karachi had said: "Then, we have army welfare trust, we have Fauji Foundation. Yes, they are involved in Banking.....they're involved in.... we've got fertilizers ....we are involved even in pharmaceuticals. We are involved in cement plants.... So, what is the problem if these organisations are contributing and are being run properly? We have the best banks. Our cement plants are doing exceptionally well. Our fertilizer plants are doing exceptionally well. So, why is anyone jealous? Why is anyone jealous if the retired military officials or the civilians with them are doing a good job contributing to the economy of Pakistan and doing well?" Siddiqa Ayesha, *Military Inc.: Inside Pakistan's Military Economy* (London: Pluto Press, 2007), p. 15.
26. Rashid Hasim bin, The Military in Business, *Pakistan Today*, March 8, 2012.
27. Muhammad Asghar Kahn, a retired Air Marshal, lodged a petition in Lahore High Court alleging large scale corruption by the senior military officers of Pakistan. The allegations related to allotment of land to military officers at throwaway price; kick-backs and commission in purchase of military aircraft and equipments; involvement of ISI in kidnapping for ransom; and corruption in military business activities. However, the petition did not succeed.
28. Lieven A., *Pakistan: A Hard Country* (London: Penguin, 2012), p.167.
29. A 2010 cable declassified by the US state department and published by the national security archives has exposed this connection. As reported, the ISI paid $200,000 to the Haqqani Network for the December 30, 2009 attack on a CIA camp on its border with Afghanistan that killed seven American agents and contractors and three others.
30. There is a tendency on the part of the retired judges of Higher Courts to look for post-retirement employment as judges of the Federal *Shariat* Court, chairman, or members of service tribunals or commissions. The keenness for post-retirement employment has been a serious impediment in the way of independent judiciary. The judges, who seek such reemployments, are likely to favour the government nearing their retirement. Khan Hamid, *A History of the Judiciary in Pakistan,* (Karachi: Oxford University Press, 2016), p. 549. Also see: Siddiqa Ayesha,. *Military Inc.: Inside Pakistan's Military Economy* (London: Pluto Press, 2007), pp. 196-197.
31. The punishment awarded to one of officer was later set aside by the Rawalpindi bench of the Lahore High Court. Army sentences two former Generals in NLC corruption case, *Dawn*, August 6, 2015, available at: http://www.dawn.com/news/1198561, accessed on January 1, 2016; Asad Malik, Court sets aside dismissal of NLC former

director general, *Dawn*, December 24, 2015, available at: http://www.dawn.com/news/1228444, accessed on January 1, 2016. Lt. Gen. Hamid Gul, former DG ISI and now a representative of an association of ex-servicemen, has demanded that a transparent and open investigation should be conducted against military officer involved in corruption.

32. Raza Syed Irfan, 'COAS green-lighted NAB action in DHA Valley scam', *Dawn*, January 11, 2016, available at: http://www.dawn.com/news/1232218, accessed on March 10, 2016.
33. Following the investigation conducted by then Adjutant General Zubair Mahmood Hayat on the orders of the Army Chief, the charged officers were asked to return all earnings accumulated through corruption. Haider Mateen, General Raheel dismisses 6 army officers from service over corruption, *Dawn*, April 22, 2016, available at: http://www.dawn.com/news/1253497, accessed on April 23, 2016.
34. Translated in English, it means "While we remained hungry, the funds have been looted by the GHQ (Pakistan Army's Headquarters)."
35. Soofi Ahmer Bilal, Pakistan in Conflict State: The Legal Aspects, *Hilal, The Pakistan Armed Forces' Magazine*, March 16, 2015, pp. 14-19.
36. The guide has been prepared to assist member States in strengthening the protection of human rights in the context of countering terrorism. It provides guidance on how States can adopt human rights-compliant measures in a number of counter-terrorism areas. The guide also identifies the critical human rights issues raised in these areas and highlights the relevant human rights principles and standards that must be respected. Basic Human Rights Reference Guide: Right to a Fair Trial and Due Process in the Context of Countering Terrorism, UNOHCHR, 2015.
37. Although the right to a fair trial is not listed as a non-derogable right under Article 4(2) of the ICCPR, the Human Rights Committee has treated the right to a fair trial as one which may not be subject to derogation where this would circumvent the protection of non-derogable rights. Even in situations when derogation from Article 14 is permissible, the principles of legality and the rule of law require that the fundamental requirements of fair trial must be respected. General Comment 32, paragraphs 6 and 59; and Human Rights Committee, General Comment 29 (States of Emergency), UN Doc CCPR/C/21/Rev.1/Add.11 (2001), paragraphs 7 and 15.
38. In the context of an international armed conflict, Article 8(2)(*a*)(vi) of the Rome Statute of the ICC explicitly states that the willful deprivation of "a prisoner of war or other protected person of the rights of fair and regular trial" constitutes a war crime. The Rome Statute also recognises that serious violations of common Article 3 of the Geneva Conventions, applicable to non-international armed conflicts, may constitute war crimes. This includes the "passing of sentences and the carrying out of executions without previous judgment pronounced by a regularly constituted court, affording all guarantees which are generally recognised as indispensable." See: Rome Statue Article 8(2)(c)(iv).
39. The Rome Statute (Article 67(1)) identifies as basic requirements: the presumption of innocence; privilege against self-incrimination; the right to communicate with legal representatives freely and in confidence; the right to remain silent without such silence being a consideration in the determination of innocence or guilt; the right not to make an unsworn oral or written statement in one's own defence; and the right not to have imposed upon the accused any reversal of the burden of proof or onus of rebuttal.
40. Justice Khosa's dissenting opinion in the 21st Amendment judgement: "compromising

justice for combating this menace (terrorism) may be a death knell for the value system of the entire nation of more than 180 million people." Omar Reema, Righting the Wrong, *Dawn*, February 16, 2016, available at: http://www.dawn.com/news/1239771/righting-the-wrong, accessed on March 18, 2016.

41. Military Injustice in Pakistan: A Briefing Paper, June 2016, International Commission of Jurists, Geneva, p. 3.
42. The Peshawar High Court (PHC) on April 5, 2016, stayed the execution of three terrorists (Fazal Ghaffar, Taj Gul, Mushtaq Ahmad), condemned to death by a military court for terrorism offences. The bench also extended a stay on the execution of death sentence awarded by military courts to three convicted terrorists Fateh Khan, Bakht Ameer and Ikramullah. *The Express Tribune*, April 6, 2016, available at: http://tribune.com.pk/story/1079429/military-trial-phc-stays-execution-of-three-convicted-terrorists/, accessed on April 7, 2016. However, on April 12, 2016, the High Court upheld the six death sentences awarded to these convicts. Akhtar Amin, PHC upholds death sentences of six terror convicts, *The International News*, April 13, 2016, available at: http://www.thenews.com.pk/print/112326-PHC-upholds-death-sentence-of-six-terror-convicts, accessed on April 14, 2016.
43. Malik Hasnaat, SC stays execution of four convicted by military courts, *The Express Tribune*, Pakistan, February 10, 2016, http://tribune.com.pk/story/1043592/sc-stays-execution-of-four-convicted-by-military-courts/, accessed February 12, 2106.
44. The Supreme Court five-judge bench headed by the Chief Justice allowed the counsels of military courts' convicts an access to Field General Court Martial proceedings and Appellate Courts record. The counsel was not allowed to take any notes or pictures, as proceedings were treated as confidential. SC conditionally allows examination of trial records, *The Nation*, April 7, 2016, http://nation.com.pk/islamabad/07-Apr-2016/sc-conditionally-allows-examination-of-trial-record, accessed on April 8, 2016.
45. In Pakistan executions resumed following the *TTP*-led attack on the Army Public School in Peshawar in December 2014. In March 2015, the moratorium on the death penalty was lifted for all 28 offences for which the death penalty is provided, including non-lethal crimes. In November, a Parliamentary Panel approved the punishment of life imprisonment or the death penalty for the rape of girls aged 13 or under. During the year 2015, more than 300 executions were recorded in Pakistan, most for murder and others for rape, attempted assassination, kidnapping, and terrorism-related charges. Available at: https://www.amnesty.org/en/countries/asia-and-the-pacific/pakistan/report-pakistan/, accessed on April 4, 2016.
46. Pakistan: "Military justice" system an affront to human rights – new analysis brief, January 6, 2016, International Commission of Jurists, available at: http://www.icj.org/pakistan-military-justice-system-an-affront-to-human-rights-new-analysis-brief/, accessed on April 10, 2016.
47. Peshawar Tragedy: Responses by the Civilian and Military Leadership in the Context of Civil-Military Relations, Pakistan Institute of Legislative Development and Transparency (PILDAT), PILDAT Monitor, December 2014.
48. Tahir Niazi, UN bodies voice objection to military courts, available at: http://nation.com.pk/islamabad/07-Dec-2015/un-bodies-voice-objection-to-military-courts, accessed on January 10, 2016.
49. Some of the infamous artisan producers in Pakistan's North West Frontier Province are licensed by the state to manufacture weapons. Siddiqa-Agha Ayesha. 1996. *Light*

Weapons manufacturing in the Public and Private Sectors: A View from Pakistan, Basic Project on Light Weapons Working paper (2), London: BASIC. While the vast majority of small arms and light weapons (SALW) originate in legal, industrial-scale production, some SALW are illicitly produced. The manufacture of SALW can be illicit in a number of ways. It may be illegal, unregulated or unlicensed. Unlicensed production may be undertaken without the permission of licensor, often through reverse engineering or other producer's design. Bourne Mike, *Arming Conflict: The Proliferation of Small Arms*, (New York: Palgrave, Macmillan, 2007), p. 66.

50. Executive Summary of comprehensive package of NAP, Pakistan Institute for Peace Studies, December 14, 2015, available at: http://pakpips.com/art.php?art=166, accessed on January 12, 2016.
51. Masood Talat, Pakistan's Relentless Fight Against Terrorism, available at: http://hilal.gov.pk/index.php/layouts/item/1943-pakistan-s-relentless-fight-against-terrorism, accessed on March 10, 2016.
52. The 1901 Frontier Crimes Regulation (FCR) and Article 247 of the Constitution disallow the police and courts jurisdiction over FATA and deny its residents fundamental political, legal and economic rights. As civilians displaced by the military operation in North Waziristan return home, they are asked to first sign the Social Contract North Waziristan, 2015. Among other undertakings, it says, "we as responsible citizens of Pakistan will be loyal to the Constitution of Pakistan, the FCR and local customs ... all the anti-Pakistan elements will be completely eliminated by our tribes". Non-compliance could mean cancellation of identity cards and passports, and seizure of property, expulsion from the area and destruction of residence. The ground reality is that colonial era FCR is supreme in FATA, not the Constitution of Pakistan. The FCR has been a part of the problem and one of the main reasons for FATA's alienation. It allows collective punishment against a tribe for individual crimes 115 years after the British promulgated it. The government should also repeal the FCR in its entirety, replacing it with the Penal Code and the Criminal Procedure Code. Revisiting Counter-terrorism Strategies in Pakistan: Opportunities and Pitfalls, Asia Report No. 271, July 22, 2015, International Crisis Group, Belgium, pp. 29-30.
53. Khan Raja Muhammad, Negotiations with TTP: An Analysis of Counter Terrorism Strategy, *NDU Journal*, Pakistan, 2013, pp. 65-92.
54. Hoodbhoy Pervez, Can Pakistan's F-16s fight terror? *Dawn*, April 16, 2016, available at: http://www.dawn.com/news/1252330/can-pakistans-f-16s-fight-terror, accessed on April 19, 2016.
55. Pervaiz Faisal, Pakistan's Military-Democracy Complex: Analysis, February 2, 2016, STRATFOR, Texas.
56. *Pakistan 2025: One Nation, One Vision*, Planning Commission, Ministry of Planning, Development and Reform, Government of Pakistan, available at: http://www.pc.gov.pk/wp-content/uploads/2015/05/Pakistan-Vision-2025.pdf, accessed on March 20, 2016.
57. Mustikhan Amhar, Pakistan: An army that owns the country, now has the courts too, 14 January 2015, available at: http://www.dailyo.in/politics/pakistan-an-army-that-owns-the-country-now-has-the-courts-too-america-nawaz-sharif-allah-taliban/story/1/1493.html, accessed on March 12, 2015.
58. According to "Fund for Peace", which publishes the annual "Fragile States Index", there are some 16 countries which could be considered failed or failing States based on extensive areas within their borders outside government control. The list includes

Sudan, South Sudan, Somalia, Syria, Central African Republic, Congo, Chad, Yemen, Afghanistan, Guinea, Haiti, Pakistan, Iraq, Nigeria, Ivory Coast, and Zimbabwe. *Fragile State Index: Fragility in the World 2015*, Fund for Peace, available at: http://fsi.fundforpeace.org/map/2015heatmap.png, accessed June 10, 2016.

59. Khalid Mahmud, 'Governance and National Security: Pakistan—a case study' in Banerjee Dipankar (ed.), *Security Studies in South Asia: Change and Challenges*, [Regional Centre for Strategic Studies, Colombo], (New Delhi: Manohar Publishers, 2000), p.132.

Bibliography

1. Abbas Hasan, *Pakistan's Drift into Extremism: Allah, the Army, and America's War Terror* (New York: Armonk, M E Sharp, 2005).
2. Abbas Hasan, Pakistan Through the Lens of the "Triple A" Theory in *The Fletcher Forum of World Affairs*, Vol. 30, No. 1, Winter 2006, pp. 181-192.
3. Akbar Zaidi S, *Issues in Pakistan's Economy* (Karachi: Oxford University Press, 2005).
4. Ahmed Ishtiaq, *The Pakistan Military in Politics: Origins, Evolution, Consequence* (New Delhi: Amaryllis, 2013).
5. Aziz M, *Military Control in Pakistan: The Parallel State* (London, Routledge, 2007).
6. Bellinger John B and Padmanabhan Vijay, Detention Operations in Contemporary Conflicts: Four Challenges for the Geneva Conventions and Other Existing Law, *The American Journal of International Law*, Vol. 105, No. 2, April 2011, pp. 201-243.
7. Bergsmo Morten and Tianying Song (ed.), *Military Self-Interest in Accountability for Core International Crimes* (Brussels: Torkel Opsahl Academic E-Publisher, 2015).
8. Bianchi Andrea and Yasmin Naqvi, *International Humanitarian Law and Terrorism* (UK: Hart Publishing Ltd, 2011).
9. Bourne Mike, *Arming Conflict: The Proliferation of Small Arms* (New York: Palgrave, Macmillan, 2007).
10. Burki S.J., *Pakistan Under Bhutto:* 1971-77 (London: Macmillian, 1988).
11. Collard Keith, *Pakistan: A Political Study* (London: Allen and Unwin, 1957).
12. Chaudhry G.M., *Pakistan Military Laws* (Rawalpindi: Federal Law House, 2006).
13. Cloughley Brian, *A History of Pakistan Army: Wars and Insurrections* (Karachi: Oxford University Press, 1999).
14. Cohen, Stephen P, *The Idea of Pakistan Army* (Washington DC: Brooking Institution Press, 2004).
15. Cohen, Stephen P, *The Pakistan Army* (Karachi: Oxford University Press, 1998).
16. Cohen, Stephen P, *The Future of Pakistan* (Washington DC: Brooking Institution Press, 2011).
17. Dormann Knut and Jose Serralvo, Common Article 1 to the Geneva Conventions and the Obligation to Prevent International Humanitarian Law Violations, *International Review of the Red Cross*, Vol. 86, No. 895/896, Autumn/Winter 2014, pp. 707-736.
18. Fair, C. Christine, *The Madrassa Challenge: Militancy and Religious Education in Pakistan* (Washington DC: United State Institute of Peace Press, 2006).
19. Fair, C. Christine, Why the Pakistan army is here to stay: prospects for civilian governance, *International Affairs*, Vol. 87. No. 3, 2011, pp. 571-588.
20. Finer Samuel E, *The Man on Horseback: The Role of Military in Politics* (USA: Transaction Publishers, 2002).
21. Fleck Dieter (ed.)., *The Handbook of International Humanitarian Law* (Oxford: Oxford University Press, 2008).
22. Gardezi Hasan and Rashid Jamil, *Pakistan: The Roots of Dictatorship*(London: Zed Press, 1983).

23. Gul Imtiaz, *The Most Dangerous Place: Pakistan's Lawless Frontier* (London: Penguin Books, 2010).
24. Grare, Frederic,*Reforming the Intelligence Agencies in Pakistan's Transitional Democracy*(Washington DC: Carnegie Endowment for International Peace, 2008).
25. Grare, Frederic Pakistan's foreign and security policies after the 2013 general elections: The judge, the politician and the military, *International Affairs*, Vol. 89. No. 4, 2013, pp. 987-1001.
26. Hanif, Mohammed, The Hamid Mir Case: 'In Pakistan, they used to censor journalists-now they shoot us', *The Guardian*, April 23, 2014.
27. Haqqani Hussain, *Pakistan: Between Mosque and Military* (India: Penguin Books, 2016).
28. Hassan Tariq, Supreme Court of Pakistan: The Case of Missing Persons, *Criterion*, Volume 4, No. 3, 2011, pp. 7-27.
29. Husain Haqqani, *Pakistan: Between Mosque and Military* (Washington DC: The Brookings Institution Press, 2005).
30. Hussain Ejaz, *Military Agency, Politics and the State in Pakistan* (New Delhi: Samskriti, 2013).
31. Hussain Zahid, *Frontline Pakistan: The Struggle with Militant Islam* (New York: Columbia University Press, 2007).
32. Iqbal Khuram, *Making of Pakistani Human Bomb* (Lexington Books: New York, 2015).
33. Jacob N. Shapiro and C. Christine Fair, Understanding Support for Islamist Militancy in Pakistan, *International Security*, Vol. 34, No. 3, Winter 2009/10, pp. 79-118.
34. Jaffrelot Christophe, *The Pakistan Paradox: Instability and Resilience* (India: Random House, 2015).
35. Jalal, Ayesha, *The State of Martial Law (*Cambridge: Cambridge University Press, 1990).
36. Jalalzai Musa Khan, *The Prospects of Nuclear Jihad in Pakistan* (New York: Algora Publishing, 2015).
37. Jillani Tassaduq Hussain, The Rule of Law and the Supreme Court of Pakistan, available at:www.aihja.org/images/users/1/files/Pakistan.national.report_pakistan.en.0.pdf
38. Khan Hamid, *A History of the Judiciary in Pakistan* (Karachi: Oxford University Press, 2016).
39. Khan Hamid, *Constitutional and Political History of Pakistan* (Karachi: Oxford University Press, 2009).
40. Khan Raja Muhammad, Negotiations with TTP: An Analysis of Counter Terrorism Strategy, *NDU Journal*, Pakistan, 2013, pp. 65-92.
41. Kukreja, Veena, *Civil Military Relations in Pakistan: Pakistan Bangladesh and India* (New Delhi: Sage, 1991).
42. Lieven A, *Pakistan: A Hard Country* (London: Penguin, 2012).
43. Maan Zahid Nawaz, Pakistan's Drone Dilemma, *NDU Journal*, Pakistan, 2014, pp. 77-96.
44. Malik I.H., *State and Civil Society in Pakistan* (London: MacMillan, 1997).
45. Malik Salma, *Pakistan in 2015: A Forecast*, Institute of Peace and Conflict Studies (IPCS) Special Report No. 171, January 2015, p. 24.
46. Masood, Maj. Gen. Talat, [Pakistan Army], Pakistan's Fight Against Terrorism, *Defence Against Terrorism Review*, Vol. 4, No. 1, Spring & Fall 2012, pp. 13-30.

47. Mir Amir, *Talibanisation of Pakistan: From 9/11 to 26/11* (New Delhi: Pentagon Security International, 2009).
48. Mirza, Lt. Gen. Zahid Latif, Baluchistan—Past, Present and Future, *NDU Journal*, Pakistan, 2013, pp. 21-34.
49. Nawaz Shuja, *Cross Swords: Pakistan, Its Army and the Wars Within* (New York: Oxford University Press, 2008).
50. Rana Amir, *A to Z of Jihadi OrganiZ.A.tions in Pakistan* (Lahore: Mashal Books, 2004).
51. Rana Athar Javed, *Biting the Silver Bullet* (Lahore: Tropical Printers, 2013).
52. Rizvi Hasan Askari,*The Military and Politics in Pakistan* (Lahore: Progressive Publishers, 1986).
53. Rizvi Hasan Askari, *The Military, State and Society in Pakistan* (London: MacMillan, 2000).
54. Sattar Babar, 'Pakistan: Retrun of Praetorianism', in Algappa Muthiah (ed.)., *Coercion and Governance: The Declining Political Role of the Military in Asia* (California: Stanford University Press, 2001).
55. Shafqat, Saeed, *Civil Military Relations in Pakistan: From Zulfikar Ali Bhutto to Benazir Bhutto* (London: Westview Press, 1997).
56. Shah Aqil, *The Army and Democracy: Military Politics in Pakistan*, (Harvard University Press, 2014).
57. Shah Niaz A, *Islamic Law and the Law of Armed Conflict: The Armed Conflict in Pakistan* (London: Routledge, 2011).
58. Siddiqa Ayesha, *Light Weapons manufacturing in the Public and Private Sectors: A View from Pakistan*, Basic Project on Light Weapons Working paper (2) London: BASIC, 1996).
59. Siddiqa Ayesha, *Military Inc.: Inside Pakistan's Military Economy* (London: Pluto Press, 2007).
60. Siddiqa Ayesha, Something's got to give in Islamabad, *The Hindu*, April 29, 2016.
61. Soofi Ahmer Bilal, 'Legal Challenges to Military Operations in Pakistan: The Case of the Federally and Provincially Administered Tribal Areas', in Yusuf Moeed (ed.), *Pakistan's Counterterrorism Challenge* (Washington DC: Foundation Books, 2014), pp. 127-148.
62. Soofi Ahmer Bilal, Pakistan in Conflict State: The Legal Aspects, *Hilal, The Pakistan Armed Forces' Magazine*, March 16, 2015, pp. 14-19.
63. Talbot, Ian, *Pakistan: A Modern History* (New York: St Martin Press, 2010).
64. Yusuf Moeed (ed.)., *Pakistan's Counterterrorism Challenge* (Washington DC: Foundation Books, 2014).
65. Ziring, Lawrence, *Pakistan in the Twentieth Century: A Political History* (Karachi: Oxford University Press, 1997).